The Prayer of Jesus

A Reading of the Lord's Prayer

The Prayer of Jesus

A Reading of the Lord's Prayer

*

Kent Gramm

WIPF & STOCK · Eugene, Oregon

THE PRAYER OF JESUS
A Reading of the Lord's Prayer

Copyright © 2015 Kent Gramm. All rights reserved. Except for brief quotations in critical publications or reviews, no part of this book may be reproduced in any manner without prior written permission from the publisher. Write: Permissions. Wipf and Stock Publishers, 199 W. 8th Ave., Suite 3, Eugene, OR 97401.

Wipf and Stock
An Imprint of Wipf and Stock Publishers
199 W. 8th Ave., Suite 3
Eugene, OR 97401

www.wipfandstock.com

ISBN 13: 978-1-62564-672-9

Manufactured in the U.S.A.   01/15/2015

Holy Bible: Authorized King James Version. Cleveland: World, 1959.

Holy Bible: New Revised Standard Version. New York: Oxford University Press, 1989.

The Revised English Bible. Cambridge: Oxford University Press and Cambridge University Press, 1989.

For Milo Milanovich
and my children

Contents

Introduction: Religion, Prayer, and the Prayer of Jesus | 1

1. Our Father | 21
2. Who art in Heaven | 48
3. Hallowed be Thy Name | 60
4. Thy Kingdom Come | 84
5. Thy Will be Done on Earth as It is in Heaven. | 102
6. Give Us This Day Our Daily Bread | 123
7. Forgive Us Our Trespasses [Debts/Sins] as We Forgive Those Who Trespass [Sin] against Us [Our Debtors] | 136
8. Lead Us Not into Temptation | 149
9. But Deliver Us from Evil | 163
10. [For Thine is the Kingdom, and the Power, and the Glory, Forever.] | 180
11. Amen. | 182

A Note of Appreciation | 187
Works Cited | 189

Introduction
Religion, Prayer, and the Prayer of Jesus

THIS BOOK IS AN explication of the Lord's Prayer—an unfolding or reading, detail by detail. A close reading of this prayer reveals the One to whom it is prayed: The Lord's Prayer is Jesus' portrait of God.

When his disciples asked, "Master, teach us how to pray," Jesus gave them a brief model prayer. It is short, blunt, and moves immediately to the Hearer of the prayer. The Lord of the Lord's Prayer answers the question, *How should we pray?* by introducing us to the Master of the Universe. Being incorrigibly superstitious, we would like to control the Holy One and harness divine power for our own projects. But if we want a verbal formula for success, we should reach for a manual on sorcery or Baal worship, not for the prayer that Jesus taught.

Fortunately, there is a deeper aspect to our nature. One's inner self belongs with God. This deeper identity prays not to get things, but prays out of longing and what St. Augustine called the restlessness that knows no rest until we rest in God. Both parts of our earthly nature—the nervous, grasping, superficial self; and the longing true Self—have prayed to Jehovah, the Great Spirit, Allah, and Krishna by countless names through countless years. Prayers for healing, peace, success, and deliverance have been answered by someone—perhaps irregularly, but indubitably. These answers to utilitarian prayer sometimes bring us to deeper prayer that unites us with our true selves and with the real Holy One.

The greatest authority on prayer who ever lived was Floyd Hutch of Picatoxin, New Jersey, who unfortunately died in total obscurity. He left no writings, letters, tapes, or other records; therefore, we will have to fall back on Jesus. Of course, the idea of having to "fall back" on Jesus is obviously silly. What Jesus has over Mr. Hutch and everyone else is, by all accounts, a quiet and palpable authority. Regardless of whatever beliefs or unbeliefs they nurse, people seem to agree Jesus was honest, courageous, and unselfish;

and he loved with extraordinary power. If that does not seem somehow divine, then at least it would be perverse to disregard a person who spoke with such compelling beauty and grace. This has been self-evident for two thousand years.

The words of the Lord's Prayer are essentially the words Jesus spoke. The two versions in Matthew (6:9–13) and Luke (11:2–4) differ, but not fundamentally. Luke leaves off "in heaven," lets "Your kingdom come" stand without "your will be done," and similarly omits "deliver us from evil" from "lead us not into temptation." The original Aramaic phrasing of Jesus might have lent itself to either Luke's or Matthew's approach to the Greek of his time and place.[1] At any rate, Jesus was a rabbi in first century Palestine, which meant that students ("disciples") would memorize his most important teachings. Prayer is at the very center of religion and directly addresses the unthinkable problems of human life. As such, this prayer must have been handed down carefully, albeit through the difficulties of translation, from the very witnesses who sat in front of Jesus.

That is my assumption, at any rate. This book is not an analysis of the text of the Lord's Prayer; it simply adopts Matthew's words.[2] I also assume that the early witnesses intended to be faithful and accurate. Implicitly, we underestimate first-century people, thinking of them as particularly superstitious and gullible. Because Jesus' contemporaries did not invent big machines that poison the air, we conclude that they were short on intelligence. But it is we, not they, who believe that money can make us immortal. It is we who serve the superstitions that technology can keep us safe and happy, and that entertainment wards off the tragedies of life. And we do worship idols, for surely we must think that God is made of wood or stone—because a god of stone cannot see what we do to each other; a god of wood cannot hear the desperation of the poor.

Any comparison of ourselves to first-century Mediterranean people must be made in light of certain facts. As I write this, not only is the world's atmosphere coughing toward catastrophe; not only are the world's economies reeling; and not only are we dodging bullets from militias, hostage-takers, common criminals, and schoolroom shooters—but one-third of the world hungers while the rest have too much; we spend our heaviest money

---

1. I am assuming that either Matthew supplies phrases and clauses the Aramaic contained or implied, or Luke cuts out parallel phrases and clauses customary in Hebrew or Aramaic poetic usage but alien and repetitious to Luke's gentile audience.

2. I use Matthew in this book because it is the more familiar version, and it is used in traditional Church services. Furthermore, Matthew's adding or including "in heaven" clarifies "Father"; "will" elucidates "kingdom"; and "evil" supplies an implication of "temptation" or "trial."

on weapons rather than on charity and education; we lie, cheat, and steal from each other instead of giving the love we all need. And fundamental to everything: we are still mortal. We awake into this insane but beautiful world and learn before long that we will die. On our way to this unthinkable termination we suffer terror, pain, and worst of all, separation. To ask God for trinkets in prayer is all right as far as it goes—this kind of prayer is contained in the Lord's Prayer—but under our intolerably tragic circumstances it is worth knowing that the prayer of Jesus offers us more.

> Wise lovers do not consider the gift of the Lover as much as they do the love of the Giver. They look more at the love than at the value of the gift; for their Beloved is far above His gifts.[3]

*

A paradox of prayer is that in its highest form it is unselfish, yet through it we can receive everything. Our complicated natures reflect a similar paradox: on the one hand we long for God from the depth of our souls, and on the other hand want to improve our dangerously powerless position in this world. We feel virtually helpless in the face of poverty, war, disease, and bad weather. The inevitable result of our desire for security and our longing for God is religion. But Jesus both fulfills and rejects religion, and so does his prayer. Jesus' harshest words were used on religious people because the desire for security and power can replace our longing for God.

To imagine a world without religion is to imagine a world without humans. We might want to assemble all the true believers on earth, transport them to some remote island, and let the ferocious know-it-alls fight it out to the last fanatic. But then the rest of us would take up the fight ourselves. We have been lording the religious truth over each other for thousands of years, killing on principle and in the name of God, and there is no reason to suppose that we will ever stop.

Religion is about life and death. As you are reading this right now, someone in the name of Jesus is bending over a dying child, brushing flies from her eyelids, propping her head up to give her a sip of water, perhaps laying the hands of prayer upon her head; and someone else believing the same creed, invoking the "father in heaven," is butchering people with knife, grenade, or bomb. Religion gives life, and religion takes it away.

Religion is inevitable and unavoidable. The word "religion" means the rituals, practices, rules, and institutions we often deplore; but it also means

---

3. Thomas á Kempis, *Imitation of Christ*, 110.

spiritual longing. After many years of practicing psychotherapy, Carl Jung observed that spiritual longing is as strong as the desire for lovemaking. This second sense of the word "religion" also includes our experiences and intimations of something greater than we are, or of something great within. It refers to our love for that reality, our love for God. We cannot help wanting the security, power, assurance, and strength that come from religious communities, religious ceremonies, and religious belief. But there is more. A young Native American did not graduate to adulthood until he or she had gone upon a spirit quest. Many of us spend a lifetime pursuing—or avoiding—such a quest.

Most of the people in this world are simply trying our best to do the right thing, to raise our families well, to turn in a decent account of ourselves, and to get through the inevitable troubles and tragedies of life. Therefore we are easy marks for anyone who comes along claiming to know what they are doing. Their self-proclaimed knowledge is their power. We are easily sold on the idea that we are sinners in the hands of an angry God, that we are born with an inner evil that suits us only for hell, and that we need to listen to an authority tell us how to get out of trouble, how to live and believe and think and act. Such authorities are confident, persuasive, even charismatic. Their self-assurance masks the malevolence and illusory origin of their power. But when a healer comes along who teaches us that God knows us, that the poor and the powerless and the sick and those who mourn are already the favored children of a heavenly parent, that God is not vengeful or jealous, and that the kingdom of this loving One has no boundaries and excludes no one for any reason, he is killed by the authorities. He is in fact crucified. But first he teaches us how to pray.

Prayer is our hope and comfort. Prayer expresses and to a degree fulfills our longing:

> O God, thou art my God; early will I seek thee:
> my soul thirsteth for thee, my flesh longeth for thee
> in a dry and thirsty land....
> Because thy lovingkindness is better than life,
> my lips shall praise thee....
> My soul shall be satisfied as with marrow and fatness;
> and my mouth shall praise thee with joyful lips:
> when I remember thee upon my bed,
> and meditate on thee in the night watches.[4]

All the creeds are idle beliefs and gilded opinions if there is no Great Spirit, no Master of the Universe. Religion is a curse apart from the love of

---

4. Ps 63:1–6, KJV.

God. Religion has built on the compassion and mercy of the human race, constructing hospitals and preaching justice and mercy, and has given us meaning and hope. It has also bloodied nearly every country and every imagination on the globe. Anyone who has worked under religious authorities knows what hell is: it is heaven, with religious authorities in charge. Religion is human, so we have to expect both good and bad. You don't refuse the air when it is all there is to breathe.

We are repelled by bad religious behavior, but we are not willing to give up on religion. We are still trying to keep faith in some way. Most of us are looking for religion that is honest about our spiritual experience and not narrow, closed-minded, fearful, hateful, or self-righteous. We are on a spirit quest, and we need not be turned aside by religious people.

Really, there are no religious authorities. The experts disagree. Beware of anyone who invokes "the biblical point of view," as if there were only one, or as if Bible truths come up off those thin pages pure and un-interpreted. Anyone calling down biblical infallibility is merely claiming his own. Wise people humbly seek the truth, and foolish people think they have it. "Blessed are the poor in spirit, for of such is the kingdom of heaven."[5]

Part of the human condition is our vulnerability to power. Military power intimidates, kills, and commands us. I once lived in a German village where NATO tanks on training maneuvers would roll out of the woods at dawn and crunch the streets and sidewalks like chalk. The word "intimidating" was made for tanks. Missiles and bombs fall out of the sky on us as we go shopping, and in some places squads of weapon-carrying militias murder us because they feel like it. If another country has a nuclear bomb and we haven't, its leaders can tell us what to do. Ships, planes, missiles, tanks, and military vehicles comprise a major environmental cancer that poisons us, and our grandchildren. We are probably still breathing fumes from the Battle of Jutland.

Political power sometimes commands military power; certainly it commands us. We get or lose our rights to travel, speak, and even eat from the decisions of politicians. Our health care and our educations depend on them. Whenever they decide to do something reasonable and humane, we are as grateful as puppies.

Police power keeps order, protects us from criminals and ourselves, and reduces traffic mayhem. Like soldiers and politicians, police officers regularly give their lives for us. But police power in the wrong hands can reduce us to cowering knaves and generally have a good old time with us if it wants to.

---

5. Matt 5:3, KJV.

The force of law is meant to achieve justice and is better than lawlessness, given human nature; but it is a human mechanism. The force of law can release us from tyranny, but it can also be used by cunning, greedy, and unscrupulous people to get what they want. In a court of law, the outcome can depend not upon the fairness of your claim or your innocence, but upon whether you hired the craftier attorney. The judge has power to put you in prison, though all the tribunals of heaven rise up and cry, "Shame!" As King Lear implies, it is not love but rich clothing that covers a multitude of sins. The thief in baggy jeans who crowbars his way into a jewelry store goes to prison, while the Armani-suited executive takes his leveraged profits to the bank.

Economic disasters teach us the reach of financial power. A few individuals can conspire to make money in a way that drops the bottoms out of the world's goosy markets, sending millions out of work and into the streets begging—and there is not Thing One that we can do about it but suffer. And complain.

This brings us to religious authorities. Most religious people are only trying to get to heaven; they are not all sanctimonious goons. The sanctimonious goons are those who assume authority for themselves, be they preachers or common civilians. The point is that all earthly power is the same. Jesus did not threaten the scribes and Pharisees only because they were self-righteous: it was their power that made them self-righteous and it was their power that Jesus rejected.

Power divides: rich from poor, us from them, the righteous from the unrighteous, the living from the dead. Power's illusion—that we are not all mortal and that we are not equally children of God—divides us from ourselves. It separates us from God. But love unites. Jesus, preaching the love of God, denied boundaries, meaning that he un-deified power and authority. The righteousness he preached—which, he said, must be greater than the righteousness of the Scribes and Pharisees (the religious authorities of the day)—is the righteousness of love.

Now, Reader, I must ask your pardon while I interrupt this consideration of power, authority, and love. My telephone is ringing with unusual urgency.

Author speaking.
Bonjour.
French? To whom have I the honor—?
You may call me simply Jacques.
Jack?
Not "Jack," you simple man. Jacques.
Your last name please?

Introduction

Calvin.

John Calvin, the second greatest theologian of the Reformation? Egad!

Second greatest? What can you mean, you small midget man?

With all due respect, Sir, you are no Luther. To paraphrase Mark Twain, you are somewhat the lightning bug compared to the lightning.

Sacré bleu, *you vulgar idiot!*

I mean no offense, Sir, only that—

Have you not read, imbécile, *St. Paul's teaching that all authority is ordained by God? The law and its authority are meant to keep the incorrigible human nature—exemplified in all its ridiculous obscenity by yourself—from committing even worse outrages than this book you are writing! Why do you write such a book, eh? Do you expect movie rights?*

Sir, again with all due respect, I doubt that Paul was speaking for God in this case; and I reject the idea that God's law is the same as human law.

Oh, we "reject," do we? Who are you, insect, to reject the words of Jacques Calvin or St. Paul, eh? I am wasting my time.

Here now, this is my book. Why are you interrupting?

I am trying to protect the world from your anarchism!

Dr. Calvin, surely love is not anarchy.

Ah! I have heard that before, a thousand times. Love!

Love, indeed. You are French, no?

You are insolent. To speak to Jacques Calvin in such manner! There ought to be a law!

There probably is, Sir.

Listen to me—

Pardon, my phone's battery is low.

No, no you don't!

Bocoo pardons, Your Honor, but we're out of juice here. Feel free to call back at a more convenient time.

Sacré—

Click. Dear reader, I would like to allow Dr. Calvin to present his idea fully, but due to the regrettable limitations of modern technology, it will not be possible. With the reader's indulgence, I shall return to our discussion of power. Dr. Calvin has issues with authority.[6]

My last point is that the constant victims of power and authority are the poor. But God loves the poor, Jesus said. "Blessed are you who are poor," according to Luke's translation.[7] Possibly the most often-used words in the

---

6. The caller must have been an imposter. The Reformation theologian and political leader would have introduced himself as *Jean Calvin*, not *Jacques Calvin*. The author of this book is sometimes confused and gullible. [Editor's note.]

7. Luke 6:20, NRSV.

world—the Lord's Prayer—are also the most ignored, because they lower the world's power into proper perspective. To pray the words of this prayer is to accept the poverty, powerlessness, and privilege of the human condition. As such, they are words of hope such as the world can hardly conceive. The prayer of Jesus describes God, who loves us, forgives us, and observes no human boundaries; and if I may paraphrase St. Paul in this case, no power or authority on earth, or below or above the earth, will prevail against God's love.

*

Prayer is at the center of religious faith; doctrines, statements of theology, and tests of religious correctness are at the outer edges. We experience the presence of God in prayer; and we bring to prayer not only our fears, sickness, wrongdoing, guilt, hopes, and happiness, but also the ideas we have absorbed from our upbringing and indeed from all over the world. In prayer, we are not on trial before God for those ideas, most of which are inevitably erroneous. As the writer of an ancient prayer put it, "I am like a green olive tree in the house of God; I will trust in the mercy of God for ever and ever."[8]

*

Why should we pray at all if, as Jesus said, God knows what we need before we ask? Prayer is a conundrum and a mystery. Reason refutes it; experience affirms it. Prayer assumes that God exists; it assumes that God is in some sense a person and cares about us, hears us, and intervenes for us. None of these assumptions is reasonable, yet those who pray know all of them to be true. Even the doubter in us gives God the benefit of the doubt during emergencies. "There are no atheists in foxholes," soldiers used to say.

You can't figure it out. There is no point in waiting to pray until we are sure it makes sense to pray, or until we have learned to do it right. Just bull ahead. "The Spirit helps us in our weakness; for we do not know how to pray as we ought, but that very Spirit intercedes with sighs too deep for words."[9] Prayer is an answer to prayer.

People have prayed for thousands of years to innumerable deities, believing that they have been heard. Today Christians and Jews and Muslims are praying each to his or her own conception or—more likely—misconception of God. So we are still praying to millions of deities, in part of our

---

8. Ps 52:8, KJV.
9. Rom 8:26, NRSV.

own devising. Presumably behind all these variations and misconceptions, the one God, Master of the Universe, Great Spirit, Allah, hears and replies. Maybe most of what the soundest believer prays is rubbish. God, through all the ages, has not objected. Three thousand years from now if there are still human beings, our present day Christianity might look as primitive as the worship of Obduh. But God answers us now. At all times and places human conceptions of God are inadequate and misleading, anthropomorphic, perverted, idolatrous, and blasphemous. As the heavens are above the earth, so God's thoughts are above our thoughts; and even if a set of holy scripture were to have been word for word dictated by God and literally true and inerrant, we would still misunderstand it, variously interpret it, wrongly translate it, and kill each other over it. Prayer rests on the indulgence and magnanimity of God. When we pray, we can be ourselves. Are we dreamers? Very well: perhaps God is a dreamer too.

*

No qualifications are needed for this prayer—not knowledge, or purity, or piety. What we must bring with us when we pray is our poverty. Our need is our permission and our qualification. The worst false boundary regarding the Lord's Prayer is the notion that there are any boundaries at all. There are none. We are in. The God of Jesus will not evict us for anything.

All of us can use teachers and guides. Nevertheless, the Lord's Prayer interprets itself, so that we are not overly dependent upon those guides (and writers.) That is, each petition works together with the others. The prayer's construction is wonderfully tight and unified. For example, we cannot understand "give us our daily bread" as meaning "give us everything we want," once we have prayed "Our Father." We may let the prayer speak for itself.

For many people, the authority of Jesus is in his words. When some of those words strike us as true, or as having the beauty of truth, those words have authority. I, the writer, have no authority in this book apart from my words. If anything said here turns the reader to the Master or to the prayer he taught us, then they come on good authority.

Of course, in terms of your own qualifications, you will have to be a sinner. By the traditional word "sinner" I mean someone who hurts him or herself and others. I mean that we lie to ourselves. We are alienated from ourselves, from other people, and from God. People think of infractions like smoking or theft, or their thoughts turn to sex, when they hear the word "sin," but sin is something more serious: sin refers to separation from God. It is enough for now to think that "sinner" means someone who is imperfect.

Do not read farther if you are not a sinner. In fact, don't do anything. We would like to stuff you and preserve you as a specimen.

*

This prayer, when prayed from the soul, will purify our desires. One can hardly ask more victory from life than that.

> Seek ye first the kingdom of God, and his righteousness;
> and all these things shall be added unto you.[10]

*

Two thousand years of Christians praying this prayer have believed that Jesus, the author of the prayer, came back from the dead. Can the Lord's Prayer be prayed without believing in the Resurrection and in the divinity of Jesus? Yes.

The first people who prayed this prayer did not think of Jesus as God, but as their teacher. Too often we are told that the way to become acceptable is to have the right beliefs. I am not saying that it is insignificant to believe that Jesus was raised from the dead; I am saying that *we do not have to believe any of the Christian beliefs, or understand any Christian doctrine, to pray this prayer.* When the disciples prayed this prayer the first times, they understood nothing. So we should not worry. We may enact the posture of prayer any way we wish—kneeling with folded hands, sitting or standing, eyes open or closed—but we may imagine the heavenly Father's posture toward us as welcoming, arms outstretched.

Men of conscience in Jesus' day could not stand the idea that God's love is for everyone. Even today, many who preach to us the Love of God want to make sure we think like them before we can have it. Forget that. We can leave our creeds and our consciences at the door.

In fact it is vital that we do this; otherwise we cannot really pray "*Our Father.*" We do not need to worry about our shortcomings or anyone else's. If we are barring someone else, we are refusing to go in ourselves. This prayer shows the heart of God. It assumes our salvation, not our damnation. Jesus gave his prayer to the just and to the unjust.[11]

*

---

10. Matt 6:33, KJV.
11. Were the disciples not sinners? Was Peter not present? Judas?

Introduction

Jesus said, "In your prayers do not go babbling on like the heathen." The heathen "imagine that the more they say the more likely they are to be heard. Do not imitate them, for your Father knows what your needs are before you ask. This is how you should pray."[12]

> Our Father, which art in heaven,
> hallowed be thy name.
> Thy kingdom come.
> Thy will be done in earth, as it is in heaven.
> Give us this day our daily bread.
> And forgive us our debts, as we forgive our debtors.
> And lead us not into temptation, but deliver us from evil:
> For thine is the kingdom, and the power, and the glory, for ever.
> Amen.[13]

> Our Father in heaven,
> hallowed be your name.
> Your kingdom come.
> Your will be done,
> on earth as it is in heaven.
> Give us this day our daily bread.
> And forgive us our debts,
> as we also have forgiven our debtors.
> And do not bring us to the time of trial,
> but rescue us from the evil one.[14]

> Our Father in heaven,
> may your name be hallowed;
> your kingdom come,
> your will be done,
> on earth as it is in heaven.
> Give us today our daily bread.
> Forgive us the wrong we have done,
> as we have forgiven those who have wronged us.
> And do not put us to the test,
> but save us from the evil one.[15]

Rendered literally from the Greek, it reads:

> Father of us the [one] in the heavens: Let it be hallowed the name of thee; let it come the kingdom of thee; let it come about

---

12. Matt 6:7–8, REB.
13. Matt 6:9b–13, KJV.
14. NRSV.
15. REB.

the will of thee, as in heaven also on earth; The bread of us daily give to us today; and forgive us the debts of us, as indeed we forgave the debtors of us; and not bring us into temptation, but rescue us from evil.[16]

Our own language changes, our understanding of Greek is not fixed and certain, and one language cannot be put exactly into another. Yet in any translation, one point is clear: Don't talk too much.

But what is too much? Is not God infinitely patient? Would God not be happy to sit back and listen to us say, "O awesome God, we just come before You on this beautiful day to just lift up our hearts to You, O Lord, and we just want to bring before Your awesome throne, Lord, our thanks and we praise You, Lord, we just praise You, and we know you are an awesome God and we just lift up praise to You for being an awesome God, and we know that you are our God, and You tell us in Your Word that You are a God that answers prayer, and You, Lord, are just a God . . . " At some point the Lord becomes a God who looks at his watch.

Now, it feels ungracious to criticize another person's prayer, but Jesus himself did say that we should not heap up empty phrases like hypocrites. Many people say prayers like the one above with sincerity and in all holy simplicity; but there is a better model. The kind of prayer I imitated does not ring fully true because it is not quite honest. Here is a good prayer: the young Martin Luther, riding terrified through a violent lightning storm, cried out, "God help me! I will become a priest!" No church language, just the honest words of his heart. Luther did not say, "Oh wonderful and awesome God, I just praise you for this lightning, and I just praise you for your awesome power, and I just lay before you my concern . . . " Who would talk to someone they respect like that? Sloppy repetitions and patronizing chatter are insulting.

God is probably not sensitive to insult from us, whom the Lord loves wisely and indulgently, but, as Luther said, with the warmth of a furnace. So undoubtedly Jesus warned us against praying like this not because we have to fear the wrath of an irritable and impatient divinity, but because when we talk like this we are not really paying attention. Therefore we are not really present, which means that we miss God's presence. We blather on automatic pilot in times of prayer only if in those moments God is not real to us. When we realize that the Master of the Universe, the Eternal, is listening, we say nothing in vain. Jesus implied that we may receive the immense gift of prayer: why not use it?

---

16. Marshall, *Interlinear Greek-English New Testament*, 20.

But there is another issue here. The "many words" feed our superstition that we customers have the power to manipulate the Manager. The more we say, the more control over God we have; the more reverent we are, the more likely God will give us what we want; the more we flatter, the more God will provide. Jesus calls this heathenish, in the contemporary translation, or "gentile" (*ethnikoi*) to an audience of devout Jewish disciples.

The essence of paganism is the belief that we can control divinity; but the essence of Jesus' prayer is that we must ask. "We are beggars," Luther wrote the day before he died.[17] No one likes to be a beggar, because it is a completely powerless position. We want security and predictable outcomes; but in fact we are flat broke, empty-handed in front of God, and if we think we have any power over the Creator of a universe containing two billion galaxies, then our unmindfulness is as self-destructive as it is comic. But God loves the poor.

*

"I believe; help my unbelief!" is a short prayer, right from the heart. A father who wanted Jesus to cure his son utters it in the Gospel of Mark.[18] He is willing to do anything for his boy, even risk acquiring a belief he knows nothing about. In exchange for the cure, he offers himself. He offers to change. This is the prayer of a man willing to be a beggar. He offers no prayers, praise, hospitality, or promises. His deep inner Self has recognized the voice of Jesus, and he pushes his everyday self across the table like a pile of chips. This is a prayer of faith and love.

To pray the Lord's Prayer is to give ourselves, because we signal our willingness to be a person we do not know we are, someone else's child. If God is our parent, who are we? If we ask what that boy's father asked, what might we receive? What might we become?

When I pray the prayer of Jesus, I start to become someone I do not know, someone I take on faith. Will I start to believe odd things? Will I act like a fool? Will I embarrass my friends and family? On the other hand, my genuine Self has heard the call to step out of its grave. I learned who I thought I am—my everyday self—from the people around me and from my fears, desires, jealousies, and pains. The world has told me who I am, though I know better deep down inside. Augustine confessed, "thou wast within and I was without." Do I have the courage to trust my real Self? I can deny my true Self, whose voice is the way of the heart; or I can deny

---

17. Luther, *Works* 54, 476.
18. Mark 9:24, NRSV.

my everyday false self—the prudent, responsible, law-abiding, successful, cowardly heathen whose secret middle name is Despair, and whose future is nothing. Traditionally, the Christian word for this future is "hell," but I prefer the Eastern phrase, "the wheel of birth and death" because I like the hamster image it evokes. I do not think that this is what God wants for us. Jesus said, "I am come that they might have life, and that they might have it more abundantly."[19]

*

The Lord's Prayer is short and plain, and we cannot make an impressive oration out of it. It does not give us half a chance to be religious. Some people have the dubious gift of being able to say monumental prayers, like applications for vacancies in the Trinity. But the prayer of Jesus simply asks. It assumes the straightforward love relation between God and us. We would rather receive a few heartfelt words from a loved one than a greeting card containing a paragraph of clever commercial eloquence. We do not feed our children according to their oratorical skills.

But elsewhere in the New Testament, we are told to "pray without ceasing."[20] Is this not a contradiction to Jesus' instruction to be brief?

The brevity of the Lord's Prayer does not mean that we should shut up, but that we *can* shut up. It says more about simplicity and directness than about how much or how often we should pray.

*

The simplicity of the Lord's Prayer prevents us from saying things that are not prayer. Sometimes we lecture God; sometimes we try to impress other people—one usually entailing the other. "O Lord, we are gathered here on the third anniversary of the founding of this great institution by the late governor of this state, Gerald Bunch, author, milliner, and polar explorer"—possibly interesting facts but unnecessary if the heavenly library stocks an almanac. Those who wait in the antechambers of the One Who Loves Us do not lecture, do not humble themselves to the highest heaven, and do not make a show of their piety before men. Ask as if the Lord knows what we need before we ask.

*

19. John 10:10b, KJV.
20. I Thess 5:17, KJV.

"Brevity is the soul of wit." The little word "wit" can refer to humor, to intelligence, and to one's mental faculties in general. We have to concentrate—keep our wits about us—in order to say something meaningful. We have to pay attention, and prayer is attention paid to God. Centuries of Christians have *repeated* the Lord's Prayer in church without attention, but no one can really *pray* it that way.

If words were as expensive as beer we would pray less and make it count. Thoreau wrote that his greatest gift was to want but little. Wanting and needing are not always the same. To feel our lack of what we really need is a gift of enlightened living, and our essential need is for God. Attachment Theory in psychology says that children's need for affection is as important as their need for food. The essential purpose of prayer is to realize our attachment to God. Blessed are those who know their need of God.[21]

*

Why did Jesus spend so much time in prayer? We are told that Jesus went off by himself to pray. Martin Luther could spend hours in prayer; Pope John Paul II began his day with long prayer, kneeling like a rock, someone said. Surely they were not heaping up empty phrases.

They knew something I don't know, because I do not pray for several hours at a time. I have trouble keeping my mind on it for ten minutes uninterrupted. I suspect that most of you readers pray as I do more than as John Paul did. Perhaps the Lord's Prayer is meant for people like us. Sometimes you and I might find the idea of a monastery or convent attractive: we could pray for hours at a time with no other cares in the world, and finally learn how to do it. But monks and contemplatives do not talk about the ease of prayer; they lament its difficulty. All of us lead lives of distraction.

I think that is a reason the Lord's Prayer is so short. Those who need to ask how to pray can start small and keep it simple. The tendency of beginners is to pray their prayers like all other distractions, not really concentrating, not really present, not really remembering who else is present. "Simplicity, simplicity, simplicity!"[22]

Henry David Thoreau gave some good advice on prayer, though it was not meant specifically as such. "I think we may safely trust a good deal more than we do," he wrote in *Walden*. "We may waive just so much care of ourselves as we honestly bestow elsewhere."[23] Might we not pray like this?

---

21. This paraphrases the NEB translation of the first Beatitude (Matt 5:3).
22. Thoreau, *Walden*, 88.
23. Ibid., 9.

Might we not begin simply and pray from the heart?—until minute by minute, year by year, our prayer becomes meditation, and meditation becomes contemplation of the Timeless Presence, and the hours come to us like gifts from eternity.

Meanwhile, let us begin by praying for our daily bread and for the feeding of the world, and ask that the very name of the One who loves us most be cherished. The prayer's brevity teaches us to pray simply and from the heart. "Suffer little children to come unto me, and forbid them not, for of such is the kingdom of God."[24]

*

Can there be communication when we do not hear back from the other side? Normally we should not hear an audible voice answering our prayers. If we do, it is either a miraculous event or we have been nibbling mushrooms from our backyard.

Many are familiar with an inner "voice" of promptings and impressions that we sometimes attribute to God. Our minds can mimic the Holy Spirit, and when these promptings clearly follow our desires and fears or go against humane ethics, we can reasonably suspect that the inner voice comes from our own brain. On the other hand, that inner voice or internal "genius" as Emerson and Thoreau called it, might be the deep mind of our true Selves and perhaps it connects us to God. Thoreau wrote, "No man ever followed his genius til it misled him."[25]

The trick is to distinguish between one's inner Self and the noise of false selves. William Faulkner said that the only subject worth writing about is "the human heart in conflict with itself."[26] From what we call the heart issues greed, lust, fear, hatred, and all the desires to which we are attached. And also from what we call the heart comes our true sense of who we are and what we must do; from this heart comes the certainty of love. One is illusion or delusion, and the other is truth apart from which no other truth would matter. The authentic inner voice brings an almost unearthly peace and clarity of intent. It is the wellspring of courage. If this inner Self does not speak with the voice of God, what does?

Awareness of the other side of the conversation might be a way to "pray without ceasing." If only we had voice catchers to filter out delusions

---

24. Luke 18:16, KJV.
25. Thoreau, *Walden*, 211.
26. Faulkner, *Nobel Lecture.*,3.

and leave only the Breath of the Eternal! We can rely on the voice of love, and be skeptical of the rest.

The voice of God might speak in our prayers themselves. If the Spirit of God helps us pray, then those prayers are the voice and presence of God, even if we do not hear promptings or phrases. Do we feel that we are being heard? Perhaps the very attention of God is the voice of God. And this is the ultimate goal of prayer—to unite us in God.

*

Prayer can be another name for worry. A constant stream of prayer can be nothing more than a compulsive burble of anxiety put into words—talking to oneself, like rocking back and forth in one's own mental world. All right, but if someone is addressed, then perhaps someone listens, even to this neurosis. Nevertheless, it is probably wise to meditate on this kind of inefficient prayer—that is, to sit quietly and become aware of the stream of anxious verbiage, watch it, accept it, and let it go by. It might be well to make a little pledge to oneself, or to God, that we will pray without worry to the best of our ability. It is surprising how the sense of someone listening can assuage anxiety: the key is to cut the chatter enough to listen for the Listener.

*

Another general characteristic of the Lord's Prayer is even more important than its brevity. It is the plural number of its petitioners: give *us our* daily bread; forgive *us our* trespasses; lead *us* not into temptation; deliver *us* from evil. While hardly noticing, I am led away from the usual intended beneficiaries of prayer: me, and a few specific others for whom I intercede in prayer—individuals in need of healing, for example, and perhaps groups of people at war or in danger of starvation. The Lord's Prayer brings us all together, asking nothing for ourselves alone nor asking anything that excludes ourselves.

This feature is essential to the prayer. As will be discussed, the prayer is located in the kingdom of God, in which there are individuals but in which there is no isolation: it is a kingdom of love. Love is the most important known characteristic of the One to whom the Lord's Prayer is prayed, and it is at the center of Jesus' preaching, ethics, and actions. It is both the premise and the goal of the Lord's Prayer. The prayer moves us toward its own fulfillment by putting "us" in our mouths in place of "me," and by compelling us to say "our" instead of "my." At the same time, there is no "them;" there is only "us." What I want, I become willing to wish for us all; what I need, I realize that we all need. The love of God is a grace that binds us together; or rather, the love of God awakens us in the family of God.

*

Prayer is a human being speaking with God. This is not a precise definition. Precisely speaking, we can pray to an orange. We can pray without having a specific hearer in mind. In fact, probably most prayer is superstitious babble to an idol—by which I mean an attempt to influence an imaginary or poorly-conceived deity. Pagan prayer is an attempt to get what we want. The Lord's Prayer is an attempt to get what God wants, an attempt to heal our wishes. The prayer of Jesus replaces our idols with God as described by the prayer itself.

How often should we pray? Until we understand that we have been heard. If there is a rule here, it is to pray as much as we need to.

I doubt that the purpose behind praying for our wants is only to satisfy those wants. The wants might be not the goal, but the vehicle—not the end but the means. If we are to pray even though God knows what we need, another purpose must be at work. God is using our wants and needs to communicate with us.

We cannot help having some kind of notion of God. Fortunately, the Lord's Prayer corrects some wrong ones. Primarily, God is not an angry, bad father who makes hellacious demands on us and hates our happiness. We are God's beloved. We become aware of the closeness of God with the prayer's first word.

*

A good deal of what follows rests on my idea of the human predicament: We wake into a world of joys and difficulties, and eventually understand that we will die. Given sufficient love, we mature fairly well under the circumstances, but without enough love, we warp. Either way, we develop ways to cope with pain and mortality. Sometimes these coping mechanisms and defenses succeed all too well. They bulk up and distort like monsters and control us. Ability to put fear on the back burner becomes a deep tendency to deny truth and reality, for example. Adaptations become a hard shell.

Another shell is the outward face we have learned to put on. When Abraham Lincoln was called two-faced, he remarked that if he had another face, he wouldn't wear this one. But nearly all of us have at least two faces, and the one we usually wear has been fashioned by people telling us who to be: parents, school, church, advertising, government, and friends.

Still another layer of the shell over us is conscience. Some basic human instincts, such as aggression and the urge to reproduce, made our species successful in competing against saber-toothed tigers, wooly mammoths, and Dallas Cowboys. We have learned to beat the brains out of human competitors. But success has made our species so numerous that these winning traits have put us in danger. To survive now, we must control these traits—suppress them, civilize them. So we are taught that some of our urges are wrong. To an extent, this is good. The world is a better place because we do not steal whenever we want something, or kill whenever we get angry. We learn to make outside rules internal; we police ourselves. But we internalize not only basic humane prohibitions; we are taught to internalize a variety of other things as well. Neurotic parents teach us to be ashamed of intimacy, for example; and our society might teach us that it is wrong to set slaves free. Some rules vary from society to society, time to time, and place to place. In Connecticut it is considered ill-mannered to scratch in public, whereas in some other states there is nuance and ambiguity attached to the concept. All of these rules, for good or ill, we take into ourselves and they become parts of the role we act in life. They become aspects of the everyday self we put on. Soon we believe that this outward face is our face, and that the conscience society has drilled into us is the Voice of God.

That everyday face or self becomes hardened by despair and fear. We have limited power in a dangerous world. Our adversaries have seemingly unlimited power: I am thinking of disease, war, and chance. Our own desires—for life, affection, and enjoyment—are unlimited also, which makes our lack of power to fulfill them painful. In our weakness we despair, give up, and live the seemingly safe life of our everyday self. "The mass of men lead lives of quiet desperation."[27]

We have turned into the policemen that we placed over ourselves, and we project onto the heavens a feared and hated imaginary god who is just a bigger version of the same cop. We have become the bogus self we learned to be, and we make a big bogus god—a Great Frowning Elder, perhaps, or a Hypocritical Evangelical. And the sweet Green Bay Packer within us is held underfoot by a demanding and unsportsmanlike bully.

We develop an artificial self that is different from the forgotten original Self. Some forms of religion address the artificial self, with its fears, rages, projections, and neuroses. But Jesus, as well as leaders of other generous

---

27. Thoreau, *Walden*, 6.

spiritual traditions, addresses the deeper Self, and appeals not to our learned desires and fears but to our longing for love and union.

The everyday self that "worships God" is not who we really are. Our artificial self creates an artificial god and the whole show is nothing but smoke and mirrors. Its tyrannical idol is not the Holy One of Jesus. That is why we need the description of God offered in the Lord's Prayer.

Accusations of sin and worthlessness do not call forth our better Selves, but love and respect can. I have learned this from thirty years of teaching and ministry. We know our shortcomings very well, but we have to be reminded of our worth—and most of us respond courageously when we are loved and valued. We become willing to risk the danger of stepping outside our defended everyday self; we are willing to endure the temporary pain of growth. The ultimate result of growth is awake-ness, or "enlightenment." In this state we can seek and be our true Selves; we can love and accept love; we can know our Eternal Beloved.

Love is what gives life its worth, and love is the only thing that can really address our limitations, wounds, and mortality. The most righteous thing is love, so "God's righteousness" is not policed correctness but unconditional love. Love heals us, helps us live and grow, and makes us able to love. Love saves us. One is not worthy or unworthy of love. You do not love your children because they are smart, obedient, or beautiful. I assume that God's love for us must be even greater than the love of whichever human being has loved us most. What if God's love is simply the principle of the universe? To awaken to reality is to know this love: enlightenment is waking up in the kingdom of heaven.

In what I have said throughout this Introduction, some will recognize echoes of the New Testament, the theology of Martin Luther, the psychology of Freud and Jung, the philosophy behind the Upanishads and the *Bhavagad Gita*, and especially this statement by Thomas Merton: "There is an irreducible opposition between the deep transcendent self . . . and the superficial, external self. . . . We must remember that this superficial 'I' is not our real self."[28] We can learn a great deal from what Thoreau might call the confluence of Walden Pond and the sacred waters of the Ganges.[29] There is nowhere, East or West, that God does not love us. There is no one for whom God is not *Our Father*.

---

28. Merton, *New Seeds of Contemplation*, 7.
29. Thoreau, *Walden*, 290.

1

Our Father

THE FIRST WORD OF the Lord's Prayer is subversive: it undermines all power on earth, especially religious power. "Our" means everyone. The word is all-inclusive, because there is no word or phrase in the prayer to limit it. We can claim that "our" means only Christians; we can claim that it means only Protestants; we can claim that it means only The Church of the True Bible Word; we can be blockheads. But to limit the word is to contradict the actual prayer and to claim an authority and power that Jesus does not give us.

"My" denotes possession, which is the basis of power. It relies upon impassable boundaries, or exclusion. I keep *you* out of what is *mine*. What is *mine* makes *me*. But it is a goal of the major religions to transcend that superficial *me* rooted in possession and exclusion and power in order to reach the true Self, which is rooted in commonality rather than exclusion, *our* rather than *my*. Paradoxically, this means not losing our selfhood but gaining it. Our Self is larger than we thought.

Think of this prayer as being handed to you somewhere else in the world. You are living in a forest by the side of a mountain, and you know nothing of civilization, or of human history outside of your valley. You know nothing of what scholars think they know of first-century Palestinian religion, or sects, or rabbis. All you have is this text, beginning with the world "our."

All of us are in this position. We look at the text, we know that "our" means us, and we pray. It is the same everywhere, for everyone.

A biblical text in the hands of scholars is like a ball of yarn in a litter of kittens: someone or other has disputed the authenticity of every word of the prayer except "Father" (the most problematic word). Fortunately, the whole prayer is contained in this word.

The beginning of the prayer addresses our deepest terror: Am I alone? With two words Jesus answers the question of our vast, deep, star-filled nights: "Our Father" means we are not alone. It can be a startling experience to realize that someone is with us. Possibly we have believed in a false isolation that permits us to violate ourselves and others. This belief or despair gives rise to a sense of separation that drives us to be selfish and therefore self-destructive; it creates the possessiveness, insecurity, jealousy, and rage that can make life miserable. Down through history we have projected such personality traits onto God as well; therefore Jesus is going to jolt us out of some Old Testament preconceptions of God by a word substitution—"our" for "my"—that should boggle our minds. Many of Jesus' contemporaries would have considered this word criminally offensive if the circle of "our" were drawn too large. The very first word of the prayer gets us into difficulty if we want to make restrictions, draw boundary lines, and decide who is in and who is out.

We should be quick to rule out a wrong understanding of this phrase, namely, that God is ours—as if we could keep the deity in a magic lamp to bring out whenever we want something, or whenever we wish to persuade people of our piety. Americans are individualists, and we believe in possessions. Therefore, whether we realize it or not, we sometimes think of God as our particular and personal possession. "My god is an awesome god. Your god watches Lawrence Welk."

If we picture our next-door neighbor as also having a magic lamp, we can more easily understand why the possession idea is wrong. Does God love that neighbor as much as God loves us? Is God personal to him or her? Would God forgive our neighbor's sins? Is our relationship to God of higher quality? We could replace that next-door neighbor with any political candidate of a party opposed to ours, and ask the same questions.

If our answers to any of the above suggest inequality between ourselves and somebody else, we might have an eentsy little problem. The Lord's Prayer helps to cure that problem.

*

"Our" is the doorway to the Lord's Prayer. It is
- an assurance of the grace of God
- an assertion of God's love
- a reminder that God is sovereign, and that God's way lasts

- an assurance that we are not alone
- a friendly recommendation that we love our neighbor

Taking these in order, we first have an assurance of God's grace. "Our Father" relates us to God. The term "father" has the effect of pinning that relationship into our minds. It is like a family relationship; it cannot be broken.

> "Home is the place where, when you have to go there,
> They have to take you in."[1]

So is the Kingdom of Heaven, because we are part of God's family. Jesus told us to pray this way, so it is not a presumption on our part. Jesus could have used the words "King," "Master," or even "Friend"; but this is a relationship that cannot be broken—certainly not by us. We cannot arouse God's anger to the point of our being made no longer God's children. This is reassuring to those of us who are imperfect, and it has deep and startling implications. One of them is to put people who draw religious boundaries out of business. That is one reason why authorities considered Jesus an enemy.

So even if we sin, God is our Father, a parent—even if we commit infractions against the rules, and if we fail to love. God remains our parent; we can still go home.

Nobody can get in the way of that parent-child relationship. We do not need to worry about whether we think the right thoughts about God: our doctrine can be impure, we can be in error, we can be uninformed, or we might simply disagree with the beliefs of whatever branch of the Church we have wandered into. Troubling as this point of view has always been to some religious professionals, it is an immense comfort to ordinary people. It should even prove to be of comfort to religious authorities, because most if not all of them are wrong. They have to be, because they all disagree. In fact, you could define "religious authority" as "one who disagrees with other religious authorities on points of theology." "Religious authorities" is a comfortable oxymoron. Such people are often in error, but seldom in doubt. Doubt is an embarrassment to the self-righteous "saved." But no matter how much we doubt, and no matter what we doubt, we can still pray the Lord's Prayer, and therefore say "Our Father." Do we make our children think the right ideas in order to stay our children?

God's grace saves us, and God's love does not depend upon conditions. I suppose that relying on this steadfast love leaves us less to do. Lots of religious theory is generated in order to relieve boredom. The most intense

---

1. Frost, *Collected Poems*, 43.

doctrine, the most burning true believers, can be found in the world's most boring places. But Christianity has a better cure for boredom: love thy neighbor. We can invest our time in thinking right, or we can invest it in doing good: I do not suppose we are flush enough to do both.[2]

The heart of the Christian faith is God's love. It is the heart of the Christian understanding of God. So the prayer Jesus taught us is an expression of that love, an exercise of the child's relationship on our part, and also the keynote of Jesus' proclamation of the Kingdom of God. "Our Father" is the leading statement of the prayer's description of God. It puts all other religious thought and action into perspective. Everything else should be tested against this primary statement.

Here we arrive at the necessity to consider that phrase, "concept of God." Our knowledge of God cannot be primarily conceptual. It is imaginative and sometimes relational. God is larger than a thought and cannot be a mere object of thought. The Master of the Universe is larger than any idea of God. We base our imaginations of God, along with whatever concepts we conceive, upon our parents. To have grown up with bad parents affects how we conceive of and imagine God, whether we know better or not. An angry, tyrannical parent tends to put us off from God, whom we can only with great difficulty resist thinking of as a tyrant. If parents are bad, then we tend to want nothing to do with God, whom Jesus in this prayer refers to as "Father."

The Lord's Prayer allows us to imagine Jesus' picture of the Father, and not our own. Jesus' picture is positive; it is what every child dreams of and no child fully gets. This picture delineated by the prayer is of a father who nourishes us, forgives us, and protects us. The Father of Jesus is both the ideal father and the ideal mother. While Jesus uses the word "father," what we see of Jesus' Father comes through this prayer and through comparisons made in parables and figures of speech: God is portrayed as a woman finding a lost coin, a shepherd searching for and even sacrificing himself for a lamb, as bread, as water, and even as a mother hen. In fact the pictures Jesus shares of God show anything but a harsh, tyrannical, jealous Nobadaddy.[3] The murderous Old Testament figure that Mark Twain so vividly excoriated is not represented in Jesus' words, or in Jesus himself: that figure is represented by the religious and imperial authorities, of whom Jesus was an innocent victim. In the Garden of Gethsemane, Jesus does not succumb to the will of a tyrannical father, but makes his Father's will his own, which

---

2. It is noble to do right. It is nobler to think right, and no trouble. (Apologies to Mark Twain.)

3. "Nobadaddy" is William Blake's name for the false, tyrannical god sometimes pictured in the Old Testament.

in his case means assuming the role of God himself—and that is a role of acceptance, suffering, and renunciation of power and authority.

That Jesus substituted "father" for "God" or the unpronounced Hebrew name "YHWH" is one of the most significant elements of his prayer. Jesus opted away from some Old Testament images of God, which (alternating with loving images such as we see in Psalms and Hosea) sometimes invoked associations with the worst human fathers imaginable: punitive, violent, unpredictable, demanding, and heartless. What does this new designation mean? What did "father" mean to Jesus, and what was the picture Jesus meant to pass along to us?

Human femininity and masculinity can be misleading when applied to God as pictured by the Jesus of the gospels. The portrait we have of Jesus of Nazareth contains elements of what have been stereotypical masculine characteristics, and stereotypical feminine characteristics. While masculine in gender, he was not the stereotypical unfeeling or domineering male any more than God is the typical earthly father.[4] The gospels' portrait of God in Jesus includes and transcends both genders, so "father" could imply "parent."

The parental figure of speech suggests the idea of family, but it replaces our experience of family with our deepest wishes for family. It restores our childhood view of mother and father, the view we cherished before we awoke

---

4. In Western culture, females are typically considered to be more religious, more prone to prayer, and more interested in spirituality. Women are typified as nurturing, whereas men value self-reliance: but Jesus is the Bread of Life, draws the little children to himself, feeds the multitudes, forgives, heals, and touches the sick and unclean. On the other hand, Jesus, like a first century soldier, was willing to say that his teachings would bring not peace, but a sword; and the exorcisms described in Mark's gospel picture a world at war, with Jesus as the high command. Still, this power comes from love, like the care of the best parents for their children, and is for us, not against us. The typical male is assertive and authoritarian, believing in physical force; but such traits characterize Jesus' enemies and killers, not the one who says "Come unto me, all ye who are burdened and heavy-laden, and I will give you rest." (Matt 11:28, KJV) Jesus travels with many people in the social fashion that is often associated with femininity, though sometimes more in "masculine" fashion he goes off alone—but that is to pray, a more typically "feminine" activity. Females tend to accomplish their purposes more through talk than through physical action, and we see Jesus teaching throughout the gospels. His physical actions—excepting the driving of money changers out of the Temple—are healing, touching, and distributing food. Creativity is considered to be a feminine characteristic: Jesus creates new social relations that change the world; he invents stories. Females tend to emphasize bonds of feeling, while men typically prefer to act independently; females are more empathetic and compassionate than males: "Do to others as you would have them do to you;" "Greater love hath no man than this, to lay down his life for his friends." Men hold in their feelings like good Romans, but the shortest and one of the most potent verses in the Bible is, "Jesus wept." (Matt 7: 12, NRSV; John 15:13, KJV; John 11:35, KJV)

to the humanity of our parents. The familiar term *Abba* or "Papa" does this. Our earthly siblings and parents and children might be as maladjusted as we are, but the phrase "in heaven" (or the word "heavenly") puts our idea of family into the mode of imagination. Under God's wise and kind parentage, we all have a new family, one that is being perfected by the Holy Spirit. The child-parent relationship will not be broken; we will not be deserted by the parent who, like the loving father in the parable of the prodigal son, takes us back, holding out his arms and letting us weep on his shoulder, while he weeps too.

But let us take up the idea of God's authority. I usually think of authority in a bad light, as something basically illegitimate and aimed against me. Authority prevents me from doing what I want, generally because what I want is a comedy of errors. We fail to realize that getting everything we want usually entails acting like childish idiots, directly or indirectly. What we do has consequences against other people and we seldom think far enough to envision those consequences. I would like to go to the nearest Mercedes-Benz dealership and take one. The authorities prevent me from doing so, and therefore I resent anything having to do with authority. I do not realize that if we all went to those dealerships and tried to take a Benz, the shortage of Benzes would immediately make itself felt and the streets would be full of weeping humanity. However, I am not arguing in favor of authority. Whether they are just or unjust, necessary or intrusive, our reactions to them mold our idea of authority and so influence our notion of the authority of God.

Jesus conceives of God's authority as essentially in our favor. And the power behind God's authority is love, not force. It is truth, not coercion; mercy, not punishment. It changes things by creating rather than by destroying. The power and authority of God in Jesus is gentle and irresistible, like that of an ideal parent, "full of grace and truth."

Authority in God does not refer primarily to what we are prohibited from doing. Certainly there are prohibitions, but that is not the essential authority of a parent. The fact comes first: this is our parent. In other words, God's authority means that God's love for us will win out. The idea of "father" uses the cultural situation of Jesus' times: the father has the authority in the family. But that authority commits the parent to us in love. Our Father is on our side; when we are embattled, we know the Father's presence as the sound of rescue, "the horn of my salvation." *If God be for us, who can be against us?*[5]

The point is that our heavenly Father's authority will prevail. God wills only goodness for us. This evil-ridden world is pockmarked with tragedy

---

5. Rom 8:31, KJV.

and horror, but God's authority outlasts everything. Our relationship with this world and this life will be broken, but our relationship with God will not; and what God values, what God wishes, will last. "Goodness is the only investment that never fails,"[6] and that is because God is our parent, the mother and father that we wish we had and wish we were, only better, infinitely better, now and forever: "There is nothing in death or life, in the realm of spirits or superhuman powers, in the world as it is or the world as it shall be, in the forces of the universe, in heights or depths—nothing in all creation that can separate us from the love of God . . ."[7]

When we kill and destroy, we act on our own authority; i.e., on no authority. God's authority is an assurance. Things are very bad. We are surrounded by heartless men with accurate firearms; they shoot our mothers, our children, our wives, and our husbands. This is an era of terrorism, random violent rages, and threats of war all over the world. We have become each other's enemies, and show no remorse or mercy.

But we are not alone. "Our" is a reassuring word, as "my" would be terrifying. "My" would mean possession as well as solitude: God would be my own; but if God is ours, then I am not in possession. Once we break through the selfish desire to have God all to ourselves and exclude our wrongheaded neighbor, we receive the assurance that we are not in hell. The picture of hell painted by its greatest imaginer, Dante, shows multitudes of people, but not in each other's company. The essential isolation of each person in hell is more terrifying than his or her individual heinous punishment. But as long as we can pray "our" and "Father," we are not alone. Jesus is always opening his arms and bringing in the family. The alienation and separation of sin are overcome. In sharing the love of God, we receive the full measure of it ourselves: we no longer need to hoard like insecure children, sitting alone in corners. The hand of Jesus reaching to us with a solid carpenter's grip is somehow the hand of God; it is "our Father."

Who are the *us* implied? Is it our family, our fellow Americans, our local church? The family Jesus has in mind is the family of faith, the children of God in the arms of the Church. *Extra ecclesiam nulla salus* (outside the Church there is no salvation). All right. Keep in mind, however, that Jesus' idea of the Church and your and my ideas might not match. Are Episcopalians or Pentecostals included? Are Hindus, Buddhists, or Muslims? What about atheists? Is that pastor who preaches snake handling included, or the liberal who wears chartreuse clerical shirts? Jesus dismissed all these considerations because his Kingdom of God has no boundaries. It is not an earthly

---

6. Thoreau, *Walden*, 213.
7. Rom 8:38–39, REB.

kingdom, with borders. It would not be God's kingdom if it had boundaries. So it is fine to think of the "our" of the Lord's Prayer as including only the Church—as long as the Church includes everyone. In Matthew's gospel, Peter is given the keys of the kingdom of heaven, and the authority to bind and to loose, and then is told to go get everybody.

I think this would be a healthy principle to adopt: None of us will be there until all of us are there—until everyone is given their welcome, their chance to enter the kingdom of heaven. We must grow to tolerate the idea of everyone finding an open door if they want it. I do not insist that this principle is correct, only that it is less prone to aggressive error than some others I have heard. It is a good principle to act upon. A minister read a letter from a parishioner to us on a recent Sunday morning. The parishioner began her letter by regretting that the minister was not going to be in heaven with her. His answer, which at first might have sounded cheeky, was, "Well, then it wouldn't be heaven, would it?" But he did not mean that he is such a swell individual that heaven would be tarnished without his presence, but that hell is the place with a gate. Not only are heaven's borders open; it is among us already.

Therefore "our Father" is a gracious reminder to love our neighbor. The kingdom of God is completely voluntary in that those who awaken to it want to be there. Perhaps there are some who choose to remain asleep: the choice is theirs, and perhaps God does not make their choice for them. It would seem that if the kingdom is love, then those who hate would not want to be in the kingdom any more than they would belong there. The more unselfishly we love, the more awake we are, and the more heavenly our home. Those within the kingdom love each other as our heavenly parent loves us. Again, the more unselfishly we love, the happier we are. We can detest our siblings and be miserable, or we can love them and be happy. Why not start now? In fact Jesus says, "Start now. Here is the kingdom." The difficulty of starting now is monumental, of course. Perhaps that is why things are so slow.

As the kingdom of God is within and among us already, perhaps hell is also. The first person singular is the hell in which each of us dwells. It is a hell that Christianity wishes to empty. It is difficult to pray "our Father" without meaning "my Father," but when we say "my," first person singular, we do not pray Jesus' prayer. Praying the prayer that Jesus gave us, not our own edition, begins from the very first word to purify our desires. It enlarges and develops our capacity to love. In the praying, the prayer becomes its own answer.

The prayer begins to free us from ourselves. It secures us in a family. It asks for shared daily bread. It asks for the forgiveness that comes as we forgive others. It wants *us,* not just you or me, to be saved from temptation and delivered from evil. It prevents us from confusing freedom with individualism.

The most preventable disease from which we die is absence of love, and this can be illustrated at all stages of life. An infant dies if not held; a child turns destructive without love; an adult becomes depressed and ill and crazy without a friend or family or someone to love; and without God's love at the end, we could be doomed to the final isolation, the ultimate individuality, which is no existence at all. We never have had existence entirely by ourselves, no matter what we might think: our distinct personalities are made real and developed only in relation to others.

I would imagine that the only reason some religious hermits survive decades of isolation more or less whole is that they have the company of God. Probably most of them go at least a little peculiar. Jesus does not ask us to fight our battles alone. Our greatest enemy—ourselves—has been put into the hands of others; and this power has been dissipated among all whom "our" includes. By making us speak correctly, God calls, gathers, and enlightens the children of His dreams.

The more expansive our conception of "our," the larger our imagination of God. If we imagine a god of kindred, tribe, or nation only, we suffer the consequences of serving an idol. The idol of a tribe or nation is a very jealous god indeed, angry and demanding, brutal and hard to please, a Big Jerk. So we become little jerks; and it is very difficult for jerks to include and love other people. The Bible points out that those who worship idols become like them. We conform to the god/God we worship; let us be deliberate.

A larger vision of God sees vast multitudes as God's children. God becomes the Creator, not a ticket collector. The prayer directs our attention outward immediately. Only this way can we make the proper address to *God*, the Master of the Universe. Awe and respect and praise are contained in this word "our." The sorrow and evil we cause, we cause through our selfishness and the desires with which it infects us. Looking outward puts us on the road to health.

From the start, everything asked in the Lord's Prayer is held in common. Nothing is mine; everything is ours. We can have it all, or we can have nothing. The condition of having it all is that we share. Share the abundance, or lose the last bit finally. "To those who have, more will be given."[8] Everything or nothing.

There is only one God in the universe and it is not our superficial, false selves. Each of the world's great religions in its own way tries to overcome

---

8. Luke 8:18, NRSV.

selfishness and its resulting pain and destructiveness. In Hinduism, Buddhism, and Taoism we have the way of union with reality through discipline, awareness, and mindfulness; the way of service to others; the way of non-attachment to the illusory objects of desire; and the way of emptying the false and isolated self in order to realize the true Self that is one with the foundation of being. Islam teaches submission, the taming of the selfish will. Old Testament Judaism is constant and merciless in its persecution of idolatry, the tendency to place our own false and invented gods before the One. Christianity in its harsher forms teaches that the idol with which we try to replace God is ourselves, cruel and jealous beyond belief; in its more generous forms, Christianity preaches an expansive love that values others no less than we are to value ourselves. To the degree that our religion is a way to get what we want, we are trying to keep the idol of our false self in the way of God. This self is false because it has been constructed of desire, opinion, fear, hatred, and illness. But the word "father" gives us our true place in a reality so kind that its best image is that of an ideal family.

The word "our" helps us to work out a problem in the New Testament pertaining to this prayer. Luke (in most authoritative manuscript versions) has simply "Father;" whereas Matthew has "Our Father." Keeping the implications of "our" in mind, we see that this minor discrepancy is no discrepancy at all, concerning meaning. "Father" implies "our" rather than "my": even if we did not correctly understand the whole idea of community and sharing, we could see that the rest of the prayer uses "us" instead of "me." So Luke, handling a word or phrase that was a translation from Jesus' Aramaic (a language descended from Hebrew), casts it into the same meaning that Matthew did, only a little more economically.

Did Jesus use the Aramaic word *Abba*? It is a familiar name, like "Papa" or "Dad," that would be used as a form of address within a family, rather than a term objectively denoting a man's legal or biological relationship to his child. This "far surpasses any possibilities of intimacy assumed in Judaism. . . "[9] No one can be certain that Jesus said *Abba*; however, it is a reasonable guess, consistent with the relationship Jesus assumed between God and God's people. Though we cannot take for granted anything beyond or behind the Greek texts of Matthew and Luke, there are benefits that accrue from conceiving of a very familiar form of address, not the least of which is humility. The name "Papa" is used by children. When we come to God, we are not five-star generals, business executives, or religious authorities; we are children. Remembering this prevents some mistakes. The familiar term also suggests and fosters a sense of the love between parent and child.

9. Kittel, *Theological Dictionary of the New Testament* I, 6.

Our Father

Matthew writes "Our Father in heaven," while Luke has simply "Father," with no "in heaven" appearing except in relatively few of the old manuscripts. Possibly Luke considered this to be understood; at least equally possible is that Jesus' original version was simply "Father" or "Our Father," and Matthew added "in heaven" or "who art in heaven" because his Jewish background made him sensitive to addressing God with maximal deference. Why not use whichever version we wish? They are both in the New Testament.

There was no biography of Jesus, existing like some solid object for the gospel writers to examine. Matthew and Luke had to collect and sift a verbal bushel of reports, sorting what they wanted to use for their readers and what they did not want to use, deciding what was reliable and useful and what was not, and perhaps most difficult of all, placing things into a sequence of events—a chronology, a story. Each gospel is incomplete and partial, undeniably inspired but certainly human at the same time. Scribes then copied manuscripts by hand for more than a thousand years, so there might well be a problem or discrepancy, an error, here and there. Fortunately, the love of God does not depend on the ideas of Christian theologians or biblical scholars, or even on the Bible itself.

The problems of what to make of Jesus, for whom we had no categories, comparisons, or precedents, and how to reconcile the early Christians' experiences with what we thought we knew about God, are not surmountable by the human mind. It seems to be our nature to try, however, even at the risk of mistaking our attempts for the reality they try to explain. Faith will seek understanding. How the gospel writers tried to represent Jesus is a version of how people in the Western traditions tried to represent God, and they came up with a similar variety of answers. Do not try to represent God at all, says Islam, not in pictures, statues, or icons. Judaism enacted a similar impulse: do not even pronounce the holy name, and as for that name, say only that our God is who God is ("I Am That I Am").

Most of Christianity has gone a different way, with its profusion of artistic images, philosophic descriptions, and theological definitions. It is natural that Christianity should do this, because for a Christian, God has been experienced as personal, and has already been represented in very concrete terms by Jesus of Nazareth. These are human and earthly terms. Jesus himself spoke of God in many ways: as a shepherd, a vine, a woman searching for a coin, a dove, an unjust judge, a loving father of a prodigal son, a vineyard owner. Jesus uses abstractions: the Way, the Truth, the Life. He makes inanimate comparisons: a door or gate, for example. In the Old Testament there are many images:

> The Lord is my rock, and my fortress, and my deliverer; my God, my strength, in whom I will trust; my buckler, and the horn of my salvation, and my high tower.[10]

Non-human images of God are risky business, because in Old Testament times many idols were non-human—a Golden Calf, a tree, or a stone—just as now our idols are cars and electronics.

Some language about God recorded in the Old Testament suggests a form for God beyond all comparison and precedent. The prophet Ezekiel received a vision of God, which he very carefully recorded, giving the exact time and place of his experience. This is how he remembered what he saw:

> As I looked, a stormy wind came out of the north: a great cloud with brightness around it and fire flashing forth continually, and in the middle of the fire, something like gleaming amber. In the middle of it was something like four living creatures. This was their appearance: they were of human form. Each had four faces, and each of them had four wings. Their legs were straight, and the soles of their feet were like the sole of a calf's foot; and they sparkled like burnished bronze. Under their wings on their four sides they had human hands. And the four had their faces and their wings thus: their wings touched one another; each of them moved straight ahead, without turning as they moved. As for the appearance of their faces: the four had the face of a human being, the face of a lion on the right side, the face of an ox on the left side, and the face of an eagle; such were their faces. Their wings were spread out above; each creature had two wings, each of which touched the wing of another, while two covered their bodies. Each moved straight ahead; wherever the spirit would go, they went, without turning as they went. In the middle of the living creatures there was something that looked like burning coals of fire, like torches moving to and fro among the living creatures; the fire was bright, and lightning issued from the fire. The living creatures darted to and fro, like a flash of lightning.[11]

Notable to this description are the phrases "something like," "something that looked like," and "like." Nearly everything described is preceded with one of those qualifiers. Ezekiel saw something that was not anything he had seen before, and he knew he was not looking at a lion, ox, or really four creatures at all, but "something like" those things; and in or from their midst came an illumination that looked like—yet was not—coals of fire, or

---

10. Ps 18:2, KJV.
11. Ezek 1:4–14, NRSV.

torches. In other words, he knows he is groping for comparisons and words; he is not able to say *literally* what he saw because God was presenting him with a mask, with symbols, with appearances. A human being cannot look straight at God, as God is, without the intermediaries of visions, appearances, and the things of this world through which God becomes visible to us. A direct vision of God would be too much for us, and it would not be containable in our limited minds. So, just as Jesus told parables—stories of comparison—to convey a point, so God gives us some kind of face that we can experience and fit into our brains. The idea of God as Father is one such face.

It seems to me that any image of God, whether it be as a man or as a woman, a father or a mother, or a hen searching for her young, is temporary. It is optional, flexible, interchangeable. It is an example of planned obsolescence. When Jesus referred to God as "father," he gave us a symbol applicable to this particular use. It was a way of saying that we are inseparably God's, that God cares for us like a parent, and perhaps that God also has authority in the way a father has authority in a first-century Mediterranean family. This authority is the final appeal in resolving disputes; it establishes rules of conduct, and gives definitive directions regarding the lives of children. But the difference is that this father is "heavenly."

Though many people have a difficult time imaginatively relating to God because their bad earthly fathers have gotten in the way, one tends to imagine God somehow. The Lord's Prayer seeks to heal our imaginations. It replaces the nightmares of our childhoods with our gentlest and bravest dreams. The image of God—the face suggested by the Lord's Prayer—is that of the Beloved, the Lover of our souls—the One who is not domineering, violent, unpredictable, uncaring, demanding, or abusive. He is the One who gives everything, gives his very life for us, and for our faults and selfishness returns only unfailing love, like some wonderful, perfect, *heavenly* parent.

This Father is noble and pure and good enough that we wish his very name to be revered—one whom we trust so much that we wish his will to be done everywhere at all times, one who gives us all we need, one who forgives us in the same cheerful and complete way we forgive others when we truly do it, and one who shields us from temptation and evil. This is the perfect father of a dream, the Father whose dreams we are.

This is the Father, as Jesus knows him. That is why Jesus loved without limit and without boundaries, and why Jesus could teach and heal. Knowing such a Father, can we not do the same? Can we not heal each other's imaginations, teach the wisdom of love to life's wounded, and live perfectly aware of the kingdom of God? For the survival of humanity, there is no alternative.

There is a stunning revelation in the eighth chapter of Luke. In that chapter we have a rising crescendo of "mighty works" by Jesus. Luke has put together four reports of Jesus' actions, and has arranged them in such a way as to illuminate their significance. In Luke 8 we start with the mention of women who accompanied Jesus and the disciples—perhaps a miracle in itself, considering the times—and then we move to Jesus teaching by telling parable stories (The Sower, The Lamp); then we see that Jesus opens up the concept of his family, beyond blood ties. From there we have three miracle stories (or four if we separate the last two). First Jesus calms a storm. After that, Jesus cures a demon-possessed man whose case had been impossible. And then we get this final occurrence, in which Jesus and his disciples enter a town and are met by a crowd waiting to see the renowned rabbi and healer. Among the crowd is a man whose station as leader of the synagogue puts him above the others socially and economically. As a religious leader, he is dignified and has his place to consider. But he does something shocking: he humbles himself in front of his townspeople by throwing himself at the feet of Jesus. A leader of the synagogue should not act like this; furthermore, he should retain the critical stance of religious authority in the face of this popular preacher who seems not to respect traditional differences among people. But he not only falls at Jesus' feet, he "begs" Jesus *to come to his house*. You can bet that leaders of synagogues did not commonly invite itinerant preachers, with their students and even female hangers-on, to enter their houses. But he *begs* Jesus. He wants Jesus to help his twelve-year old daughter, who is sick to the point of death.

This is Luke's picture of a father. It must be one of the most moving pictures of a father ever written. The man has abased himself, completely disregarding his dignity. He would do anything for his beloved child. This picture of a father's love should be applied to the Lord's Prayer. The father loves with complete abandon.

But there is more. Now Jesus is going to the man's house. Crowds walk with him, pressing around him, and someone in that crowd touches Jesus. Touch is important. It is an unclean woman—considered "unclean" in terms of the religion's purity laws—because she has a flow of blood, an unceasing hemorrhage. She comes up behind Jesus merely to touch the edge of his robe, hoping for a cure.

Mark tells us that she has spent all her money on doctors, who have been unable to cure her. (Luke, himself a physician, appears to have left out this uncomplimentary detail, though it is present in some ancient manuscripts of his gospel.) The woman is desperate; she also, like the religious man's daughter, has a life-endangering illness. So she touches a rabbi!

Jesus halts. "Who touched me?" The crowd expects an outraged rebuke. The poor woman, "trembling," pushes toward him and falls at his feet. She confesses that she did it. She says that she has felt a change inside her. Now people know for certain that an unclean woman has touched the rabbi.

Jesus' first word is: "Daughter." He says, "Daughter, your faith has made you well; go in peace." Then Jesus moves on. Imagine how the people must have hesitated a moment, for one last look at the woman. "Daughter."

Jesus comes to the house and enters it, but is told that the girl is dead. (You can almost hear the father's wail of anguish.) Jesus enters the room where the girl's pale body lies stark and motionless on the bed. Only three disciples and the parents are with him. A dead body is ritually unclean. If possible, this is worse than a bleeding woman. Jesus takes up her hand and says, "Child . . ." She breathes, and sits up. Like a parent, Jesus says that she should be given something to eat.

Jesus has called the woman "Daughter," and has called the girl "Child." Now we know what "Father" means in the Lord's Prayer. "I and my Father are one."[12]

*

In calling us not servants of the Almighty and Everlasting and Omnipotent God, but children of the heavenly Father, Jesus tells us that we are born of mystery. Abandon what you know about everything, including fathers, as you enter. "Father" for "God"?

The strangeness of that word for God must be recaptured. We employ it all the time if we pray the Lord's Prayer, and we have become used to it. We are accustomed to the Almighty God being our Father! God becomes so close with that word that a true and complete experience of it in all its paradox and impossibility would spring us into a Zen-like awakening. It could bring us to a reality more familiar and final than we can imagine. The word "father" is closer than reason or the historical record permit.

What I mean is that for Jesus, the Father was the perfect and only genuine reality. Jesus' Father did not give him everything he wanted. Here is the most abusive father on record, if we want to figure it in our own terms: He committed Jesus to an undeserved death, (according to Christian doctrine) heaping upon him for good measure all the sins of the world. Jesus experienced a oneness with the Father beyond all human experience; and at the same time felt "forsaken" upon the cross. Our categories of kindness, abuse, indulgence, and the rest do not fit in this case. A person with a benevolent

---

12. John 10:30, KJV.

earthly father is just as lost here as someone with a ragingly abusive one. Jesus' term *Abba* seems quite understandable, but it is at the same time an utterly alien word. We have no equivalent in our heads; there is no concept for this, only the immediate relationship, as was the case with Jesus.

Christianity is at home with such paradoxes as the majesty and immediacy of God, and the tragedy and beatitude of Jesus' relationship with the father. We are faced with both the terrible remorselessness of the sacrifice of Jesus, and the joy of Jesus' oneness with the Father. If such paradoxes were not at the core of Christianity, the Christian faith would be a mere brew of human knowledge and experience, at best an apotheosis of wisdom and wishes. But to be a Christian believer is to trust that there is a transcendent but present, and more real, world than the one we usually see—the usual world that logic is made to work on and figure out. Paradoxes can jar us out of this less real world, reminding us of the higher reality, the higher dimension, where "Father" is no longer so absolutely nonsensical when the word is applied between God and us.

What is stranger than being children of the unknown? What is truer? We hardly know our earthly fathers, except in the limited and fantastic ways that children know their parents. We do not know the young man who was our father, the man who courted our unknown young mother; and we do not know the internal father, his fears and worries. He surprises us by bringing home an ulcer one day. If we do not know our mother and dad, how then shall we know the Ancient of Days? Yet the Holy One is our Father.

This idea of God as Father is Jesus' most radical teaching. From it comes all the Christian faith with its theology, its goodness, and its questions. In this word is the pathos and tragedy of the crucifixion on Good Friday and the beautiful life and appearances of Jesus afterward. Everything in our Christian belief and practice, and in our theological arguments, must be tested and measured against this one teaching. From this one word, "Father," comes Christianity's creeds, ethics, and understanding of sin, forgiveness, and salvation. In this word is the mystery that Jesus presents to each of us.

From this word also comes our understanding of eternity. In the religion of Jesus, though it is too intimate to be called a "religion," eternity is not an abstraction, something with which philosophers are more at home than the rest of us. Eternity is familial and intimate. We are children of the eternal. Being children of the eternal, and travelers in time, we ourselves are a paradox. The rest of the prayer might be understood and prayed in this light.

We do not know "eternity" as a concept; it makes no sense. Eternity has to be in The Eternal somehow, in God, in a way similar to Jesus saying

"I am the resurrection and the life." I am eternity, he says. We are eternity's children.

If we kept in mind that we are made by and for eternity, we would change the way we act. Ethics tend to be based on the following appeal: Remember that you will die someday. But perhaps we should say, Remember that you will live forever. In the *Iliad* and the *Odyssey*, the Greek gods struggle with each other and yet ultimately have to get along. All they do is done with the knowledge that they will have to live with each other forever. None of them is going away anytime soon. If we would think of ourselves and each other that way, we might hesitate before committing the petty, nasty, and unforgivable things we do and say to each other. Nobody is going away.

*

A theological interlude. It is time to have fun again, to live again. Let us consider the doctrine of the Trinity—the basic Christian mystery that experiences God as One in three "persons": Father, Son, Holy Spirit. According to this doctrine, God is not an isolated figure. God is somehow relational: One, yet not single. Something about the essence of God is social: "God is love."

Jesus prayed. Yet when a person somehow experiences Jesus alive, it becomes virtually impossible to think of Jesus as a human being only. It becomes natural to associate Jesus, in some way however unclear, with the supernatural and with divinity. It is interesting that we have made rules for God. Philosophically, we might insist that "God cannot break his own laws." I wonder if God knows this. The ultimate logical insistence is that "God cannot be God and not-God." "What is the sound of one hand clapping?" is a famous Zen *koan,* or riddle meant to awaken a person to enlightenment. "Jesus prayed" might be a Christian equivalent.

God does not have gender; God is like a king and like a dove, and like neither; God forsakes and God is close; God is a woman searching for a coin and God has the wings of an eagle, but is neither beast nor human; God counts every hair on our heads but God also leads his very, true, human son-like self to the cross; God dies and God is eternal: confronting the fact that *our idea of God is not God* can be shattering. Actual experiences of God tend to shred our ideas and break our idols.

After an experience of God, we employ reason in an attempt to make the experience intellectually manageable. Theology is talk about the ineffable. But as our images of God are not God, so our theologies are not divine. The rational willingness to consider irrational reality is necessary in contemporary physics and is respectable there, even geeky cool. There might be alternate universes. A particle can be located but its speed cannot be measured; or if its speed is measured, then it cannot be located. To maintain what Keats called "negative capability," to hold one's own ideas in suspension, is both a reverent and a rational point of view. Such a willingness to simply look at our experience regardless of whether or not it makes sense right now enables us to grow. Our intellects were made or evolved for something: they keep us operational in this world; they check raging emotions and self-destructive psychoses. But these intellects of ours—which Mark Twain suggested that the Deity does not sit up nights to admire—should be able to recognize their own limitations. "My thoughts are not your thoughts," Old Testament prophecy reminds us.[13]

With the human mind we have a useful tool when applied to its proper objects. God is not one of its proper objects. Our *arguments* about God are proper objects of logic; our *assertions* about God are proper objects for debate; our ethics and our philosophies and our science are proper objects of the mind. But God is not an object of the human mind. We can try; it seems to be our nature to try; but God in all God's intimacy with us is outside the circumference of our mental universe.

We are floating in our own indefinability, and from that unsteady platform we attempt to get a fix on God. From minds reeling in the fog of existence we project a God we call immutable, all-powerful, good, and all-knowing. Ultimately it does not all hold together: one dead child contradicts calm assertions about the nature of God.

It is at least as difficult to explain what we call the good in this life as it is to explain the bad. How can one logically deduce our happiness from the universe out there?—the unimaginably vast stretches of intergalactic distance punctuated by black holes and stupendously violent flame, beautiful from a distance but infinitesimally miniaturizing the human world.

> When I look at your heavens, the work of your fingers,
> and the moon and the stars that you have established,
> what are human beings that you are mindful of them,
> mortals that you care for them?[14]

But the fact is that we do experience God. Despite the overwhelming logic, God does take note of us, and sometimes we cannot help but conclude that God does care for us.

---

13. Isa 55:8, KJV.
14. Ps 8: 3–4, KJV.

The answer to our philosophical and theological questions is the love of God. Perhaps, as Pascal says, the heart has its reasons, that reason does not know.

So where does this discussion put us? I think it places us in Jesus' prayer like little children in the presence of God. Prayer is difficult to understand, perhaps impossible to understand. But as Karl Barth said about preaching, it is both impossible and necessary. We do not understand God or God's relationship to the pain of this world. But we go on living; we go on praying. Perhaps we will find the answers and understand it all one day, and perhaps not. Live and pray.

*

I have implied skepticism about the power of the rational mind to solve the problem of pain, or to approach very near to God. However, this skepticism presents its own problems. How can we recognize the limitations of reason without putting ourselves at the mercy of anyone who wants to claim historical inerrancy for his Bible, or who insists that unquestioned obedience to the Pope or Church doctrine is what God requires of us? Could someone not say that biblical inerrancy is a mysterious truth beyond reason? In other words, are we not to use reason at all, as our faith seeks understanding? I think the answer is that we can and must use reason to refute reason; we use logic to refute bogus arguments. The doctrines of the Trinity and the Incarnation are not arguments; the claim of biblical inerrancy is.[15]

*

---

15. Inerrancy is an argument with steps leading to a conclusion, and the steps can be examined, the conclusion standing or falling depending upon whether the steps were valid. For example: "St. Paul says that all Scripture is inspired; inspired means inerrant; therefore all Scripture is inerrant." Each step is false, as is the unstated premise, namely that everything St. Paul says is inspired. First, Paul's claim does not cover the New Testament; furthermore, he admits that at least some of what he writes does not come from God. Second, "inspired" does not mean "inerrant." Third, if Scripture claimed it was inerrant, the argument would be self-referential (like a Cretan saying "All Cretans are liars") and therefore without meaning. Fourth, the entire reasoning process here is circular: St. Paul is inerrant concerning Scripture because St. Paul is Scripture and Scripture is inerrant. Therefore the conclusion here is invalid. An argument was implied in the claim for inerrancy, but the argument *as argument* was invalid. The Incarnation, on the other hand, is not an argument but a claim. It is as if the Incarnation were an axiom, beyond or behind proof; but inerrancy is subject to proof or disproof.

For Jesus, prayer realizes a relationship. Maybe our relationships with God are miniatures of the Trinity idea; that is, we are estranged from God, and at the same time essentially related to God.

Jesus' concept of God is clearly implied by Jesus' own intentions: God is benign toward human beings. God means to do us only good. God is love. Not all religions have made these assumptions. If you have to appease a god by sacrificing children, or your intellect, the god so appeased cannot be unfailingly good-willed toward us. But Jesus has us ask that God's will be done and God's kingdom come. We are to trust that these consummations are good, and in our favor ultimately. We are not risking anything contrary to our interests when we place the future in God's hands. God is good. Our trust is all wrapped up in the love of God; and for that our best evidence is Jesus. Our best understanding comes not in thinking about it, but in praying this prayer.

*

Since Jesus probably used a word that some might translate as "Dad," or something even less formal, we might ask whether we can use this word for God. That is, are we willing to use it? Can we consider God to be a Dad, in view of what happens in this world? What "Dad" would let his children starve? What kind of father would let a child be born with an impairment; what father lets his children be shot in the streets of the world, or lets them die of cancer and tuberculosis and AIDS and polio? This is our Father? We're going to call someone like this "Dad"?

All my life I have been trying to answer the question of why, if God is merciful and loving and all-powerful, there is suffering in the world. I do not have an answer. But it occurs to me that ultimately we might be asking the wrong question again—or the answer might come in a different mode, perhaps a mode so different that the words "problem" and "answer" would not apply.

What we hope most from God is unconditional love; in fact we hardly dare hope for it. We know that if God were to demand correct behavior, if sins were counted, all of us would be sunk. Sometimes we substitute trivially correct behavior and correct theological opinions for our hope. But of course we have no claim upon God's leniency just because we do not smoke or swear, nor should we be so certain of the correctness of any beliefs as to be confident that God will save us because we are right. Actually, the idea that God will save us because we are right is hilarious. Let me be the first to apprehend all of God's purposes and make up a comprehensive and fully correct theology. If only I had the time.

We must rely on God's unconditional love. Jesus, Paul, Augustine, Luther, and Wesley all tried to face down the notion that God places conditions on us. The Gospel, the Good News, is that God loves us unconditionally. We know in our own human relationships that this is the only love that counts, or is worthy of the name.

However, we do not love God unconditionally. If He would shape up, we might love Him a little more. Feed the world's hungry. Bring justice down like a river, and righteousness like a rolling stream, preferably without us having to do the grunt work but acting in a purely advisory capacity. He should cure cancer finally. Then we'll talk. I do not like suggesting the possibility that we are to love God even if God has faults—but why not? I do not like the idea that what we consider faults actually are faults, because Christian teaching from Sunday School through seminary has inculcated in me the idea that God is perfect in all ways that we consider perfect; but look at the evidence. Why should we love God? Why should God love us? The great mystery—an even greater mystery than the universe itself—is love. Love that loves only a worthy object is not love. Why and how do we love God? With all our heart, mind, soul, and strength. That is how to pray.

My brief discussion of the problem of evil must appear facile to anyone for whom this question refutes the existence of God. In *A Grief Observed*, C. S. Lewis does not attempt an intellectual solution to the problem of pain; instead he suspects that the answer will actually come in another key, clear and palpable, something like hearing a chuckle in the dark. If we can entertain a similar suspicion or hope, then perhaps we could defer a rational discussion of this problem in favor, for now, of simply talking to someone—God—about our hurts and asking why God has forsaken us, why God allows this pain, or whether God will do anything about it.

*

By directing our attention away from illusions and toward the imminent lover of our souls, the Lord's Prayer brings us toward love of God. Pity those who have no love for God. A great power of God's love is that it awakens that in us which heals, even saves us. In this sense we become perfected even while we are imperfect—"at the same time saved and sinners," as Luther put it.[16] The lotus blooms in our soul, nothing can uproot it, but it is still barely coming to blossom.

By using the word "heavenly," Jesus assumes that God loves exquisitely, perfectly. We are selfish, afraid, jealous, sick, and weak in so many ways.

---

16. Luther, *Works* 25, 336.

We know that we fall short of loving as we ourselves want to be loved. And yet we are images of God, because we love. Our love of a person, whether child or sibling or spouse or lover, gives him or her ultimacy: we love him or her without holding back. We might say that we know intellectually that everyone falls short; but although we might love with our eyes open, we do not love with reservations. So we are completely unlike, and completely like God, as objects of love. We are creatures, not the Creator; yet we are also made in the Creator's image.

Paul, Augustine, and Luther preached that God's gracious love is the primary fact, and our reformed thought and behavior follows after it: we respond to love. The opposite idea is that our good behavior makes God merciful to us; but that is bribery and not love on our parts, and it does not work. It is like washing our car in order to make it rain. The way to reform the world is for everyone to awaken, to realize that God loves us without reservations and without boundaries. We respond badly to tyrants; but a child always looks for a parent's love, and that love can be transformative. An answer to the evil that we commit is already present; it is within and among us.

God's love for us poor, mourning, wandering creatures sounds like madness. Would not God want such madness in return? As Emily Dickinson says, "Much Madness is divinest Sense."[17] Love is not love unless it is sheer abandon.

Let those love God rationally, who wish to be loved rationally themselves. Let those love God with reserve, who want to be loved reservedly. Let us love God as we ourselves would be loved.

*

When we begin the Lord's Prayer we enter a mystery. We abandon what we know. We abandon our small world of desires when we say "our" in the prayer's way; we abandon what we know and expect concerning God when we say "Father." We are praying to Jesus' father.

If we are praying to Jesus' father, we are placing our most profound, life-and-death trust in Jesus. It feels much safer to pray to our own father, made bigger by the inflating power of thousands of years of superstition, wishes, and fears. We would like to have a predictable father, because if humans hunger after anything consistently, it is control. But by praying to Jesus' father, we trust Jesus more than ourselves.

---

17. Dickinson, *Poems*, 278.

I do not think we realize the extent to which we trust Jesus. We use Jesus' model prayer to pray for our needs and our deliverance from evil. We pray *to* and *with* One whom Jesus exemplifies. The more open-heartedly we pray this prayer, the less we pray to an inflated version of our false selves. Jesus is our guide, our rabbi, and as we use this prayer Jesus becomes our savior. Is not the image we build of the Father an image of Jesus?

The personhood of God is the real surprise here. The intensity and abandon of God's love does not seem to belong to a deity. The Lord's Prayer is, above all, prayed to a person. This is the baffling mystery. Here is the Creator of this universe, the unapproachable Light, the Physicist and Mathematician whose codes we only begin to understand, or think we do; here is vastness and immediacy combined, whose greatness is most obvious in the care we feel surrounding us in the smallest things. Here is the Old One, the Great Spirit, the Nameless—listening.

*

"In heaven" can be a figurative way of saying that God sees, hears, and knows everything concerning us. God's perspective is from "heaven." To be seen, heard, and completely known by a loving parent would be to have a perfect parent. How many of us have sometimes felt that our mother or father did not really listen to us, or see us for who we actually are? But "he that planted the ear, shall he not hear? he that formed the eye, shall he not see?"[18] The kingdom of heaven, Jesus says, is the dwelling-place of love: God perfectly sees, knows, hears, and loves.

*

The Lord's Prayer is terse and compact, but if one had to summarize it or compress it further, "our Father" might do. That phrase contains all of the prayer, although one might not know why until the rest of it is understood; that is, the rest of the prayer assures us that the word "father" refers to the kind of father shown in Luke 8. But beyond introducing and summarizing the prayer, "our Father" provides an assurance that disorients the mind. Jesus has given us permission to call the Master of the Universe "our Father."

Our galaxy, the Milky Way, is one hundred thousand light years across. Light moves fast. The sun is 93 million miles away from us and its light takes only a few minutes to hit us. But a beam of light would have to pack a lunch, a big lunch, if it wanted to go from one edge of the galaxy to another. The Milky Way contains about two hundred billion stars. That's "billion," as

---

18. Ps 94:9, KJV.

in the number of calories in a Big Mac. There are more galaxies out there than there are stars in the Milky Way. Light reaching us from some of those galaxies is several billion years old. If we can begin to imagine a universe that is several billion years old, and vast enough for light from its beginning ("Let there be light!") to be still out of our sight coming toward us, then we can begin to appreciate the awesome majesty of our Creator.

A note on the word "awesome": A half hour ago a salesperson on the phone wished me "an awesome weekend." This person is not seventeen. He is probably fifty. Awesome. That wish should have terrified me. What if this person gets his wish? Yes, "awesome" is overused. That is unfortunate, because here, in describing the universe and the Creator of the universe, is where the word ought to shine. I have tried replacing the word "awesome" in the previous paragraph with all the superlatives I know, such as gnarly and tubular, but all of them fall short.

Our words fail to describe God. Our concepts fail. Even our imaginations fail. A dark, starry night can teach us more about God than all the theology books in the world. This God—even those words are absurd, as if there were other gods—this God is our Father. Why should we ever be afraid, mean, selfish, or discouraged? But we are. I think we usually are. And so we need the rest of the prayer.

*

There is another way to look at the "our" in the Lord's Prayer. We can ask, as happened somewhere under the Galilean sun, "Who is my neighbor?" Jesus' reply should yield an answer to the question of who are meant by "our, " "we," and "us" in the prayer. The interrogator was a young student of the religious law, or "lawyer," who wanted to know whom we are to love. Jesus had just told him that the two great commandments are to love the Lord your God with all your heart, soul, mind, and strength; and to love your neighbor as yourself. So who is my neighbor? Whom am I supposed to love—family, friends, people who live around me, co-religionists, fellow citizens?

To answer, Jesus told the parable of the "Good Samaritan,"[19] whose details are familiar but whose point is often misunderstood. A man traveling to Jericho is jumped by thieves, who beat and rob him. A priest crosses to the other side of the road to avoid touching this bleeding man; another religious man does the same. Then a Samaritan— someone who Jews shunned and despised—kneels down and examines him, washes his wounds, carries

---

19. Luke 10–37.

him to an inn, leaves money to pay for his care, etc. When people hear this parable they often think Jesus is answering the lawyer's question by saying, "Anyone in need is your neighbor." But that is not Jesus' point. He asks the lawyer, "Who proved neighbor to the man who was robbed?"

He has turned the question around. Jesus instructs the lawyer to be a neighbor. A neighbor is one who acts lovingly toward another: *you* be that kind of person. The original question was misconceived and misleading. Don't ask who your neighbor is; *be* a neighbor.

Applied to the "we" in the Lord's Prayer, this parable would suggest that the only limits to whom is meant by "us" are set by ourselves. There are no inherent limits. Again, there are no boundaries. Only the ones we invent.

We might apply the Golden Rule to the Lord's Prayer. That is, we could pray for those whom we wish would pray for us. It is probably all right if the most we can honestly say is "my family," or "my friends Chad and Jeremy." The size of the prayer seems to be up to us. It is a prayer no matter how large or small. If by "our" we mean all Christians, those we wish prayed for us as well, then that is the kind of Lord's Prayer we pray. If we would want all humanity to pray for us, then let us pray for them.[20] I do not know about you, but I could use all the prayer I can get.

But we are to pray honestly, whatever we mean.

> Lord, who shall abide in thy tabernacle?
> Who shall dwell in thy holy hill?
> He that walketh uprightly,
>   and worketh righteousness,
> and speaketh the truth in his heart.[21]

If our heart is agonizing over our family—or perhaps tonight over one person for whom we are filled with fear or joy—then we should pray with him or her in mind. We pray this prayer for anyone who is in our heart now.

Perhaps to enter the kingdom, we must bring someone along. If so, we would probably find that it is they who will have brought us.

The word "our" can be considered a possessive without denoting something belonging to us like a watch. We can speak of "our birth," for example, a phrase which uses "our" to designate ourselves. Our body and our mind have no "us" to belong to: rather they make the "us" that exists. Our mother and our father are not our property; the word "our" designates a relationship. In these three ways, "our" suggests not what we possess, but what

---

20. This begins to sound too much like work. Fortunately, we do not have to pray for anybody who God does not love.

21. Ps 15: 1–2, KJ

we belong to, or what we are. In these senses "our" can identify to whom we belong. So we could say that the first word of the prayer establishes our identity. Who is that man? "He is Simon, son of Jonah." Ah. Who are we, then? Children of the living God. Saying "Our Father" is like showing the other side of the coin of our own name. "Father, it is I."

When I say whom I mean by "our," I declare who I am. It is as if at the outset of the prayer we must tell the Father who is calling, and in this way we remind ourselves. There is no place in the prayer to give a name; the only place to describe myself is in the first word. I believe that God knows me as an individual. But it is not enough to know God in my own way. I call upon the understandings of my brothers and sisters to help realize the Lover of my soul. Who am I to this Beloved? Am I a friend? Then the faults of a friend will be forgiven. Am I a lover? Then the wrongs of a lover will be forgiven. Am I a brother or a father? Then the betrayals of a brother or father will be forgiven. If I am a Christian, the sins of Christianity will be forgiven. But if I am a human being, with all others, then the dark acts of a human being will be washed whiter than snow, and the vast abyss of a human heart will be filled.

We could turn it another way. How would we like some sinner to pray for us? I mean some poor girl who has not gone to church since her mother took her thirty years ago, and who drinks herself to sleep every Friday night, who feeds her scruffy cat leftovers from TV dinners, and who has given up on keeping healthy and washing her hair and on hoping ever to be loved and happy—in other words, someone whom God loves so madly there are no words for it—how about that person? Would we like her to pray for us? Would we like someone God loves to pray for us?

For whom would we like to pray? Whom do we wish we could love? In whose heaven do we want to live? The larger the answer, the larger we are becoming inside, and the closer we are to the kingdom of God.

Or maybe not. Maybe God made this immense, vast, beautiful universe, with its wheeling galaxies and flowering nebulae, its stars so pure in whites and blues and reds that they seem to sing together—so that afterwards there could be a little heaven for Rotational Methodists, or a heaven with only my friends and a few relatives in it, together with only those people who, like me, believe that the buckles on our shoes must be made out of pewter not brass, and that cigarettes must be smoked from the reverse end just as it says in Deuteronomy, that the word *homousias* was spelled with two m's in the original manuscript, and that there will be a thousand years of peace between the end of the world and when Jesus comes back. Whoa, or is it a thousand years *after* Jesus comes back and before the end of the world? Oh, man.

So, when we come to the first word of the Lord's Prayer, we are exercising. We are expanding. How small do we want God to be? Small enough to make out of wood and place in our living rooms? In praying this prayer from the heart, we are making our vision of God, and ourselves, larger.

*

Jesus gave this prayer as a pattern for what form prayer should take:

- address (Our Father)
- adoration (hallowed be thy name)
- confession (forgive us our sins/debts/trespasses)
- thanksgiving (for thine is the kingdom, power, and glory)
- intercession (give us . . . forgive us . . . deliver us . . .)
- petition (the "us" above also implies "me")

(The acronym ACTIP is a way of remembering these elements of prayer, which also constitute the basis of worship services, aside from the reading and preaching of the Word and the celebration of the sacraments.) So there might be no significant difficulty created by having two different versions in Matthew and Luke. Some Christians insist that both versions were given by Jesus—so we can preserve the idea that the Bible is literally, factually, and historically infallible. Other Christians conclude that either Matthew or Luke, and probably both, worked over the version of the prayer they heard: Luke stripped it of Semitisms, to make it more understandable to his gentile audience; and Matthew added things like "who art in heaven" out of his Semitic (Middle Eastern, specifically Jewish) tendency to make sure the divine name and concept are treated with sufficient adoration and respect.[22]

The Church has prayed and taught children Matthew's version for more than two thousand years. Using the received text of Matthew—"who art in heaven"—we might wonder:

- What or where is heaven?
- Is God there?
- And if God is there, does that mean God is not here?

---

22. And then someone later added to Matthew's text the doxology that the Church was already using to end the prayer during services—"for thine is the kingdom and the power and the glory forever."

2

Who art in Heaven

"Who art in heaven" means that God is beautiful. To those mystics who have seen the face of God, the sight is of beauty beyond anything on earth, beyond expression or comparison; it is of light brighter than the sun, though it does not blind. This is the Father in heaven.

Where is heaven? Most of us would point upward. But Jesus pointed around him, figuratively: the kingdom of God is within you and among you.

The point is not that heaven is flat around us like a pancake, but that our idea of location regarding heaven is inadequate and misleading. Here we are dissuaded from thinking of heaven in a localized way. To ask *where* is to miss everything and to end up nowhere. There will be a contrast later in Matthew's version of the prayer—"on earth ... in heaven"—that will suggest location, but certainly at this point in the prayer, "in heaven" is meant as a modifier for the noun "Father." "In heaven" describes God; it does not locate God.

The word "heavenly" is applied to food, romantic interests, and peace at Christmas. But what does it mean when connected to "Father"? Goodness comes to mind. Here the traditional image of heaven is useful. "Heavenly" means blissful and pure—free of all the evil and grime of earthly existence. Beauty is associated with this term, as the picturing power of this word-image establishes itself in our imaginations. We see pale blue skies and white clouds.

But we know there is no place in the clouds where heaven has its location. That was the popular picture until the airplane, and it still is useful in giving us an idea of the peace and beauty behind the idea of heaven. But earlier ideas of heaven were actually more credible than that relatively recent notion. Milton's idea in *Paradise Lost*, for example, is that heaven is a vast place outside the created universe. The same idea holds for the book of Genesis, where heaven cannot be in or above the clouds, because the firmament where the stars are placed really is firm: it is a surface backed by water. For the people who first read Genesis, space was water, because water was the best available symbol of chaotic, un-ordered stuff. When in the story of Noah's flood we read that "the fountains of the great deep were broken up, and the windows of heaven were opened," we understand that Earth is in a kind of bubble of air. Overhead is the vast weight of water. Open the windows and let some in, and the earth is flooded. Likewise below: the water comes up when the hatches are "broken." So not in the water, but above the waters—above the universe—God resides in heaven. "Heaven" in that usage is not the same as "the heavens," which means the firmament, the surface upon which stars are placed in their courses.

"In heaven" can also denote power, but we must be careful here, because nothing is so susceptible to human abuse than power and the definition of power. Our ideas of power are completely erroneous, in Jesus' view. We are impressed by money, fame, force, and hardware. The essential power in the kingdom of God is love. God has the physical force to blow aside our hardware and explosive power, but those abilities of God are not necessarily what Jesus considers to be *power*. Jesus showed power in healing, preaching, and obedience—all of which originated in the love of God.

Contemporary physics—which considers such exotic ideas and phenomena as black holes that gulp matter and light into someplace where they cannot get out, a pre-universe "singularity" in which everything that expanded into our universe was smaller than a dot, and which also is toying with the idea of multiple universes—suggests that "heaven" might be more mental and personal than we have been able to imagine it before. If matter is energy, can energy be thought? Is the whole shebang in the Mind of God?

Thus the question, "Where is heaven?" becomes the question, "What is heaven?" As Jesus' prayer is predicated on God's being our Father, not simply our inventor, heaven must be where God is. Perhaps God himself is heaven, and the kingdom of God is the recognition of our existence in God. I say "perhaps" because this is blatant speculation on my part. I am only trying to snatch the idea of heaven out of geography and cosmology. We know virtually nothing of the kingdom of heaven, aside from Jesus himself and how he acted and what he taught on earth, including his parables of the kingdom and this prayer. To define heaven is to get closer to talking about the nature of God, and heaven is our relationship with God. Without God there is no heaven. The Lord's Prayer, love for God and each other, and the beauty and goodness we perceive in our lives, are experiences of the kingdom of heaven. It is among us and within us. We might as well ask, "Who is heaven?" as, "Where is heaven?"

This is not as difficult a turn of mind as it might seem. One can think of a person as heaven—not just "heavenly," but heaven. In *Paradise Lost*, Adam says that where Eve is, is paradise.

To be in heaven alone seems a self-evident contradiction. The relational aspect of heaven is its essence. At the risk of sounding moony, one could say that heaven is a place of the heart. But then we would have to define "heart" as the true Self, the image of God, the indwelling Spirit. And the heart, which loves, cannot be the heart without a beloved; so the heart implies relationship and community. We are back to "heaven."

If relationship is the key to the kingdom, then we can surely trust whatever heaven is—trust God. That is why to love God is primary; if we want to "go" to heaven, we need to want God. Heaven is our heavenly Beloved.

*

The word "heavenly" is a strange word in this context, because it not only almost infinitely expands the idea of father; it also limits that idea. We cannot expand the "father" element too far. If "heaven" is a metaphor, a figure of speech, then so is Father, and this expression reminds us of that. It is well to remember that Psalm 63 imagines God as a great eagle: "in the shadow of thy wings will I rejoice."

When we push the logic of the expression, "heavenly Father," the metaphor fails. "Heavenly" and "father" are contradictions. A father is first of all a physical engenderer—but say "heavenly" and we lose that first requirement of fathers. Yet in another sense, God is a more physical creator than our earthly fathers, because God made *all* the earthly stuff from which we and our fathers were made. So we have an expression that is both a contradiction and the most literal truth—a contradiction in itself. That is, we have a mystery. We pray to Someone both unknown and known.

Here is an important element of prayer: this phrase "heavenly Father" reveals something essential in our relationship with God—the unknown. We pray in large part with our imaginations. We virtually pretend to talk to someone. This cannot be literally true. God is closer than that. Language is not needed, except by us.

For a while, using our imaginary picture of God, we forget that this Someone is the Creator of the Universe. It is necessary that we do this. We both remember, and we must forget, that we are praying to God. We could not pray at all if we remembered that thought too often. Or we would punctuate every phrase with exclamations of surprise and alarm or adoration. Or we would grovel like guilty mutts. How do we dare talk to the Master of the Universe, the Great Spirit?

Yet the Lord's Prayer would have us imagine that we are speaking to a father. We could not pray if we had to substitute direct knowledge for the image of God the Father. Mystics who reach a relatively direct experience of God speak little if at all during that experience, nor can they speak of it adequately afterwards. "Heavenly" Father reminds us that we pray on the bridge of our imaginations.

This is not to say that we pray nonsensically, because the imagination conveys a kind of truth that the intellect is not built to handle. The Lord's Prayer educates our imagination about God, shapes its picture, and expands it. The imagination is the vehicle of our compassion for others; without it we would not be able to identify with people's suffering. Through the imagination we can feel what they feel, and out of this empathy we pray for the health, safety, and happiness of others. But also, in pulling the picture of our heavenly Father away from our rational minds, Jesus causes us to approach God with the mixture of familiarity, confidence, and awe that only this mysterious "Father" can call forth.

The person with a fully concrete picture of God is an idolater. The person of unaided intellect conceives of a cold cosmic watchmaker. The person of simple sentimentality prays to a pal, as a child talks to a stuffed animal. But Jesus stretches and fills the imagination with an intimate mystery. We remember that we are mere humans; we remember that we are God's children.

The mystery of the Hearer of our prayers reminds us that prayer itself is a mystery. Our unknown Self is speaking to the unknown. In reminding ourselves of this we issue ourselves a warning. Here is an experience larger than ourselves. Remembering this would alter and educate our expectations. For one thing, we might cease to apply economic terms to prayer. Do we *get* anything for it? Is there a law of diminishing returns for prayer and its supposed benefits? But prayer begins from somewhere in us that is invisible to ourselves, proceeds by an invisible route, and reaches an invisible destination—a seemingly vast and opaque reality.

If I say that prayer has no power, I might sound as though I am quibbling over semantics—that is, it is God, not prayer itself, who has power; but this clarification is important because it confronts the dilemma of unanswered prayer. We imagine that when we do not get what we ask for that a problem exists. Possibly the power of God comes into question. Or to avoid that problem, we try to apologize for God's lack of response: "God knows that what we wanted wasn't best for us"; "God will not interfere with nature, and we would have brought natural consequences down upon ourselves";

"God will not interfere with the laws that make our lives possible in the first place." Maybe God's answer was "Later," rather than "No." Maybe the answer was "Nuts!"

All this misses the point. Not all of us have been delivered from evil; we have not been kept from temptation. Probably many of us have felt that prayers have been answered, and we know there are times that we actually have been delivered from temptation and evil. But there is something vaguely crass and insulting about praising God for answering our prayers, when the unfortunates of the world are more or less within earshot. Didn't God hear their prayers? Didn't they pray? Are they evildoers? Yes, God has healed our child, and we should give thanks. But why is there sickness in the first place?

The petitions of Jesus' prayer have not been answered, except fragmentarily. We do not have our daily bread. Yes, you and I might have our daily bread right now; but if "we" means more than upper or middle class Americans, the prayer has been ignored or refused. A third of the world is undernourished, and has been for these two thousand years. Did the people who died in the most recent typhoon not say their prayers? We can say that God meant some greater good for them—in fact we trust that is the case—but we are talking beyond our knowledge. We are exercising faith, or wishful thinking. On the face of it, the Lord's Prayer has not been answered.

Therefore we are praying in faith, not economically. We have not gotten returns in the coin we wanted. Bread, safety—where are they? Still asking. Still waiting. Still praying. It is as if Jesus, in the form of his body on Earth, the Church, were still saying the prayer for the first time—one long address to the heavenly Father in and for His kingdom, until it comes.

Here is an essential element of the mystery of prayer: waiting. As an economic transaction, prayer has kept us waiting too long. But as a faithful action, the waiting must be somehow essential. The Church has dedicated a whole season, Advent, to waiting. We think about the importance of waiting every year. Either waiting is a significant spiritual exercise, or we are chumps.

If the Lord's Prayer puts us into an attitude of asking, it also puts us into an attitude of waiting. We have been waiting, oh, how long? Well, how long has the Father been waiting for us? As if it were all right for God to wait, but not for us to wait? Perhaps waiting is a godly act.

We do not like people who are just takers. Most of us know at least one person who is flattered by our attention, who has gotten used to receiving gifts from us—and who never reciprocates in any way, just expects to receive. That may be ourselves relative to God. But perhaps one thing we can give to God is our patience.

By patience I do not mean simply sitting apathetically. I am referring to faithful waiting, to expectation, to unhurried confidence coupled with urgency, to gratitude, and to doing all we can to create the goodness we await. Advent. Eventually we are waiting not for the benefits brought by the Savior, but for the Savior. It is not the exotic trinkets Dad brings home from his trips to Cleveland, but Dad himself.

In that way, prayer seems like our work, but it is God's gift. We pray to God, let it be once or a thousand times; let it be a glance, or a perspiring obsession. We repeat our prayer until we understand that God has heard. We speak—God hears—what an answer! We asked for our daily bread, but we received God. We will never be hungry again.

In this prayer, we will be asking for God's success: God's kingdom to come, God's will to be done, and God's name to be hallowed. These successes have not come. Presumably God would not need our prayers to bring about these things. But the prayer says otherwise. These things—God's kingdom, will, and holiness—we may conclude to be actually human items. They make sense only in human terms; they are irrelevant to God. Therefore we are asking for conformity between our ideas of God's power and God's actual power. We are asking for a shift in our perspective and a movement of our wills.

Such a movement would bring us closer to God, rather than leaving us where we are, with deep-seated beliefs that alienate us from God. We pray, "thy kingdom come," not: "My ideas be borne out. My theology proved correct. My way certified to be the right way. For mine is the kingdom and the power and the glory, amen."

This is an answer to the problem of evil. How can God be good, powerful, all-knowing, and caring, and also allow evil and suffering in the world? Answer: Father, thy will be done. The answer is not a solution to a puzzle. The answer is to address the mystery behind the whole problem, and to address our mystery with the trust of a child.

The Lord's Prayer also breaks our idols. Ask God to do God's will? As if God needs us, needs our prayer? I thought God was the toughest guy on the block. Maybe in thinking this way about God—not necessarily incorrectly as far as that goes—maybe in our whole picture of God, we have been pagans. When Jesus strode into the Temple in Jerusalem and turned over those moneychangers' tables—it was we who sat at those tables. And we still do.

I know that I am speaking harshly. I would include myself in these indictments except that I mean well. In any case, I fall back on the fact that Jesus gave us this prayer. He did not do it out of sarcasm, but to help us. He assumed that we need help.

The other side of the coin is that we do have wonderful moments. This morning I went to a service, a weekday morning service at a church I do not attend, and found myself among only five other people, and of course the little service got around to the Lord's Prayer. But in saying the prayer with those other frail people, single-minded and humble and together for that minute or two, I realized why the Father we address is called "heavenly." People saying this prayer—burdened with unanswered requests and surrounded by illness and danger and terror—are momentarily in that kingdom. It is a mystery, and it is not a place, but now and then we can be there. In this prayer, together, we are there.

*

The New Testament is not a book about passive people, who pray and then sit back and wait for God to do cool stuff. The people in the New Testament are always on the go. They are the busiest people in literature. Jesus is constantly on the move, constantly teaching, healing, walking, suffering, telling stories, eating and drinking, and, thank goodness, fishing. His followers were if anything more energetic, as Jesus promised they would be.

That is why Luther said we should pray as though everything depends upon God, and work as though everything depends upon us. Of course, prayer itself is work.

We seem not to have much choice about praying. Humankind is the praying animal and one way or another we pray all the time, hoping to be within earshot of whomever or whatever we vaguely fancy. We play to invisible judges, feel the beads of anxiety before the statues of childhood beliefs, and wryly comment to whomever we wish we could believe in. We pray to idols. But Jesus wants us to talk to God.

Our deepest expressions might not look like prayer, but then again neither does what we sometimes do in church look like prayer. That is, the most typical failure of community prayer is that we forget to whom we are talking. The way we sometimes speak to God in public prayers can be amazingly cavalier: self-conscious instead of God-conscious, crowd-conscious instead of intent. We want people to think we are pious, witty, profound, poetic, right, and intelligent; and so we blather disrespectfully, strike attractive poses, lecture God, and just talk. "O FatherGod, here we are this beautiful morning, concerned about so many things but grateful for the Mud Hens' victory yesterday, in need of comfort and good cheer but knowing that God helps he who helps herself, cheerfully calling for the best from each other but soberly understanding that all of us are flawed and all fall short, verily, of the glory of God, the great Author and Finisher of our faith, grateful for that faith and for the blessings of climate, reveling in your revelation in nature . . . " This is piling up empty phrases. God probably does not pay by the word. Those who pray this way have their reward—from the people to whom they pray.

In how we speak, do we presume in ways that a child would not presume upon a parent, or a servant presume upon a king? Jesus redefined the idea of servitude when he wrapped a towel around himself, filled a bowl with water, and knelt to wash his disciples' feet. The Christian servant is a volunteer, not a slave economically or by statute; Jesus said, the greatest among us are those who serve. In the Christian sense, the concept of "servant" works only after we have entered the kingdom where all things are made new. So would the greatest among us—big enough and strong enough and loving enough to seek voluntarily the will of God—speak like a foolish egoist in the presence of the One we would gladly try to make happy?

It would be nice if we ourselves were simply happy to be here, in God's presence. Beyond that—for we do not always, or even often, approach God in happy frames of mind—we must be honest. We must be transparent, not conscious of what anyone else might think, except insofar as we are teaching other people to pray. One can understand why Jesus advised his pupils to go into a room alone to pray.

Prayer might be simply quieting oneself, as when meditating, in order to listen. In a Quaker meeting, a group of like-minded people still themselves and pay attention; but in a more common church service it is difficult to achieve a half-minute of silence before the desire for entertainment takes over. At this point of lamentable necessity, it is especially urgent to recall who we are and in whose presence.

There are public occasions—worship services and funerals and weddings and inaugurals—in which it can be our duty to pray out loud as a voice for a community of people. Is it wrong to prepare beforehand? When we know we are going to ask a parent for something, we consider it ahead of time. But sometimes we assume that God inspires only spontaneous prayer, rather than prayers written out, as if God does not work when we get to our desks. "Teach us how to pray." Jesus' answer assumes that something can be learned, remembered, and applied. He did not say, "Never mind—just open your mouth when the time comes." But we pray repetitious spontaneous prayers filled with stale, mimicked phrases and subculture words that really mean "umm" and "er." If we were in the presence of an important person, or our own parent, we would not ramble or address someone else. Should we treat our most beloved carelessly?

*

Let us consider results of prayer. If prayer somehow connects to results, then the results are changes. I mean they are changes to nature, and/or to things as they are. That is why it is easy to confuse prayer with magic, and to think in terms of exercising spiritual muscle and to talk about "the power of prayer." We are asking God to make changes, and to do new things.

Answers to prayer are not natural reactions of the material world. They are new creations: out of nothing, something new has been made and done. If we are given bread for the day and know it, if we are helped in our work and feel helped, or if we are healed and know that a loving and powerful Person has done it, then God has *made* something, not just bent something. The creative work of God has been done again. This is not to say nature has been violated. A poet does not violate language: he or she makes something new, and sets it down—shiny and solid, green and fragrant—right in the midst of language. God creates something new and places it in the material world.

Prayer is asking for more creation. We further the universe, we participate; and who knows who has moved whom? When we pray, we might think first whether we are asking to make the universe better, more beautiful, and more good; or whether we are asking for a drag on its movement or requesting a screech in the music of the spheres. Suppose what is created through our request were to last a thousand years. Would we be proud of it? I do not say that God would perform it, if the act were less than good; I am saying that this is a way to evaluate our desires. The appearance and presence of any new thing alters the whole of creation. We are praying to change the world.

*

On a similar note, it should be mentioned that by saying "heavenly Father," or "our Father, who art in heaven," we are putting what follows into perspective, perhaps even giving ourselves a dope slap. To phrase it in a more seemly way: The address of this prayer ushers us into the divine presence. "Remember, before you ask," the beginning tells us, "that you are praying to heaven, and through this prayer you have stepped before the Living God. You are in the Lord's holy presence. What will you say? What are the desires of your heart? To God all hearts are open, all desires known, and no secrets are hidden. Do you wish to confirm these desires by making them into requests? Are these requests what you truly wish to place in front of God?"

Before our requests, we ourselves are placed into the light of God's countenance. What a treasure this prayer is. If we can pray it in the faith that

God will supply the specifics, then it is a great gift to be able to say simply in this prayer, "Give us what we need, forgive us, protect us; thank you."

Jesus' first words are also a reassurance, and a kind of authorization: call the Holy One "Father." Set your hearts at ease. Remember: "heavenly Father." Then your hearts will be pure. When you say "heavenly Father," you speak in love as you speak in reverence.

The first words of the Lord's Prayer condition us, take us through a portal that shapes and cleanses us. Only, the prayer must be intentional. Words do not purify us if they are repeated by rote. That is why it is good to meditate on the prayer itself, to think about what the words mean, and to feel their cleansing power moving through us. As we meditate, the prayer teaches. Then it does great work in us. We ourselves are the results, the miracles, wrought by this prayer.

*

A brief note on honesty. We are adults. Adulthood can be defined as pretending. A young child, young enough to use the name "Papa" unselfconsciously, does not pretend except on purpose, playing a game that everyone knows is a game. But adults have become pretenders to such a degree that we do it without thinking. It is our second nature. We believe our own acts. Yet within us sometimes there is a little voice that whispers, "You are not who you're pretending to be."

Jesus would have us drop the pretense. We begin by addressing God as "Papa," and we are children again; or rather, we become again the children we really are. Without that, how should God answer our prayers? "Who's asking?" God might say. "Is this the big shot?—an act I've never bought. Or are you wearing the mask of Romeo today? Or is this the responsible Christian adult? Or perhaps the cool dude today? Whom shall I send the answer to, which costume?" Therefore Jesus said, "Suffer the little children to come unto me, and forbid them not: for of such is the kingdom of heaven."[1]

*

The Lord's Prayer is an individual prayer, but it is also, perhaps primarily, a communion, a communal activity. It was first given not as a private prayer but as a group prayer: its references are plural. Are we all praying to the same Father? Do we all imagine the same God? Any one of us, on different days, can have different notions and impressions of God. Some of us might picture a mother; some picture a king, a shepherd, a general, or a

---

1. Mark 10:14, KJV.

sentimental friend. How can we say the same prayer if we are all addressing different listeners, most or all of whom are imaginary? Is the visible communion a crowd of people divided by a common prayer?

We are not as divided as we might think. The Lord's Prayer unifies our desires. This unification makes us one not only with each other in the Church, but makes us one with all humanity. The more we are unified, the more we are praying to the Holy One and not to an idol. These are not churchly petitions, but requests basic to all human life. Our individual and passing desires are left out of this prayer. So here the human race is one people united in our need.

The prayer prayed communally cleanses our image of God. In a group of humble, earnest sharers of this prayer, many brassy and terrible pictures of God get blown off like chaff. In a group of needy people, those helzapoppin' images do not work. But the humble petitions of the Lord's Prayer help to create a community, and that very community works. This prayer unifies its pray-ers in honesty, supplication, gratitude, simplicity, and love, and so fulfills itself by helping bring to fruition the kingdom of God. Something different and unified can be made when people pray this prayer together.

*

Should not a heavenly father have heavenly children?

Who are we, saying this prayer, addressing God, our heavenly father? This is a fiercely compact prayer. Excavate toward its implications, and we find that the roots are very deep. The reverse side of this phrase, "heavenly Father," is an earthly, ethical side. The phrase is an identifier; it identifies the Father and it identifies us.

Do we act the part of heavenly children? The whole prayer is entailed by the first words. Do we give daily bread to others, do we forgive, do we perform God's will; do we try to avoid temptation and do we refrain from doing evil? Do we hallow God's name in thought, word, and deed; and do we wish for the kingdom of God to come within us?

No, we shoot off our mouths like the hypocrites we are and falsely identify ourselves. The Lord's Prayer can be a penitential statement with a high degree of implied irony. But we are not going to call our Father anything other than heavenly, no matter what we are. The prayer summons us to be more than we are, and better than we are. If we take this name upon ourselves, we encourage each other to live up to that name, and to be children of our heavenly Father.

We might remember our shortcomings, but we must not remain fixated upon them. Love fills us desolated children and makes us strong. To approach God in penitence and gratitude is not the same as slinking up to God in guilt. If we are mere children, we are children of the kingdom and children of the heavenly Father. Let us remember, Jesus has conferred this name on us. Jesus knew human nature; Jesus knew we are seriously damaged, ethically challenged, and only marginally sane. So the first phrase of this prayer confers grace upon us. With that grace and in its light, we begin.

3

Hallowed be Thy Name

Martin Luther wrote, "In all the Scriptures I know of no other passage that denounces and dooms our life more than this petition."[1]

That statement comes under Luther's title, "The worst and most harmful people in Christendom."[2] He means you and me. He means people who think, "I am so good at heart; I mean so well." He means people who are disappointed in, or disapprove of, other people—those other people who do not go along with our beliefs and practices even though, "I am willing to share my very heart" with them. Well, says Luther; we should be terrified by our own prayer.

Luther was not kidding. The man was known for his stand-up routine, but in this case I am sure he did not crack a smile. He really meant that people of good conscience are the worst kinds of people. He says,

> Note well that it happens when these people become convinced of their piety, when they have a good opinion of themselves, when they discover that they pray more, fast more, and perform other good works more and that they are endowed by God with more understanding and grace than other people.... They soon forget that everything they have is a gift from God. Now this is bound to lead to judging, condemning ....[3]

All sin comes from this forgetting. By sin, Luther does not mean infractions. There is a branch of Christendom that specializes in spotting

1. Luther, *Works* 42, 33.
2. Ibid,, 30.
3. Ibid.

infractions. That branch is rooted in your heart and mine. A while ago I heard a reasonable, personable, intelligent, and highly literate man say, "He drinks? I had thought he was a Christian."

The story of the Fall of Man is the Bible's way of saying that all of us are flawed, incomplete, ill, in progress, weak, fearful, and untrustworthy. By that I do not mean that we are secretly thieves and murderers, but that we are closet policemen. We are on the watch for sin—other people's sin. And we are very liberal in this regard; we do not have a narrow definition of sin. Just about anything other people do falls under our generous rubric. Those of us who really exercise this mentality to the fullest are almost willing to define sin as "that which is different from what I do," and likewise they define heresy or error as "that opinion which differs from mine." Sometimes carefully religious people preach the infallibility and inerrancy of the Bible—the Bible as *we* understand it. In that way, we become infallible ourselves. Luther says this righteous attitude is the foundation of all sin.

Again, he means real sin, not infractions, like drinking or swearing or fornication; nor does he mean violations of civil law, like speeding or vandalism. He means real sin: that which separates us from God. The Wizard of Oz and the police can take care of the other things. But when we lose our sense of total dependence upon God—or to put it less abjectly and more essentially, when we lose our sense of relatedness to God—we are dealing with sin proper and only God can save us. When we think we are saving ourselves, when we think we are in any way better than others—then we are in the grip of sin. We believe this illusion of saving ourselves, or righteousness, when we lose our awareness of God.

A friend of mine was out taking some photographs last week at night along the banks of a river, and fell into a sinkhole. It was pitch dark, raining, windy, and forty degrees. As he put it, the mud just "gripped" him and he could not get out. Trapped for hours, he thought he was a goner. Finally someone came along, hearing my friend's now-weak cries for help, and managed to hold out a branch for him to grasp, and my friend was saved.

We get saved, and then, as Luther continues, "there are two kinds of people. There are some who recognize and deplore that they do not fully hallow God's name, who earnestly pray that they may do so, and who take seriously their wretchedness."[4] These people understand their total dependence upon God for salvation. The other kind think that they were the primary actors: they persevered; they cried out; they grabbed the branch. They enlisted the otherwise oblivious passer-by. They deserved to be saved; they earned it.

---

4. Ibid,, 34.

These two kinds of people are easy to separate in a little parable, but not so easy to separate in ourselves. Many of us will readily admit our own "wretchedness," in Luther's terminology, and even pray to God in paroxysms of guilt and inadequacy—then go out and judge others in all the subtle and blatant ways available to the human mind. We are always willing to police other people. This proves our repentance to be only theoretical. In practice we rarely repent; we boast. And we are the incorrigible ones. We are the righteous people who kneel beside a felon and give thanks to God that we are not like him. In contrast to the light and love of God, we are all felons. But those who do not realize and admit that they are as felonious as anyone else are those who are really lost.

Frankly, we are a bunch of liars. The really pious among us admit that all of us are sinners, because we are "fallen." We even quote Scripture (like the devil) and say, "All have sinned, and come short of the glory of God."[5] So it must be true. However, this is a theoretical understanding only. We then go out and show in every way imaginable that we are better than somebody else. We are God's attorneys. Somebody must uphold God's standards. No better people than us. "Surely ye are the people," Job would say, "and wisdom shall die with you."[6] Perhaps the hard shell of spiritual illness is denial of reality, and lying to oneself.

Where does this self-deception come from? The story in Genesis tries to answer that question, picturing a pair of first humans losing recollection that God is the single reality; and they forget that they are related to God. In their short-sightedness, they reach for some small item that promises something they desire; and then they deceive themselves about their condition, namely, that they are visible to God. They hide. When caught, Adam points to Eve and says, *she* gave me the fruit. In hiding and in blame we exercise our flabbergasting power of denial. We avoid reality, ourselves, and our fears.

If, as the sacred scriptures of India say, we are lost in a world of illusion, then we are the chief agents of illusion because we delude ourselves. We choose illusion. Why? We wish to avoid pain, including the pain of growth. Adam and Eve would have grown if they had been willing to awaken to life in God's sight. And we choose illusion because we fall for our desires. To fall for desire is to fall away from awareness of God—not that we forget that God is watching and we will be punished—but that we fall away from our highest joy, which is life in the love and light of God. We become attached to our desires and the objects of our desires. No one has found the explanation

---

5. Rom 3:23, KJV.
6. Job 12:2, KJV.

for this; it seems to be a given, and so the biblical tradition calls this original sin.

This is serious stuff because in thinking of ourselves as alone, we are "stealing God's name." The name of God means God's honor.

> Hence, he who uses the name, not for his neighbor's benefit, but in contempt of him, robs God of his honor, usurps God's honor, and arrogates to himself the nature and virtue which are God's and not his.[7]

And so such people, undoubtedly you and I from time to time, "blaspheme God's name more shamefully with their respectable lives than all others do with their evil lives."[8]

In this way the core of Christianity, preached by Jesus, Paul, Augustine, Francis of Assisi, Luther, and Wesley, reverses the way we look at things, particularly when it comes to righteousness. Human righteousness is the enemy of God's righteousness. We, the righteous in our own eyes, are always the worst. We are not aware of our plight, our actual lack of control, or our need; and for all this we have a delusional sense of security.

This is all crucial because "hallowed be thy name" is what Luther calls an unlimited petition. It includes all the others. "If anyone were able to hallow God's name perfectly, he would no longer need to pray the Lord's Prayer."[9] Everything else is included in this petition. To hallow is to cherish.

But we must pray this petition, unless we think we are all set—"right with God," in the ludicrous phrase of Old Time Religion. Being convinced in our minds and consciences that we are right with God is like saying, "I'm a gerbil. Praise God!" But we are not gerbils; we are children of the kingdom of God, which is within us and among us if we would only brave the pain of breaking with our illusions and waking up. The first step of realizing that we are loved is somehow conceiving that we are in a relationship: we are not alone. To have a heavenly Father is to be related to God, and to be loved. To have been created means to be loved. "All men are blasphemers of God's name, some to a greater, others to a lesser degree, even though the arrogant saints refuse to believe it."[10] Luther's term "arrogant saints" is a great one. It is one worth remembering. We can always haul it out and use it on someone.

Luther also points out that when we pray this petition, we imply and admit that God's name is not yet "holy in us." The first petition is therefore

---

7. Luther, *Works* 42, 30. The two quotations following are also from this passage.
8. Ibid,, 31.
9. Ibid,, 33.
10. Ibid.

crucial because it "accuses," in the terminology of St. Paul—but perhaps we could say instead that it reveals; it shows us where we really stand and what we really are. By praying it, however, we are confessing. This humility is the only realistic attitude with which to approach God. "Blessed are the poor in spirit." What at first feels like a painful realization opens into awareness of God's love.

So there is good news. The gospel, or good news, is that we belong in this heavenly kingdom. We are not merely despicable worms deserving the wrath of an imaginary terrifying god. Luther hammered at the nastiness of righteousness in order to prepare us for the real heavenly Father's unmerited and unlimited grace, reminding us that God taught us this prayer because he wished to answer it. Take heart. We are better off being the worst sinners in the world and confessing it from our hearts, than being the most righteous people in the world and believing we are "right with God." Following the little rules that make us "right with God" is stuporficial: we can do it half asleep, and it's superficial compared to actually awakening.

There is a profound truth in the idea of being "born again," but it is not what popular religion tends to aim at. The first birth, physical birth, was an awakening into a new and at first painful world: the comforting warmth of the amniotic fluid is left behind with a shocking chill, and light stuns us; now we must grow or die. Being "born again" must be as fundamental and astounding. It is not simply to remain the way we were except more obedient and ceremonial, less prone to stealing and swearing. The new birth must be an awakening into a new world, or it would not be a new birth but a mere change of clothes. What redeems the great tragedies of ancient Greece is their sudden burst of light. The first instance of it is agony—no wonder we want to deny and cuddle in the warm water of our illusion—but then we become not a somewhat improved being but a new being. Now we are aware; we are awake.

*

A note on conscience. Luther distrusted the conscience. We like to think that God planted the conscience in our heads, or hearts; but it was put there by human beings. Conscience is a human invention. We are taught the contents of our individual consciences by our parents, teachers, governments, and other human agents. Conscience is a thing of this earth and pertains to this earth. It cannot rise above the earth, and it does not rise above its own causes. It is not pertinent to salvation.

The conscience is necessary for civilization. Criminals with no consciences are the worst kind. But the conscience can be placated with phony goodness, and it can accuse the most innocent of children. In the American Civil War, more than seven hundred thousand people died—at least seven million in terms of today's population—and most of them were fighting for their consciences. Half were on one side of the questions, half on the other. Heartless violence is carried out today by people of conscience. You not only die for the sake of your conscience; you kill for your conscience. Conscience might guide you, but it will not save you. For salvation—meaning health and wholeness, meaning life in God's light and love—we cannot trust our consciences; we trust the One who loves us.

In our daily life we have to follow our consciences if we want to do what is right in society. But in the kingdom of God, we are saved not because our consciences say so, or because our consciences have quit knifing us—but because God loves us and proved it by Jesus' death for us and his resurrection. We are baptized into that certainty, a certainty that often does not feel or think like a certainty.

*

The initial wish in the prayer is not for benefit to ourselves—or so it first seems—yet this wish, come true, could supply most of what we need. "Hallowed" signifies pure wonder and praise. Here is our exclamation of joy, of appreciation. It is well that we repeat this exclamation in a regularly recited prayer, because we exhibit a phenomenal ability to forget it otherwise.

Consider something as common and ordinary as a gray squirrel. I have been watching one. She is going about her business with energy and skill, frugally collecting nuts for the winter. She fixes a walnut between her forepaws, used like our hands, and rotates it, milling off the shell with her teeth. The fragments fly in all directions. Her legs shift a little now and then to achieve better balance or comfort; the fluffy plume of her tail provides a steady counterweight. Why should such a creature—studying me with casual wariness as she eats—why should she exist at all? Why, from the universe of gasses and light and rock, should anything exist, let alone this fuzzy wonder that climbs and dashes and chatters and saves for the winter? Why even the gasses and light? This squirrel might as well be a star.

Yet we go on day after day—the only creature, we assume, with the power of reflection—never thinking how strange, how beautiful, how terrible this stupendous achievement called creation is. We plod ahead with our complaints and preoccupations and short-sighted enmities, rarely thinking that we live in an impossibility, or that wonder is our proper response. Wonder and reverence. "Hallowed be thy name!" To "cherish" God might mean, in the words of the Westminster Shorter Catechism, to glorify and enjoy God forever.

A consequence of such periodic lucidity on our part should be shame at how we disgrace and violate this splendid creation with our unawareness, our selfishness. Thus we profane the name of God. But let that not block our adoration. All of the prayer follows from this hallowing, as the other nine Commandments follow from the first: here is the Lord our God, our heavenly Father. Adoration is the first mode of the prayer.

*

We might wonder whether "hallowed be thy name" is not actually a petition, but simply a statement or an exclamation, as the previous section implies. If so, the petition would read, "hallowed *is* your name." However, the indicative mood is not used; rather the phrase is in the conditional or subjunctive.[11]

So the subjunctive, or conditional, mood replaces the indicative in Jesus' prayer, and it seems safe to assume that there is a reason. We ask God for his name to be hallowed. Very odd, when you think about it. Ask God that God's own name be hallowed: respected, honored, praised, appreciated, adored, and cherished?

A couple of points might be noted here:

- If God made us hallow his name, all warfare, greed, selfishness, cruelty, and pollution would cease.
- We cannot hallow God's name.

Let us take up the second point. Many of us memorized the Gettysburg Address back in grade school. Or we look forward to memorizing it soon. Lincoln said, "We cannot dedicate, we cannot consecrate, we cannot hallow this ground. The brave men, living and dead, who struggled here, have consecrated it far above our poor power to add or detract." We say, "How true."

How much more true, as applied to God! Since when can human beings hallow God's name? From a standpoint outside the kingdom of heaven, we see ourselves as puny, and lacking the power and will—much less the know-how—to hallow God's name. Who and what are we, to hallow the name of the Creator? From an unloving point of view—"unloved," I might say, describing not how things are but how our illusion feels—we are infinitesimal beings scrambling and snarling across the face of a befouled Earth.

---

11. I have been getting a good deal of mail about my use of the word "subjunctive," and I want to make it clear that the word is not off-color. It is merely a grammatical term referring to a condition contrary to fact.

Individually we might be well-intentioned, but as a species we are termites on steroids.

But to ask that God's name be hallowed is to ask that God show forth the right hand of divine power in the human heart. It is safe to imagine that God's name is hallowed by "fire, and hail; snow, and vapour: stormy wind fulfilling his word,"[12] for they please God.[13] But we are also praying,

> Kings of the earth, and all people;
> princes and all judges of the earth:
> Both young men and maidens;
> old men and children:
> Let them praise the name of the Lord:
> for his name alone is excellent:
> his glory is above the earth and heaven.[14]

This is to ask nothing short of a new world. Jesus called that new world the kingdom of God, and that is our clue as to how we can hallow God's name. The kingdom of God is within and among us through the presence of the Holy Spirit, shown in love. It comes down to a very simple equation: "hallowed be thy name" = love one another.

There are other ways. The name of God is a representation of God among us, not God himself. That name, or representation, is what we wish to be hallowed in this prayer. But surely we do not mean simply the words "God," or "Lord," or even "heavenly Father." In Christian theology, the intermediary, or representation of God on earth, is Christ. The first way to hallow the name, the intermediary, is to believe or value Christ. It would be to realize that God was in Christ, reconciling the world to himself.

There are two ways to believe in Christ, each one half of the whole. One is to confess and believe in our hearts that Jesus is God's son, and that Jesus and the Father are one. That is a static belief. The active side of this belief is to live the life and teachings of Christ. It is hard to do one without the other. We cannot love our enemies without believing that such a command comes from the highest good—from God, we might as well say. We cannot believe in Jesus as Christ if we keep his love to ourselves. Belief in Christ is an active condition: it is to live the *way* of Christ.

So—to refer to a passage in John—how do we hallow the name of God? How do we "work the works of God"? By believing in "him whom he has sent."[15]

12. Ps 148:8, KJV.
13. Gen 1:10, KJV.
14. Ps 148:11–13, NRSV.
15. John 6:28, KJV.

But Jesus could not have meant this, someone might point out. When Jesus referred to the name of God he meant neither *Abba* nor himself. He would have meant the name of God as written—with only consonants—in the sacred books, as one honors a king by bowing at his name or by treating his messenger with deference and honor. A Hebrew name is, in a sense, a messenger. Other cultures have attached more significance to names than our current mainstream American society does, so it is difficult for us to understand this idea of hallowing a name.

But not every American is mainstream. Recently some Lakota people raised a complaint about some strip clubs being called "Crazy Horse." These nightclubs feature ceremonial dancing that is done not for the purpose of motivating a war party but for the purpose of entertaining customers. The Lakota consider the name Crazy Horse to be sacred. Crazy Horse and Sitting Bull led the Sioux and Cheyenne attack on George A. Custer, whose soldiers had been shooting their people. Some time later, Crazy Horse was assassinated while in U.S. Army custody. To raise the name of Crazy Horse is to evoke a martyr and to remind people of a vast and remorseless tragedy that is personal to many Lakota.

One wouldn't expect a strip club to be named "Saint Peter's" or "Mary and Joseph." However, there are a lot of establishments around here named "Prince of Peace," "Lord of Lords," and "Divine Savior." How do we decide whether they hallow or desecrate those names? Do we judge by intent? Do we judge by purity of ideas? Do we judge by how they act?

Hallowing God's name is not merely a matter of not using the word "god" when we are angry or surprised, although it is that, too. We are careful with the name of someone we love or honor. But we take God's name in vain when we invoke it as a tool; that is, when we invoke God's power for our selfish purposes. We dishonor God's name when we treat God like a magician. All prayer prefaced by an assumption that God is a genie is foolishness. Every attempt to wield God's influence for unloving goals trashes the name. Prayer is about accomplishing God's will. To honor God's name is actually to address God when we use the words "Father in heaven," and not some imaginary useful brute who will deliver us that Mercedes-Benz and squash our enemies.

To hallow the name by which we are called as God's children, we should be "gentle, merciful, chaste, just, truthful, guileless, friendly, peaceful, and kindly disposed toward all, even toward our enemies."[16]

*

---

16. Luther, *Works* 42, 28.

Hallowed be Thy Name

This petition is the reverse side of the commandment against taking God's name in vain. We take that name in vain if we use the word itself for purposes other than those for which it was given. Worship, prayer, and some theology are proper usages, but it is difficult to think of others.

But to "take in vain" is a problematic expression. We do not speak like that any more. What does "vain" usage of something mean? It does not mean primarily to use a name in an angry or dirty way, but in a careless way, and especially in a meaningless way. We do this when we say "oh my god," for instance. But we also use God's name vainly when we use it in an attempt to invoke God's power.

This name is above all other names. Despite it being a word, not a proper name, "God" is used as a name, or as a placeholder for a name, and it is unique. This name in prayer is a name of power, a channel through which God's power might operate. We use the name wrongly when we think of God's power as being primarily a kind of force. The New Testament attempts to show us the errors of our concept of power. We think of God's power in human terms, differing from our use of force only in scope. To confound those expectations, God appears in a stable rather than a palace, dies rather than kills, blesses the poor, and forgives the humble.

Yet we constantly invoke God's force. What if we loved our enemies, and used prayer as a way of doing that? What if we invoked God's name on their behalf?

Sometimes we try to govern God along the lines of our damaged desires. We should distinguish desire from longing. Our deepest psychological desire is for love, and when this is unavailable we substitute desires for titillation or flattery or power or entertainment. These desires result in compounded illusion and ultimately in destruction. That deepest desire is actually for God, for a relationship with our heavenly Father. This need should be distinguished from the desires that clamp us to the wheel of futility, by substituting the word "longing." To the Romantic poets, longing is an intimation of infinity. It is a kind of evidence. Such longing cannot be fulfilled by satisfaction of short-term desires. Therefore when I say it is foolish to pray our desires, I am thinking of desires in the limited, illusory sense; we have not yet awakened to the depthless pain of true longing. No other pain is like this pain. As to filling our desires, more and more short-term satisfaction will never fill us. "Our heart is restless until it rests in you."[17]

So unless we ask for God's will to be done primarily, rather than for the satisfaction of our desires, we take the name in vain. Note that I am saying "desires," not "needs." This prayer addresses our needs. To use God's name

---

17. Augustine, *Confessions*, 3.

in a hallowed manner is to submit our needs, rather than to assert our wills. We in the West have always been good at asserting. Our use of this prayer should not be assertive but humble.

All invocation of God's power must look forward to the next two petitions: "thy kingdom come, thy will be done." Not to do so is to take God's name in vain. We could shorten that to say, "to take God's name." That is, to take it for our own, to use it for our own desperate and illusory purposes. But if we leave it with God, we are applying it to our Father in heaven, not to a genie with Popeye forearms or to a towering Nobadaddy who will stomp our enemies like bugs.

It is natural for us to take God's name in vain. We are blasphemers, crying out for what we want; to pray our desires is the natural direction of our flawed impulses. God's kingdom brings the fulfillment of our needs, which is to say it fulfills our longing, but it is probably the enemy of our desires—or at least of the tyranny of those desires over us. Our desires clamor unceasingly, and they refuse to serve God or even to let God be God. Our desires place themselves in the positions of gods, and we serve them abjectly. But the Lord's Prayer intends for us to regain our position of children of God rather than remaining slaves of desire. To hallow God's name is to call God "Father" again.

*

Everything I have said assumes that there is something wrong with us, but whether the fault is essential or superficial remains an open question. Where did the fault come from? Is human nature fallen? Is the story of Adam and Eve literal, historical fact; is it an imaginative truth about human nature; is it a false and misleading fable? Is human nature fundamentally good, fundamentally bad, a mixture, or none of these? We get somewhere when we understand ourselves to be unawake or unaware. Our faults can be seen as a condition of somnolence.

We offend each other carelessly, and we misunderstand each other's intentions. Does this not mean that there is a flaw in our condition somewhere? Why do we not see each other clearly? How well do we see ourselves? Henry David Thoreau, surely one of the most sublime people in American letters, wrote, "I never knew, and never shall know, a worse man than myself."[18] For him, this was clarity and not despair. Which of us can see inwardly this well, and not judge? In any case, we remain mysteries to ourselves. Perhaps this is a kind of original sin.

18. Thoreau, *Walden*, 74.

Hallowed be Thy Name

The history of Israel and Judah can be seen as a sort of parable or image of the apparent mixture of good and bad in the human personality. King David was especially loved by God, for whom the great king was "a man after his own heart."[19] David did what was right in the eyes of God; however, he also committed a deep and inexcusable crime or two. David's son Solomon presided over the greatest, most opulent era of the kingdom of Israel. He was considered to be very wise, yet eventually he was drawn aside by some of his foreign wives to worship "Astarte the goddess of the Sidonians, Chemosh the god of Moab, and Milcom the god of the Ammonites."[20] Nor did the king walk in God's way or do what was right. As punishment, the Lord gave Solomon more wives. Those kings displayed the best and worst in human nature.

Then the nation itself split, becoming a visible symbol of the divided realm of the human self. After Solomon, the twelve tribes of the great kingdom of Israel were divided among three kings: Jeroboam, Rehoboam, and Styrofoam. The division resulted in centuries of hostility among the tribes, and their piecemeal conquest by outside forces.

By Jesus' day, the division had been frozen in permanency for centuries. Judah and Benjamin were considered by the Jews to be the true and faithful nation; the other ten tribes had become a people called Samaritans, whose worship of God had fallen into error and incorrect practice. (That is what gives the Parable of the Good Samaritan its unsettling force.)

Perhaps we could think of human nature this way. The whole entity is somehow divided. There is a dark closet—or a magical forest—somewhere inside, where God's child lives. It is not the conscience; it is a place deep in the heart, where the pain and draw of longing are felt. Here the voice of God is still heard, and this child still speaks and acts. But there are roiling kingdoms at the surface, constantly at war like Israel and Judah. They are all parts of a once-holy nation, and perhaps they will become a holy nation again. It will not be in an earthly kingdom, but rather in the kingdom of God, that human nature will be made fully sacred or whole. It will not retrieve an earlier earthly glory, but will attain a higher, heavenly glory, in the light of our heavenly Father. Our ignorance will be dispelled; the mystery of who we are will be revealed. What is dark in us will be illumined. We dead will awaken. This is what we pray for in the Lord's Prayer.

*

---

19. I Sam 13:14, KJV.

20. I Kgs 11:33, NRSV. Milcom is now an internet company in southeastern Wisconsin.

"Hallowed be thy name" also has the sound of an ultimate and radical wish—what theologians would call "eschatological," pertaining to end times.[21] This petition is eschatological in the sense that God's name certainly is not hallowed now. If God's name were to be hallowed by all people in the world, history as we know it would have reached its end: the kingdom of God will have arrived on earth. In this way, "hallowed be thy name" expresses not only willingness, but the desire for the end of things as they are. The Lord's Prayer arises from the awareness that the world is tragic. Let the new world come.

How widely do we wish this petition to be answered? Would we like God's name to be hallowed by Christians, and all other people to be destroyed when God blows up the world? Do we want everyone to become Christian, and so hallow God's name? Or do we wish all people to hallow God's name, regardless of their religion, regardless of which of God's names they use? Which of these alternatives would best hallow God's name?

*

To cherish God's name must include obedience to God's commandments, primarily the Great Commandment: "Thou shalt love the Lord thy God with all thy heart, soul, mind, and strength," and the similar one, "Thou shalt love thy neighbor as thyself." The jump from hallowing to obeying is not a long one. Certainly respect includes wanting to honor someone's wishes. Christians learn that the chief *desideratum* for followers of Jesus is love. To hallow God's name, then, involves more than ceremonial obeisance, warm feelings toward an imagined or felt deity, right theological opinions, and decent behavior. To hallow God's name means to love God and God's children. All we have to do is look within ourselves on most days to understand that pure love for either God or neighbor is fleeting. Our habits are against pure love for our neighbor. Our desires and obsessions keep us focused on what interests and amuses us, on what we want. Other people get in the way. That is why this is a petition, not a description, or even a law. The fulfillment of this petition might be an answer to nearly all prayer. Weapons would be forged into pruning hooks, justice would roll down like a river, the world's resources would be shared and fairly distributed, greed and exploitation would be no more, and the world itself would no longer be beaten and robbed by our pollutants and cravings. This would not solve everything, but it would make a new world. This petition is not a fantasy, but a prescription for survival.

---

21. This is an inviting place for me to furnish a murky, boundary-pushing pun on the word "eschatological," but an example for seriousness must be set.

Hallowed be Thy Name

*

In the preceding pages I have been trying to widen the applications of items in the Lord's Prayer to include all people; but here we must also narrow the application. That is, we are praying here not only that all creation hallow God's name, but that God's name "may be hallowed also by us."[22] And this means that you and I, as we pray this prayer, are to look into ourselves. Why is it that we who have received so much often are so forgetful? Is it human nature to take things for granted, or to assume and resent a feeling of obligation even where a gift is given freely? Is it human nature to assume, in effect, that a gift we have gotten used to was created by ourselves? It is not false modesty or morbid guilt to think of ourselves as "the worst person I know" if the thought comes from intimate awareness of our own need and somnolence.

The only reasonable conclusion of such self-examination is that we cannot heal ourselves. We cannot pull ourselves up by our own Bibles. We are impaired, somehow ill, and possibly leading lives of quiet or not-so-quiet desperation. That is why this is a petition, not a resolution. We ask God that we hallow God's name. There could be no greater gift to us than our pure hallowing of God, and we need nothing less than the power of God to do it. The first petition of the Lord's Prayer is a plea for grace. We do not pray this to ingratiate ourselves with God; we do not want to be, in Mark Twain's phrase, "a Christian for revenue."[23] To the extent that we can, we adore and glorify God, requesting God's loving force to help us. The result—God's name being hallowed by everyone—would be nothing God lacks and no addition to the name of God, but it would put us in a wonderful world. There is no shame in asking how to love. "We are beggars." Jesus turned our world upside down, giving honor to beggars, being a beggar himself—homeless, living day to day—owning only his tunic and cloak, the king of kings.

*

What is the actual name of God? Jesus replaced the Hebrew name so imbued with power, terror, and awe that it was never to be fully written or pronounced, with the most common of names, one that everyone says as a child. This is a name of love, and therefore Jesus is showing us what the highest holiness is.

---

22. Luther again, *Shorter Catechism*, 347.
23. Twain, *Autobiography*, 42.

In hallowing this name, Jesus remains consistent with the program of reversals that characterize his entire ministry and presence. He does not hallow the usual titles, giving respect to names of power and glory, but implies that the name of love we give to a parent is most worthy of praise. This prayer begins with a profound statement on the nature of God. God's majesty is such that God has no interest in exceeding kings and mythological gods as to power and glory; God's love is such that our heavenly Father continues to be an affectionate parent. The humility and love at the very core of the Christian program comes from this kind, parental name.

*

Perhaps prayer is sometimes unanswered because it is sometimes unmeant. It is easy to skim over the implications of this petition with the vague notion that we wish people everywhere to respect God. But even this vague and self-congratulatory wish is deeper than our everyday version. Normally, all we intend is personal praise—from us, individually. This is faint praise indeed. I do not say this chiefly as a way of deriding our pretentions, although if we are pretentious a course of moderation certainly is in order. But our praise is faint if it is mumbled by sleepers. For us who long for God and feel the restless emptiness or despair that come from separation from our Beloved, to awaken to the kingdom of God is to know a radical new reality of being loved. From one aware of being loved, praise is not faint. There is the faint praise of duty, guilt, obligation, or desire for revenue; on the other hand there is the real and heartfelt praise and adoration of true love.

Consider how insignificant our praise is when it comes from sluggards mumbling in our sleep, or from buzzy runarounds not really paying attention. In these states, you and I offering praise make the word "puny" reverberate with grandeur. Yet each of us is of ultimate importance to God. Think of how deeply you and I can love someone. Surely God loves each of us infinitely more.

If we needed any kind of qualifications other than love to praise God, we would be inaudible. Fortunately we do not have to be models of approved conduct or doctrine, nor are we expected to be accurate. Our sad habit is to praise some cartoon instead of God. From such a premise, praise from us is a Bronx cheer from a gang of pickpockets or a motley chorus from a churchful of sanctimonious Muppets. Lovable, I suppose, in the way children of devoted parents seem lovable to them.

To be overly thoughtful about our shortcomings is really to give in to temptation. It is a temptation to think that we do not deserve to pray, or deserve to be heard, or deserve to praise God. Jesus implies that we should realize that we are no better than anyone else, ask forgiveness, and move ahead. God's love takes care of the vast chasm between heaven and us: between the kingdom of light and the dark forgetfulness of isolation.

*

Church talk is full of the words "worship" and "praise," though I find it impossible to believe that God wants us to grovel and flatter. Such tyrannized behavior diminishes not merely us humans; it would diminish a god that expected it. Here the idol we thought was in the Bible and in our churches is exposed not as God, not the heavenly Father of Jesus. Abject worship is not what happens in a love relationship. Worship and praise—in the sense that the prayer implicitly redefines them—are acknowledgements of reality. To praise God and to worship God are to be present—to be aware, attentive, and awake. Enlightenment and worship are the same; praise and presence are the same.

In this way the Lord's Prayer gives us a portrait of God, the Father of Jesus. The Holy One is our heavenly Father, whose name when hallowed awakens us to a happy childhood. To be aware and a child is to be mature in innocence—to be an adult in the kingdom of God. The Lord of the kingdom is not our own raging, distracted child inflated large as a thundercloud; the Lord is our shepherd, a "good shepherd" who lays down his life for the sheep of his hand, the people of his pasture. The Lord is the lover of our souls.

*

To hallow God's name means "to love the Lord thy God" and to "love thy neighbor as thyself." One can hardly begin to imagine what disruption would occur if everyone did this. We might not pray this petition with much enthusiasm if we were alert to its implications, which are inhospitable to our desires and obsessions. Fulfillment of the request might put us to considerable inconvenience.

Our economic system would break down. To begin absurdly small, suppose you want to buy a car. If the car were being offered by a private person, you would now want to give him or her plenty of money for it; all that she needs, or at least all that you can spare. And she would want to give you the car. No loans. The banking system would go on the fritz in five minutes, for good this time. Is it not the point of business to buy low and sell high? Are you a coffee broker? You would give everything you could to the Kenyan growing the beans, and be delighted to sell them only for what the enterprise costs you. The systems of the world would crumble, to be replaced by what? By sharing and by adequate food for everyone? We would not need incentives, such as capitalism supplies, because our hearts would have changed. We would work hard and do good work, not to get ahead, but for the beauty of it. Success would not require force, nor a communist, socialist, or capitalist system, but good will and cheerful abandonment of self-interest. What kind of world are we talking about? The kingdom of God.

It gets worse. If God's name were hallowed on the scale this prayer envisions, *all* people would love and revere God. Consider this for a moment. Finished would be our special status, not merely as Christians, but as the "right" Christians. It is splendidly pleasant to be part of a minority when it is the only minority God likes. But if this petition were granted *en masse*, the great majority of people, whom we quietly dislike and distrust, would be elevated to our status.

The unknown majority are our slaves right now. They do our work for us, and it is very important work. They carry us on their shoulders. On those shoulders, we stretch up our arms to praise God. This petition would be like a giant Emancipation Proclamation for the rest of the world. We would be up to our necks in people, all kinds of people, all makes and models and persuasions. We would be no better in the eyes of God than the average deadbeat or theologian. The righteously correct minority would drain the world of Prozac.

Of course this idea of total equal worth expresses reality as it is—that we are no better in the eyes of God than anyone else—but our delusion has been dispelled. It has been a gratifying illusion, but it is a mean and fatal one. It prevents us from really intending, and therefore praying, the Lord's Prayer. It is simply wrong to ask that God be interested in the love and respect, and the welfare, of only some human beings. To pray this petition backwards—intending a minority instead of all people—is truly a diabolical use of the prayer and a dishonoring of God's name. *Lord, we pray that you remove our illusions.*

In the kingdom of God, we would all assume our true role of beggars. Happy beggars! Everything would be ours, when nothing is our own. The sickness of false self would be shed like a scaly skin. As winged, luminescent people we would emerge immortal into light and colors we had never been able to imagine. Joy would be everywhere, and even Presbyterians would be in love. We would not miss all that junk we had fancied to be treasure.

So we are asking for life—not merely more abundant life, but radically renewed and radiant life. Only, from this side of the divide, such a change frightens us. The dizzy gap between there and here makes us afraid and theologically correct. Better a known evil, we might think, than an unknown good. Since the unknown must be taken on trust, this petition demands that we trust God. The new life, whatever it is, our heavenly Father holds in his hands. Do we want to give up everything for that unimaginable pearl God holds out to us? Because it comes from God, we are willing. Faith in God is required for this first petition—utter abandon. We will go where God is; we will leave everything behind if need be, and count it a blessing. The first petition holds all the other petitions. In it, we take God's hand.

*

What is God's name? For Christians, one of God's names is "Jesus Christ." Such a claim sounds bizarre or impious to a non-Christian, but it is the essence of Christian belief: we can address Christ and know that we address God. In Christ, we know something of God. Our understanding of God, our childhood in God's kingdom, and our hope do not exist in the abstract; they do not exist apart from the Second Person of the Trinity. We relate to God through and in Christ. God without Christ is what? Loving? We might wish it so, but Christ assures us that God indeed loves us. Jesus gives us a picture of God, whose most awe-inspiring power is his love for us. By teaching us this prayer, Jesus teaches us about God. So for those who can embrace the teaching of Jesus, here is a name for God, a name or representation that we can hallow by our devotion—by implication hallowing the One behind the name, whose unknown name is above every name.

The prayer—that is, the text alone, in and of itself—does not require that one adopt the Christian faith. God by any name is still God; and the word "God" is not a name at all. God as described in the Lord's Prayer is great enough and loving enough not to be offended by our various names. The Supreme is in our names, and is beyond all names. To hallow God's name is to acknowledge the name above every name, even the one by which *we* know God.

*

We beggars do well to swallow our pride and recognize the Lord's Prayer as a purely petitionary prayer. Even when it does not seem to be, such as in "hallowed be thy name," the prayer is nothing but requests, begging.

If we were to see our other prayers from an outside perspective, they might humiliate us by their selfishness and presumption. The tone of these prayers is in some ways their substance. Consider two examples.

My tradition is what has been called "Mainline," as I was educated at a Presbyterian college and seminary, and liturgical, as I was raised and confirmed as a Lutheran. My college hymn, "O God Our Help in Ages Past," still brings tears to my eyes and makes me stand up straight.

> O God our help in ages past,
> Our hope for years to come,
> Our shelter from the stormy blast,
> And our eternal home.
> Beneath the shadow of thy throne . . .[24]

I love the stately, comforting solemnity of the tone, the reassuring solidity of the hymn's ponderousness. It is grand and slow, like the growth of tradition. It makes me want to pray:

> *O thou Great Presbyterian, we spread before Thee these our reasonable petitions in decency and good order. Vouchsafe to us our polity. Assure our traditions and petrify them forever in the kingdom of God. Respect our educations, remain Thou instituted forever God in God's Self, and grant Thou me a Scottish accent and all the rights, privileges, and responsibilities thereof. Amen, and amen.*

My understanding of God in that context is therefore largely cultural, so much so that when I am pulled out of a good-smelling Presbyterian church and smuggled into a contemporary service at something like a Brookwood Worship Center, surrounded by crisp, eerily beaming people all carrying well-thumbed Bibles, I feel like a disguised felon. A long-haired minister with a wireless microphone steps to a podium, the people begin nodding and amenning, and I fear that I am in danger of becoming a complete, insincere dorkwit, praying,

> *O awesome God, I just praise you! Lord, I just praise you for your awesomeness, and Lord, I just want to invite you into my life, etc.*

And so it goes interminably with multiple variations on the same, until the minister, who looks like he has just been through a car wash and blow dried, slides into the sermon, pacing across the stage in front of a huge projection screen, expounding upon a limp, gilt-edged, open Bobble. And then, of course, we all sing the praise song, "Awesome Lord":

> *I think you're awesome, Lord.*
> Refrain: *Awesome, Awesome, Awesome, Lord! Awesome, Awesome Lord!*
> *Our God is an awesome God.*
> Refrain, three times.

---

24. Lutheran Church in America, *Service Book*, 168.

Everyone here thinks you're awesome, Lord.
Refrain x 7.
Awesome Lord, Awesome Lord, Awesome Lord.
Refrain x 100.

I appreciate that these praise songs are contemporary versions of the old classic, "One Hundred Bottles of Beer on the Wall." I wish I were on a bus trip. As I leave, glancing furtively beyond the pack of people to the open door like a man underwater looking for air, the nosey grownups in the aisle assure me that they will be praying for me this week.

In the vast parking lot, trying to remember where I put my car, its color, its make and model, I try to pin down my visceral upset. The problem here is that this whole hour and a half has been one careless address to a cultural invention that is not God but something else. The impertinence of offering up this sloppy chowder as praise! Effortless clichés and smug ignorance! Let's don't kid ourselves that we are sincere: laziness is never sincerity. But somewhere a nagging voice says, *Congratulations! How right you are. So what else, Mister Theologian, is* your *mainline god? You think, maybe, you're different?*

God transcends all our understandings, and we are all more wrong than right. But many of our understandings of God are gateways. If our window is small and the sky is large, we still can pray in the light. None of us has God, but we may rest assured that God has us.

In these two examples, the limitations of our understanding are obvious. In the first, tradition drowses us into the assurance that there is only tradition, and nothing outside tradition; whereas Jesus went about bursting the boundaries of custom. In the second example, the long perspective of the larger Church stretching back through history is fearfully ignored, and we are lost in small, egocentric, me-and-God hole that if followed to its extreme, lands us in an isolation that looks very much like the Inferno. In each case, we children of God blather baby talk.

Both groups, to borrow Abraham Lincoln's words, "read the same Bible, and pray to the same God."[25] Sometimes it would seem that they are not praying to the same God—that in fact no two people pray to the same God; but our assurance in hallowing the name that is above every name that we can devise or imagine, is that we are in fact praying to the same, the One, God, and that we are all members of the same family, with the same Father in Heaven.

*

25. Lincoln, *Collected Works* VIII, 333.

God does not need our praise. God's name is already holy. If God's name were to be hallowed, would God's reputation be enhanced?

If this petition were granted, we, not God, would be changed. We are asking not for some addition to God's glories, but a change in our hearts. God's name is holy in itself (except that the concept of "name" exists only for us); we beg that it may be hallowed, that is, treated as holy and thought of as holy. This wish changes not at all the holiness of God, but it changes us. It is as if we were God's name, and "holy" means realized or made real. God becomes real for and in us; therefore, we become real. So our heavenly Father wishes us to pray this petition not for his sake but for ours. It can open our eyes to reality. "To be awake is to be alive."[26]

However, there are many aspects of each of these petitions. In another sense, we are asking for a god of holiness. We are not at the moment asking for a god of vengeance, or a god of our prosperity, or a god of national victory. We ask for a certain kind of appearance of God: sanctity. We beg to perceive God as holy; so shall we be made holy through our realization that we are loved.

In its purest sense, this petition is the ultimate prayer. Our minds are temporarily cleared, all desires stilled, as if we had achieved a perfect state of contemplation. We ask that the Holy One be Holy. This first petition is a perfect mystical moment: we are contemplating God, and only God. No desires filter in, no attributes are cooked up by humans; there is simply the pure and holy God. The Lord's Prayer starts with the goal of all prayer: union with God.

This mind- and desire-stilling might appear to be self-hypnotic praise singing, but notice that one is repetitive noise, and the other is silence. One dulls the mind; the other awakens it. This petition is a kind of tautology: Hallowed be the Holy One, Holy be God. Perhaps the Lord of the Lord's Prayer is giving us at the outset his intimate vision of God, his being-God.

The petition is also a declaration of the nature of God. There is no list of attributes in this prayer, no "gracious, powerful, righteous, glorious," and so on. Not that these are necessarily wrong, but the one petition that comes closest to a statement on the nature of God encapsulates and transcends all the attributes we know and use, in this silent tautology: The Holy is Holy, God is God. True, the rest of the prayer implies some divine attributes when it asks God to feed us, protect us, and forgive us: these are attributes of a heavenly Father. But this petition steps above or inside the "father" image, and touches the holiness of God more intimately than those attributes we have traditionally assigned.

---

26. Thoreau, *Walden*, 86.

What does "holiness" mean in the new sense that this prayer gives it? If "servant," "praise," "worship," and other terms have been redefined, surely this term has also been newly understood. Holiness here no longer means that which is removed, apart, forbidden, and therefore dangerous, like the Ark of the Covenant that can be death to touch. It is exactly the opposite: to be holy is to be intimate in the purity of a love relationship. It is the divine Self in union with our true Self. "That Art Thou," is the phrase of the Upanishads: the intimacy is beyond what we can imagine.

*

We are asking for life in this petition—eternal life—when we wish for God's name to be hallowed by us. The living and the dead will be distinguished from each other by which of them hallows God's name—that is, by those who are awake in the kingdom of heaven, enlightened by God's light and aware of God's love. Everything permanent is related to God, belongs to God, and reflects our relationship; that is, it hallows God's name. The dead clinkers floating around in space, the denser-than-iron balls of rock that were once stars but now are cold and dark—these will not praise God's name.[27] But as God is the resurrection and the life—as God is love—that which is alive will sing the music of the spheres.

*

The first petition of the prayer expresses a wish for reality. In praying this petition, we seek the truth. All that shall remain real must be related to God. "None can keep alive his own soul."[28]

Often we think and act as though we believed in our own power to resurrect ourselves, or in the immortality of our souls. Our souls are not immortal; they will not stay alive by their own power, or because they were made to last forever. They all depend on God. We are alive only in the mind of God.

We might distinguish what is real from what is temporary, or what is real from what is only an illusion because it is fleeting like a dream. That is, perhaps we could say that what is permanent is more real than that which is temporary, though both exist now. What is temporary must be part of the illusory world; what is permanent must belong to another world.

Greater reality does not exist apart from God, and by hallowing God's name we signify our reality. It is not enough merely to acknowledge God's

---

27. Yet perhaps "even the stones would cry out."
28. Ps 22:29, KJV.

existence, or to "believe in God." As James says, "the devils believe, and tremble."[29] To hallow God's name is to be happy in the knowledge that God is the highest good and the highest blessing; it is to know that we are enfolded in God's love.

We do not always live as though we believe this. What is good behavior—what is Christian ethics—but to hallow the name of God? We recognize the face of God in others. There is a family resemblance in the children of God: they have the image of God shining from their needy faces. That recognition is like honoring a king in the person of his servants and messengers. Every other human being is a messenger of God, bearing God's seal and likeness. When we love and serve these children of the heavenly Father, we honor the Father.

But we can be careless. We neglect other people; it is not simply that we commit outright crimes against them. We know of people who are lonely, afraid, depressed, or hungry. Yet we do nothing. Partly, we are not brave enough. It takes considerable courage to do good. This petition asks for the courage to honor God's name in other people.

And of course we can be good at combining crimes with neglect: when we hurt someone far away through a selfish business, national, or church policy that creates suffering somewhere in the world, we remain comfortable in our ignorance, as if our ignorance absolves us of responsibility. It is true that we cannot help everyone in need; we cannot learn enough these days to avoid being part of large, unjust forces. But could we not do better? This is part of hallowing God's name; it is not simply a little option for people with particular political views. If we all did better than we do by one person, the world would be renewed.

Perhaps the subtlest of our failures to honor God's name is to act out the prejudices and petty judgments with which so many of us were raised. Children grow. It is natural to be marred by the ignorance and neuroses of our families and friends, but eventually we become adults and need to assume responsibility for what we do. I do not know if there are Spiritual Laws, but why would not the unseen realm operate along definite lines just as the physical world does? A reasonable Spiritual Law might be: "What we do unto others, we guarantee ourselves." Failing to respect others, we fail to honor God and hallow God's name, dishonoring and damaging ourselves.

*

---

29. Jas 2:19, KJV.

Finally, we ask for vision; we ask to see. We cannot honestly hallow the name of God until we understand that God is holy. We cannot hallow the name of God out of duty or a sense of responsibility; least of all can we truly hallow God's name out of fear. We do not hallow God's name because we want to go to heaven. Perhaps that is actually the worst thing we can do: to playact our respect for God only because we want something God gives rather than wanting our heavenly Father.

We ask to see the beauty and holiness of the Master of the Universe, that we may "glorify God and enjoy Him forever."

4

Thy Kingdom Come

THE SETTING OF THE Lord's Prayer is the kingdom of God—a concept straight from Jesus and central to Christianity. The prayer might be considered representative of all prayer that praises a deity and asks for benefits. It can be prayed as such. But the prayer makes complete sense only for the world it invokes. That world is where God's presence is realized, where all delusion is dispelled: the kingdom of God.[1]

*

Problems arise. We are "born to trouble, as the sparks fly upward."[2] That is part of the contract when we come here. Around the time of birth, we are each issued a big head, tiny feet, a blue or pink blanket, and a variable set of coupons for such things as cars, romance, adventurous travel, ice cream—and mixed among the jolly coupons in an unpredictable ratio are coupons for dreck. These dolorous items are like prayer beads: we pray about them one by one throughout life, concentrating on them with fine attention to detail, rubbing them over and over again with our minds.

It seems possible for some people to go through the troubles of life untroubled. If you were one of those people, you would not be reading this book; and if I were one of those people, I would not be writing it. But in this way we help each other. If the kingdom of God were to come, we would all feed each other, comfort each other, pray for each other, and in

---

1. Or "kingdom of heaven" according to Matthew, who as a Jewish writer does not wish to use God's name.
2. Job 5:7, KJV.

some measure heal each other. The troubles of life have no explanation. It seems that we are put here to be wounded, and wounded we shall be; and we shall wound others—most of all the ones who love us. And whether those wounds come because we deserve them, because we are meant to use them to learn, because we have generated them in the past, or whether they just happen in an imperfect universe, we cannot tell. Holocaust survivor and Nobel laureate Elie Wiesel has said, "the great questions in life have no answers."[3]

We assume that in the kingdom of God no troubles will come. No children will be born into poverty, none will suffer, no one will lie, and no one will abuse another person. Even the weather will be good. We will not have to do work we don't like. All of this might be correct, but Jesus certainly did not tell us so. He said that the kingdom of God has already come amid all these troubles, these lies and diseases and crimes. God's kingdom is here alongside and within the diseased and wounded heart, alive among the questions that have no answers.

In the pain and despair of illness, the kingdom of God is present. To those unjustly in prison, the kingdom of God comes. As we ruin children's lives with our carelessness and insecurity, God's reign begins. If the world would never be just, if the questions would never be answered, if the lion would never lie down with the lamb, and if the cruel and the violent always ruled the world, the light would shine in darkness—the everlasting light. It is always Bethlehem, it is always Calvary, it is always the Resurrection and the Life, as far as we are concerned, as far as we know. This is the world of the Lord's Prayer, the world we live in. All the promises have been fulfilled. If we speak, feel, and act our prayers, we can be the answer we seek.

*

The kingdom of God is unknowable, but it is somewhat doable. In asking for God's kingdom to come, we are asking that it come to us, come in us; we are asking that God's will be done also by us, as Luther said. The reign of God is not our reign, so it is alien to our desire to know and control, but if there is anything we might control it is what we do. Therefore if we ask to carry out God's will or reign, we are stating our pledge to love. Implied is our intention to "do justly, love mercy, and walk humbly with our God;" to care for the sick, support the oppressed, feed the hungry, and do all that may achieve a just and a lasting peace among ourselves and among all humankind. We promise that as God's authority comes, we will be the

---

3. Wiesel, Press Club, Q&A.

first to obey, and this obedience means loving attention. It is immaterial that we will obey imperfectly at first: when someone enlists in the army, he or she is not claiming already to be a perfect soldier.[4] However, the point is that in praying for God's kingdom to come, we materialize our intentions rather than simply asking for a vague power to come solve all our problems, answer all our questions, and heal all our wounds.

Perhaps we are confident that these things will happen—if not in this life, then in the next. Such confidence rests on the expectation lodged in this petition. Along with the expectation, perhaps in front of it, is the intention of the petition. The requests in these petitions imply that we want help with developing the right intentions. However haltingly and partially at first, we want to prefer serving God to serving idols. We lovingly attend to God: we are present, and our awareness is upon God. We attend to God instead of attending to our artificial self and its symbols. Surely to serve God in this new sense would be to act out of our true Self, which is an image of God; but the world is such as it is because we live our false selves—the masks of selfishness and desire painted onto our faces.

*

A fellow once asked me what God is "for." I think he got the idea for his question from prayers he had heard or read. Most prayers are utilitarian—they operate on the working assumption that God is a tool for getting what we want. They bend our concept of God until we think like idolaters. God, then, is *for* something, some purpose. To be a Christian "for revenue" is nothing compared to this astounding notion.

Utilitarian prayer resembles trying to cure measles by surgically removing all the red dots, like some people's concept of foreign policy. But this prayer addresses the underlying cause of our illness. It removes our terrors by striking at their common root: our false selves. The false self is the photographic negative of our separation from God.

The Lord's Prayer asks for and describes the kingdom of God. That kingdom, rather than any earthly kingdom we could imagine and ask for, is the location of our true happiness and wellbeing. The prayer does not express our wish for vindication, prosperity, or advantages. It certainly does not ask for vengeance or power. Instead, the prayer asks for God, and for God's will; it voices our longing. To ask for God's kingdom might be to ask to go to God.

---

4. Vince Lombardi said that we should try to achieve perfection. We cannot be perfect, but in striving for perfection we can achieve excellence.

"Be ye therefore perfect, as your father which is in heaven is perfect." Matt. 5:48, KJV.

To ask for God's kingdom rather than our personal desires is not only a step toward surrender; it is a step of trust, an essential element of faith. We do not know exactly what God's kingdom is, but we do understand that it is the heavenly Father's love and grace. In praying, we begin to experience the kingdom; so again, the Lord's Prayer is part of its own fulfillment. We move away from delusion and begin to be present and awake in the heavenly kingdom. We start to practice the presence of God, and become more real and present ourselves.

In this petition, we ask for help in acting on the reality that there are "no other gods before" our Father in heaven. As this petition is enacted within us and by us, the process of "letting God be God" takes on new light and new warmth.

*

What is the kingdom of God? The prayer is structured so as to provide an instant answer: it is God's will being done. This is not a series of orders carried out like the commands of a Roman governor. This petition and the next are twins in that respect. The rest of the prayer describes aspects of God's kingdom: it is where God's name is hallowed, where our needs are met, and where there is no temptation or evil.

The cautious idolater in us wants a more specific, visual plan of the kingdom of God. Are the walls pink, white, or blue? Are there benches, and is formal wear required? What language will be spoken? What will our "spiritual bodies" be like? Perhaps everything will be uncanny, strangely familiar. But in any case, we might wish for something more concrete than an assurance that in God's kingdom we will be restored to awareness of God's love. But we have to let that wish go.

*

As we pray for the heavenly kingdom, we begin to make God's reality our reality; this is a considerable advance on our usual frame of mind. We begin to make the child's consciousness our consciousness, and that childlike consciousness might be called "Christ-consciousness." We pray this petition all the time, and saying it has become mere word casserole. So I propose some strange ways to think of this petition, in hopes that they will illuminate its foreignness and radical nature.

We give something to God. God is the beggar in this prayer; we ask for something for God. We ask for God's kingdom so that in the mystery of God, God's wish is granted. God comes to us as a child in a manger, dependent on us. If we do not pray, God does not get that kingdom. That is, God is not God for us.

God becomes powerless, so we can abandon our infatuation with power. Yes, in theory we cannot do a thing about God's kingdom. We cannot save ourselves; we cannot save the world: only God can do these things. But this petition is not theory; it is God's weakness placed on our lips. If God does not have the power, who does?

This petition should be prayed because the God we imagined has ceased to exist. This petition shatters our conception of God. God has chosen to be a helpless infant in our arms. We kiss the baby's forehead and sing a lullaby. We want God to be happy.

This petition is a battle of wills—a wrestling match—between us and God. We want the kingdom. God says No. We demand the kingdom. God says Way no. God says, Just try to get it. See if you can take it from me.

Give it here, we say. Now!

When I feel like it, God says. Which is never.

God does not want his kingdom to come. We are going to have to pray like Peter and Paul to get it.

The idea of a human being wrestling with God is found in the first book of the Bible, in a mysterious story. Jacob wrestles with the angel or apparition of God, called simply a man. Day is about to break, and the man cannot get away from Jacob, who wants a blessing. God does not want to be caught in daylight. This can happen only in the night of human sleep. The angel dislocates Jacob's thigh (ouch) and whisks away.[5] This is either a relic of some kind of primitive superstition or a profound and uncanny truth.

- Perhaps in our night of sin, embracing God appears to be a fight with God.
- Perhaps the strangest thing about God is God's intimacy with us.
- Prayer is an argument; it strengthens our insistence.
- Prayer exposes us as the roughnecks we really are. We would like to think of ourselves as good, but when pushed, our combative side arises.
- With Jacob, this man, or God in disguise, picked the fight. Hey, want to wrestle? Who, me? Yeah, you. Oof! Arghh! It's YOU!? God started the match because we would never come to grips with God on our own initiative. We are too pious; we are idolaters.

---

5. Gen 32:24–29.

- What is life but a wrestling match? The Jacob story, and prayer itself, are clarifications of life. The troubles we had—the adversity and the defeats and the body blows? Guess who they really came from.
- You think God is a myth? How does that hip feel?
- Perhaps the story is an image of internal struggle, Self against self.

We do not really want God's rule; or at best we are ambivalent. God listens to our prayer for the kingdom and waits. It is a long wait, because God will not grant that which is not truly in our hearts. Just to want the kingdom of God can be a struggle.

God hears our *real* prayer in this petition. Our real prayer runs something like this:

- *Thy kingdom come. I don't know what the kingdom is and therefore I don't mean it. I just pray this because it's part of the Lord's Prayer, which is what we are supposed to pray. Praying it is a way of making you like me, making you give me what I want, of forgiving me for being a poltroon and for ignoring the poor; and basically that's all this prayer means to me. I am earning points for heaven here.*
- *Thy kingdom come, as long as that kingdom means all good stuff for me and people I like—things like peace and harmony and tranquility and happiness—but I am assuming that these good things will not come to scruffy ethnic people and Democrats/Republicans and other substandard individuals.*
- *Thy kingdom come, but not yet. Thy kingdom come: at some indefinite future date. Thy kingdom come after I have made my money and had my fun. Definitely after my date this weekend.*
- *Thy kingdom come. I trust you, that the kingdom is the best thing for everyone, including me, so whatever it is and every bit as soon as You will, may it come. Just kidding.*

The kingdom of God arriving tomorrow afternoon might wreck the surface of our lives. But to ask for the kingdom of God is to ask for it *now*. What a risk this petition can appear to be! It requires surrendering our superficial hopes and fears, shedding our false securities, gathering up our courage, and seeking our deepest dreams. It means to ask that like Adam we awaken and discover the dream of Eve to be true. Jesus said that a house divided against itself cannot stand. It will become all one thing, or all the other, and we now dare to resolve the issue. Perhaps the result will be fundamental and astounding.

Here we might deal with a common question: Should we love God more than we love any human being? Teaching at religious colleges, I have heard young people say, "I want my future spouse to love God more than they love me." This wish might be well-intended, but it could lead to being sacrificed with a stone knife on a stone altar, at least figuratively. You are asking for someone to trust their mental voices more than their heart. Our brains can mimic the voice of the Holy Spirit, and even the devil can quote Scripture.[6] You are asking that someone numb and destroy his or her own heart.

What God wants is for us to love God with our whole heart, mind, and strength. And God wants us to love our neighbor just the same. God does not want love in degrees, either for God or for other people. The only love worth the name is flat-out. You love God wholly. You love your lover wholly. You love your children wholly. This business of loving someone more than another, or God more or less than some given quantity, is false piety. How could God want such nonsense? The human heart was created to love everyone full blast, all the time. There are no comparisons in the kingdom of God. I want to be loved with the love of God. And I want to love with that same strength. I want to be big enough to accept and offer such love.

This petition is pure sin. "Kingdom, now!" we pray. "No, I shall not," God replies. God's answer is No, isn't it? I mean, has the kingdom come?[7] So we are not taking no for an answer. We are persistent little beggars. God has said, "I don't want you to have it." In this light, most petitionary prayer is an affront, and ought not to be prayed. What if "success" in such prayer means getting what God did not want us to have? Our success in prayer is a defeat for God, an instance of God being not God, and of our wills being stronger than God's. We demand the kingdom of God, though it is not ours and God wishes to keep it. Just so, his mother asks Jesus to create wine at a wedding.[8] "It is not my time," he answers. "Do what he tells you," she tells the servants, and Jesus gives in. It is not yet time for the kingdom of God, but we request it *now*. It is not of this world, but we demand it *here*. It is God's kingdom; we want it for ourselves.

But part of this petition is its indefiniteness. We should be willing for the kingdom to come now, but "now" is not part of the prayer. There must be a value in the transformation of impatience to anticipation: the effect might be to prepare us. It is not conceivable that those who are asleep could

---

6. Matt 4:6.

7. Yes, according to Jesus, in that it is within and among us. However, this petition is also according to Jesus.

8. John 2:1–8.

be ready. Surrendering our timetable means surrendering our definition of the kingdom. The requirements of love are timeless; the nature of love is eternal. Love will wait while all lesser desires pass away.

Saying a prayer does not immediately make us over. But what is the alternative?

These ideas are meant to provide ways to consider how different the kingdom of God is. At the same time, it must be intimately familiar. We must pray for the kingdom, and we must be willing to wait forever; it has been within and among us all along.

*

This petition is a leap toward the invisible.[9] It is a petition to be prayed both carefully, and with abandon. We should be careful to understand what we are asking. We are not asking for an increase of pleasantness in our world. We are asking for another world. We are not asking for more justice, but Justice; and we are asking to do justly. We are asking not for a better life, but for the Resurrection and the Life; we are asking to live. When Jesus says, "I am the Resurrection and the Life,"[10] he causes us to see life not as a chronology but as a person. Once again our notions are fundamentally changed. Life is not the unending quotidian which we experience ordinarily; life is God, a person, a relation. Therefore, we do not wish for the known world to remain the same except with improvements, with bad people, disease, and disasters removed; we ask to stop hurting others. We are not simply asking for enough for everybody; we are asking to share. We are not asking merely for everyone's intentions to become good, but for our own intentions to become good.

We imagine peace and harmony and good weather when we think of the kingdom of God: we ask for our fantasy. This might be wrong in an ultimate sense, because as imperfect people we cannot conceive of the perfect world. But there is something constructive about imagining the best conceivable world. Our imaginations educate us. If we can learn to imagine ever better worlds, perhaps we can prepare the way for the kingdom of God in us.

Perhaps the arrival of the kingdom here awaits our arrival there. We are not ready. Our heavenly Father says, "No," because we are not ready; we would not be happy in a place for which we are not yet prepared. When we are ready, we will find that the kingdom is ready. To pray this prayer intentionally is to prepare the way of the Lord. How could the kingdom come

---

9. St. Exupery's Little Prince learns that "Anything essential is invisible to the eyes." *Little Prince*, 63.

10. John 11:25, NRSV.

to dry imaginations, narrow minds, and small hearts? It would be painful beyond belief; it would be a kind of hell. *May your kingdom come in me.*

When Jesus says, "love your neighbor," he is saying, "prepare the way." When he says, "pray in this way," he is saying, "prepare!"

*

During the Vietnam War there were incidents of infantrymen in firefights radioing to call down artillery on their own positions, because the enemy had closed in hand-to-hand. We have to realize that praying this petition is to call down fire on our own positions. Let us not pray this petition casually; because once those big shells start coming in they will blow hell out of us.

The petitions in the Lord's Prayer are like pieces of a hologram. When you shatter a glass hologram picture, each of the shards contains the whole picture in miniature. In a similar way, this petition contains other petitions. The whole Prayer is about the kingdom of God. To ask for God's kingdom to come is to ask for forgiveness and more. If the kingdom would come tonight, our earthbound desires would be weighed in the balance and found wanting. Let us make up our minds that the first victim of the kingdom of God will be our false selves. Not only is the world a mess due to our own contributions, we are messes ourselves. We are fighting hand-to-hand with the false self and we are calling in the artillery. To those asleep, the Day of the Lord will be blinding—"darkness and not light," as the Old Testament prophet says.[11]

> I will bring the blind by a way that they knew not;
> I will lead them in paths that they have not known:
> I will make darkness light before them,
> and crooked things straight.
> These things will I do unto them,
> and not forsake them.[12]

The first thing to go—why not give it up now?—will be our complacency. And along with it would go our sense of guilt. They are two sides of the same coin. They are our currency in this economic system; but the light of heaven will sear our system away. We will be absolutely poor; we will have to acknowledge ourselves as beggars, without virtue and without guilt.

---

11. Amos 5:18, KJV. "The light which puts out our eyes is darkness to us." Thoreau, *Walden*, 324.

12. Isa 42:16, KJV.

Where would we be without our guilt? In the kingdom of God. We are so used to our guilt, we clutch it like a blanket. We would hardly know ourselves without it. We constantly play to an invisible audience of our imagination. But Jesus implies that we have access to the Self: the kingdom of God is within us. We defeat ourselves by thinking that we are unfit to receive God's love, that we are unfit to love with abandon. But Jesus says the kingdom of God is among us. The world as we know it depends on idolatry and self-destruction. But Jesus says that world is impermanent.

When the kingdom comes, our true Selves will be bared to the world. Do you suppose when Jacob wrestled the angel of God, they were both attired in voluminous flowing robes, just as in our Bible illustrations? The thought makes one feel squiggly inside. We are not even close to being ready.

*

How long should we have to wait? It is not unreasonable that we become impatient for the kingdoms of our desires. We rage, we become depressed, we despair, we give up, and we learn to hate. When it is finally God's kingdom that we await, we are patient.

Our kingdoms of desire will not come. The kingdom of God is a more likely bet than the kingdom of man. The kingdoms of fantasy will never arrive, no matter how vehemently we reproach God for not ushering them in. Some of these kingdoms of ours are not too bad; they might even be influenced by what Jesus preached. At best, we want peace on earth, enough for everyone, and good will among all people. At worst we imagine a final gruesome destruction surprising our enemies, and a carnival of pleasures for ourselves. Our theologies sometimes are built upon the tension between our fantasies and the world as it is: theology is often a structure meant to explain the discrepancy between a good God and a bad world, as we define them. Systematically, we work up a notion of prayer as a way of bringing the two fantasies together. Our desires are once again the center of this cosmology: our notion of God is brought into action against the world along the lines we wish.

The dynamo within many theologies is theodicy, or the question of how a good, wise, and all-knowing God can permit the pain and suffering in this world. This is proper, but in another sense, Jesus bypasses the theodicy question (and perhaps theology as we know it), because the "kingdom of heaven" is an unknown. The most solid description of it involves love, and involves the life and work of Jesus. But we do not know what will be "done" except the will of God, and we do not know where this will be done except in the presence of God. Our deepest longing is for the kingdom of God *for its own sake*. That is, we do not wish for the kingdom because it is attractive to us: we do not look for the pleasing details that ordinarily make us desire some new kingdom, some new place in time. We do not desire the kingdom of heaven even for peace, good will, and plenty for the world's poor. We love God as the men on the road to Emmaus said: "Did not our hearts burn within us?"[13] We love God because we love Jesus, and we long for the kingdom.

*

Being Boss of the Universe is a thankless job, and we should be glad to get rid of it. We should also get rid of the concept. All its benefits are paper benefits: we have written our own job description, and the contract is printed in disappearing ink. In "letting God be God," we are trusting in the only reliable fact of the universe: the person of God. The actual kingdom of God might involve levels of physics and geometry that are over our heads. What if we made up a wonderful kingdom of glory and then found that we did not calculate the correct obloidal vectors?

The kingdom of heaven is unknown because it is new—not simply a refreshed world, but a new world. It is also a reversal of the world we know, the world whose ideas of power, wealth, and even goodness are wrong in the eyes of Jesus. "My kingdom is not of this world," Jesus told Pilate.[14] From beginning to end, the gospels imply a kingdom of reversals, where the last shall be first, those of low degree are exalted, where the dead live, and where the Son of God is laid in a feeding trough. We long for this deeply, yet we can hardly believe it. It clashes with our usual frames of reference.

So the measurements to which we are accustomed cannot describe the kingdom of God. We are unable to know it in our present state. Our senses register other phenomena. We are good at things like scratching, peeling coconuts, and chattering; figuring out the Mind of God is a stretch. But our deepest Selves have heard Jesus, and our longing has been awakened. "Did not our hearts burn within us?"

*

A note of caution. Sometimes when people tell you to put God on the throne of your life, to turn over your life to God, to surrender your will to God, they are really telling you to

- agree with them

---

13. Luke 24:32, KJV.
14. John 18:36, KJV.

- act out every bizarre impulse that comes into your head
- believe that in effect you are God after all.

The last point might seem peculiar. I mean that "putting God on the throne of one's life," to use so-called evangelical terminology, can be simply a means of elevating oneself: I snatch God's infallibility and ascribe it to myself. I am acting out God's will, so gangway, evildoers! If you disagree with me, I quote the Bible and the Bible is God's inerrant word, meaning that however I interpret what it says, God Himself is shouting you down!

How do we actually put God on the thrones of our lives? With humility. By acknowledging that another person might also have God on the throne of his or her life, and that we might be wrong. This does not do much for one's self-assertiveness and confidence, and confidence sells; confidence works—in this world. When we believe we are right, we can be inspired with the courage to do right; and we can be deluded, bull-headed, and heartless. Human activity is almost inherently ironic, entailing double meanings when least expected. We can never be humble enough. Perhaps we imagine that when we have made it into the kingdom of heaven and are given our green and gold jerseys, we can say, "I was sufficiently humble." Revenue again.

One taste, one intimation, one whiff of the kingdom of God would make us all genuinely and honestly humble. We will renounce what we thought we knew when the Day of Jubilee comes. There will be a lot of forced renunciation going on. Our house, our possessions, our country, and even our body, will be gone. Here profound skepticism and profound humility merge. If this causes hope rather than depression, we have a sign of faith. Our ideas of reality and much of our certainty as to right and wrong will disappear along with our ideas of what is important, who we are, and what we should do. We will be born again. We will emerge like babies, awed by the new light.

So it is best to keep in mind at all times that "the wind blows where it chooses, and you hear the sound of it, but you do not know where it comes from or where it goes. So it is with everyone who is born of the Spirit."[15] The works and ways of God can be as independent of us as the wind, and we ourselves as children of God are similarly hard to know and pin down. Even the wind is only a figure of speech. The kingdom of heaven is within your grasp? Try to catch the wind. We do not know very much and we tend to believe only what we know. "If I have told you about earthly things and you do not believe, how can you believe if I tell you about heavenly things?"[16]

---

15. John 3:8, NRSV.
16. Ibid., 3:12.

*

Would we be willing to give up everything we know, and simply trust God for whatever comes in its place? To pray this petition is to answer, "Yes." Where does such faith come from? From our Father in heaven, whose hand we have reached for as we speak these words. The prayer is communication in the invisible kingdom that is within us and among us, and is to come.

*

A note on what we will not give up. I have consulted Martin Luther on this. I always have believed that rather than sit and stew about an issue, you just pick up the phone and talk it through:

Ja? What do you want? I'm busy. So much beer, so little time.

I was saying in my little book here—

Little is right.

—that we are willing to give up everything for the kingdom of God except one thing. What is that one—

Righteousness.

Excuse me?

We are willing to give up everything but our own righteousness. I thought you studied my works.

I did, but—

Well, then, why must I lead you by the nose? Why is someone like you writing this book anyway? Couldn't they afford a real Lutheran? Do you think the world is needing yet another funny book on the Lord's Prayer?

Ah, Sir, they—I mean the readers—can overhear what we're saying and it's a little embarrass—

I don't care about your reputation as much as you do. See, Knobbelkopf, everyone cares about his own righteousness one way or another.

I think I am actually rather good about that, Dr. Luther.

See what I mean? Maybe you'll get an extra serving of sauerkraut in the kingdom of God, since you're so good. Everybody will give up anything for God, except their own righteousness. That's why the sins of righteousness are the worst.

Who then can be saved?

The unrighteous. Like you and me.

I am going to bail on the rest of this conversation because it is becoming personally humiliating. I was trying to say, before that ill-timed phone call, that we put such faith in our own righteousness that there is sometimes little room left over for the mysterious God whose ways are as high above our ways as the heavens are above the earth. Let me ask you: If you were to be placed right now before the Living God, in whose presence the angels veil their faces, and you were asked if you know the difference between right and wrong, what would you answer? I don't think we really do know the difference between right and wrong.

We are the material of irony, tragedy, and comedy. There is more to human history than the romance between God and human beings: there is our incessant folly, the fathomless idiocy that has made a graveyard and sewer of the Earth. I exaggerate only the humor of our condition. Nobody goes to war with the thought, "I am in the wrong and am going to create all the insult to heaven that I can." Nobody has made the great mistake of their lives thinking, "I am going to do wrong and act like a reckless fool just for the sheer pain of it." Much of the evil we do in the world, we do because we imagine we know the difference between right and wrong.

I do not deny that sometimes we guess right. We all know the solid and thrilling exhilaration that comes from a person who stands up for what is right. Luther himself did it: "Here I stand. I can do no other, God help me!" And every one of his accusers made the same stand. The very high of doing what is right makes it hard to let our righteousness go. In some cases, our righteousness is our identity. We have built our character by refusing to trade our integrity for short-term advantages. It is altogether fitting and proper that we should do this. But in a larger sense, we cannot hallow the ground we stand on. All we can do is try our best to do what is right. The world depends on people acting out of good motives. But we can never see far enough to guarantee ourselves a heavenly medal of honor instead of a pair of donkey ears. We have to be willing to walk into the house of God with dirty feet.

It is really much more serious than that. We probably perpetrate untold evil, even in our small daily decisions. The knowledge of what we have done wrong would crush us. What we have done wrong might overwhelm all the good we have done, all the integrity we have developed by standing for what is good and honorable and just; our selfishness might outweigh our compassion. We are only human, after all. But it is not so much that our evil overbalances our good; for we will be forgiven. It is that we cling to the good, and to our convictions of righteousness—even if we have made it all up. Even if we have not made it all up, and we have acted like angels, that very goodness would doom us if we held on to it as our own. A little goodness can take us a long way toward hell. Instead, may we awaken to the peaceable kingdom, where no one has earned his or her entrance. We are beggars.

*

This petition is a little apocalypse. Many readers of the New Testament conclude that Jesus believed and preached that the end of the world would come very soon, and the earliest Christians thought it might well arrive within their generation. Therefore, the ethics of Jesus, this prayer, and virtually everything else, should be seen in light of that expectation. Studies of disappointed end-of-the-world sects show that people do not give up their beliefs when the end does not come as predicted; likewise, some say Christianity has developed despite the radical errors of its first preachers, including Paul. Somehow Christianity managed to transmogrify itself from an eschatological sect into a broadly-based religion.

Eschatology—or talk about end things—has never been abandoned by Christianity. It remains near the center of the traditional faith. However, chronological expectation has left the mainstream and moved out to the fringes. Into its place has moved the idea and attitude of expectation itself. Jews celebrating the Passover are not being frivolous when they conclude each year's ceremony with the words, "Next year in Jerusalem!" Christians also live their earthly lives in an un-arrived Jerusalem, always waiting for next year. To hope for something that almost doubtless will not happen in one's lifetime is on the one hand pathetic and embittering; on the other hand this patient expectation is one of the most elegantly courageous attitudes a human being can strike.

An attitude of faithful waiting is transformative. We are changed by the faithfulness we insist upon despite the evidence and forces in place against us. What we expect governs how we act. If we expect a slam-bang apocalypse of explosions and divine fury, then we are unlikely to love our enemies or even the natural world: they are circling the drain anyway. If we expect the rule of God by which love is the only power, then we are more likely to do unto others what we would have them do unto us. We are practical: we will conform to a new order if we think that order is coming, and we will speak its language. We can be inspired. We can lift ourselves; or rather, the kingdom lifts us. Either way, an expectation of the kingdom of God is another means of expressing our faith in Jesus, and the faithful will imitate their master.

One way to pray this petition is to affirm our belief in this kingdom. We are talking nonsense if we say "thy kingdom come" and mean nothing. But if we are acquiescing in its arrival, and desiring it, we are bringing about a little personal apocalypse in ourselves. We are ending the world of quiet desperation, and opening our eyes to the kingdom of God.

That is why it is important to have some notion of what we pray for. It is all right to pray with the general idea that we can sign onto whatever God is going to bring about. But this petition also gives us the opportunity—perhaps even requires us—to examine our values. What do we live for? What might we die for? Are we fans and cheerleaders for the world order, with its particular understanding of power and success? Are we skeptics, viewing our world from the perspective of the kingdom of God? Our understanding of that kingdom dictates our perspective.

Expecting the kingdom of God makes us citizens of that kingdom. The very idea of a "kingdom of God" assumes that there is a different kingdom, not particularly of God, down here. We are surrounded by it, but if we hold a foreign passport we are not fully at home here.

> If a man does not keep pace with his companions, perhaps it is because he hears a different drummer. Let him step to the music which he hears, however measured or far away.[17]

This petition harkens us to the kingdom of God. Perhaps there is no real conflict between God's kingdom and the world around us. One of them is a dream.[18] When you dream, you think you are awake, but "only that day dawns to which we are awake."[19] The kingdom of God will arrive when we sleepers awake.

What is prayer but a realization of God in one's self?

*

The wreckage of history lies all around us as proof that no kingdom of God is coming. Even if it were, our false selves stand armed and ready at the gate. It does not look good. We might wish for a wonderful kingdom, but our shrewd side tells us that wishful thinking will not pay our bills. Nevertheless, Jesus invites us to act completely from love. This love of God generates faith, which is a Christian word for courage. The better angels of our nature have always been attracted to forlorn hopes and lost causes, perhaps because we hear some faraway music that reminds us that things ought to be better. Jesus tells us not to give in, not to sell out. We are born fighters. Why not put that to good use?

*

17. Thoreau, *Walden*, 317.

18. One can suffer in a dream. I do not say that our world is unreal, but that dreams have a kind of reality. Yet there is a difference between our dreams and God's dream.

19. Thoreau, *Walden*, 324.

God is everywhere. God's kingdom cannot arrive; it is already here. So we are praying for *this place, this world, this universe,* and *this creation* to become complete. The kingdom's arrival is nothing less than the perfection of what is not yet fully made. God is still, always, creating.

Maybe the present world is not the enemy of God's world; it is simply unfinished. We are privileged to be present at the creation. It is a long process. This world is not our enemy: the darkness that preceded it is our enemy. In this petition we ask for God's light in the darkness. Seeing the light, small but sure, we now ask for the whole dawn. Encouraged and hopeful, from our dark streets we ask for the everlasting light.

*

Perhaps the kingdom of God is a destination not wholly unknown. Perhaps we have been there. We might not have been able to enjoy fully our being there, but the experience has entered our lives like a week spent in a beautiful place that has become our heart's home. We tack up its postcards; we work the year long to earn money to return; the place becomes the residence of our spirit, giving meaning to our days. This place becomes our first love. We judge our happiness by how close we are to returning.

The return must always be a sojourn while we are on earth. We cannot live on the holiday island. But unlike a place of earthly travel, the kingdom of heaven is not the goal for our retirement; it is the place where life begins.

We sense that place to be the source of our life. We return to it in spirit; we drink from this source in our dreams. Any token from this place—dawn in the mountains, the look of a happy child, the touch of a loved one—reminds us and is a source of comfort, strength, activity, and joy.

For the Christian Church, such postcards and reminders and tokens are worship, good works, fellowship, the words of Jesus, hymns, and sacraments. The Church of course is not perfect. To require perfection of the Church is to assume that we could enjoy perfection if we saw it. To require perfection now would assume that the Church is not made of people like us, or that the Church is supposed to be the kingdom of God instead of the community of those who pray for the kingdom to come.

The Church consists of those who pray the Lord's Prayer. This prayer is the center of the Church's work, holding it together—the one work on which all Christians agree. This prayer is agreed upon not only in principle but in practice. What matters is not what we think of the prayer, but that we pray it. This prayer is given to us by Jesus: it is a holy relic sanctified by use, a garment—left at the exit of the tomb—that now clothes us. These words become the breath of life as we speak them.

The Church is the outward and visible sign, the imperfect evidence, of the kingdom of God—not in the way it behaves but in the way it hopes. The prayer is a prophecy of the kingdom, as is the Church. The Church is the Spirit of the prayer dwelling in time and history. It is no good either to have faith or lose faith in the Church. The Church is a prayer we make with our hands. Our faith is properly placed not in prayer, but in the Answerer of prayer. We hope nothing of the Church, but everything of the kingdom of God. We work in sin, we pray in sin, and we love in sin; but that which is imperfect will some day be perfected. The Church is the embodiment of the prayer, yet it is blatant evidence that we still pray imperfectly. But where else shall we go? The Church prays the words of eternal life.

"Next year in Jerusalem!"

5

Thy Will be Done on Earth as It is in Heaven.

PRAYING THE PREVIOUS PETITION, we confess that the kingdom of God has not yet come in us. In this petition we admit that we do not do God's will. The Lord's Prayer is like a truth serum; so far we have stated nothing but "the facts as they really are." Like the last petition, this one "humbles and it exalts; it makes sinners and it makes righteous people; for the Word of God always works both judgment and righteousness."[1]

We ought to consider "will." Although we would probably like to start with the will of God, we might be better off starting with our own. It turns out that we do not understand our own will very well.

Our will is the inner force driving to get or to do what we want. But who understands where our desires come from? We all have certain needs in common: food, shelter, and love. These are not distinctive. They do not articulate our individuality. It is our specific and unique set of wants that makes us who we are. It could be said that we are what we want. But where have we gotten our particular wants?

We seem to be born with them. One has preferences for certain colors, certain foods; one likes baseball and figure skating but not football and tennis. Why? To an extent these things depend upon what we have been exposed to, but deep preferences come from someplace other than early experience. Give two toddlers their first tastes of peanut butter, cheese, tomatoes, or

---

1. Luther, *Works* 42. I would use other theologians for some of this material, but then we would feel obligated to lower the price of the book.

avocadoes: the two will already prefer some of these items more than others, and both will probably have different preferences.

In order to assist the reader in understanding my theological bias, I will state here that I have philosophical issues with avocadoes. Green fruit should not be eaten. But is it a vegetable? If so, it is the only vegetable with a big stone in the middle like a fruit. The texture gives you the willies and does not belong to the fruit—or to the vegetable—or to the food—family. It is shaped like a grenade, a Shmoo, or a Civil War re-enactor. I conclude that it is not a food; it is a consequence. It is bad karma made palpable.

I am expressing a negative preference that has been with me since day one. My point is that we have likes and dislikes whose origins we cannot trace. Sometimes it is said, "She doesn't know her own mind," meaning that she does not know what she wants. Perhaps this condition is more widely true than we have thought. The word "predilection" implies that our preferences exist prior to ("pre") any choice ("election").

We are defined by our wills, but we do not necessarily know our wills, and we do not know where our wills come from. We are strangers to ourselves. It is a humiliating position, but there it is. We call it our will but it is not precisely *ours*. Then whose is it? Or *what* is it? God's will seems incompatible with our own superficial will. The will has been observed and analyzed for thousands of years, and with particular seriousness by the leading figures of the Protestant Reformation. John Calvin, though French, approached this problem with great intellectual efficiency, fundamentally agreeing with Martin—excuse me, the phone:

Yes?

'Ello?

To whom am I speaking?

Are you about to quote Marteen Luthaire again?

You bet.

Sacré bleu! *You are incorrigible!*

Who is this?

I? I am Docteur Jean Calvin.

The authentic? I am honored.

Listen, escargot: Ze will of man ees corrupt!

Thank you. But what exactly do you mean by the word "corrupt"?

It is a basic doctrine of ze Church, zat ze will is corrupt. Do we not read books?

Sir, is it necessary to speak rudely?

Ohh, ze mountain flowair is offended. Let me put it so even an 'ooligan like yourself can understand: Your will does not belong to you, but to ze devil. Sufficiently clear? Perhaps you would like me to put it on a DVD?

Interpersonal relations is not your *forte*, Dr. Calvin.

Ohh, my sensitive one!

I would like to hang up now.

But you cannot, my Pekinese. And why? Because your will is not your own. Perhaps a good thing, in your case.

Yes, I can hang up! *Bam.*

Fortunately, I still use a desk phone. I deplore these interruptions, but on the other hand they lend a measure of celebrity and timelessness to our discussions. John Calvin agreed with Luther that our wills are wrecked. They are not pure; they are neither reflections of God's will nor are they in harmony with our own best interests, so we are now our own worst enemies. Luther and Calvin did agree that the will is free, except (here is the enormous catch) where it comes to salvation. We cannot, ourselves, will the will of God.

But in all other things, our wills are free. In our daily choices, we have been given and still can retain "free will." However, Luther says—and I will not answer the phone before I make this point—"To be sure, he [God] gave you a free will. But why do you want to make it your own? Why not let it remain free?"[2]

I'll answer now.

Aha! You have quoted exactly ze correct statement from my friend and adversary, Marteen Luthaire. How did you do it? Who told you?

You are not a nice person.

Ohh. You have totally annihilated me. I cry ze leetle crocodile tears, sneef sneef.

Tell it to the Marines. *Bam!*

Now I feel guilty. Perhaps he will never call back.

Then let us carry on without him, and review. Our will has become mysterious to us and is not within our conscious control, so in a sense it is not ours. We have lost sight of its forgotten depths. Our will was free, but our desires now order it around like a toy soldier. The will used to be our deepest expression, but now it is a slave, a leaf in the wind. What was pure and single is now a mixed metaphor. Our soul is entombed like Lazarus, awaiting the call to come forth.

What does freedom mean, if not the ability to enact our will? Originally, we might suppose, will and deed were one. For God the will is still free, because God simply wills something and it is done. For us, however, that nasty factor of ability intervenes. We can will something but if it cannot

---

2. Luther, *Works* 42, 48.

be done, the "willing" is empty. In that sense, our desire-driven wills are not free.

Our deepest will is submerged under short-term selfishness, or "willfulness." We mistake our desires for our essential will. When we pray for God's will to be done, we are praying for our germinal will to break out; we are praying against our desires, but for our longing. It is inconceivable that a healthy human will could conflict with the Creator's, the wise One who knows what is good, and who made us and loves us and whose indwelling Spirit informs our true Self.

This petition confesses that we do neither the will of God nor our own will. St. Paul wrote, "I do not even acknowledge my own actions as mine, for what I do is not what I want to do, but what I detest."[3] This petition expresses repentance, as we pray to turn from our willy-nillyness toward God's will.

We ask God to take our true Self by the hand and lead it past the jealous false selves of our desires. I have said false "selves" because I think our apparent will is not single and consistent, but is more like the demoniac in Mark 5, who was possessed by a "legion" of demons. The clamor of desires is certainly loud enough to be caused by many voices. If that demoniac claimed that he was free to follow his will, it was a meaningless freedom, leading only to self-destruction. We are like that man, captivated by false freedoms. The will is not only confusing, but confused. It cannot be sorted out by logic. The Lord's Prayer works on our wills, purges our desires, and ultimately would make our wills pure and clear. The phone.

Je congratulaire, Buddy. *You have made things totally confusing.*

My name is not Buddy.

Do you not like zee name, oval?

I have a predilection against it. It is not mine.

Ah, mine, mine, mine. Is that not what we have been talking about, my leetle—

Yes, that is what we have been talking about. In the whole prayer, we are trying to trade "mine" for God's—that is, exchange superficial desires for inner longing. One is opposed to God's will; the other is the breath of the Eternal.

*

---

3. Rom 7:15b, REB. Or in the KJV, "What I hate, that I do."

This petition could be a meditation on the divine will. During the Civil War, President Lincoln wrote a memo to himself that was discovered after his death and named "A Meditation on the Divine Will."

> The will of God prevails. In great contests each party claims to act in accordance with the will of God. Both *may* be, and one *must* be wrong. God can not be *for*, and *against* the same thing at the same time. In the present civil war it is quite possible that God's purpose is something different from the purpose of either party—and yet the human instrumentalities, working just as they do, are of the best adaptation to effect His purpose. I am almost ready to say this is probably true—that God wills this contest, and wills that it shall not end yet. By his mere quiet power, on the minds of the now contestants, He could have either *saved* or *destroyed* the Union without a human contest. Yet the contest began. And having begun He could give the final victory to either side any day. Yet the contest proceeds.[4]

Lincoln was one of the great minds of his or any other time, and he was at the center of the "contest" that caused seven hundred thousand American deaths. So one would think—as did he—that if anyone should perceive the will of God, Lincoln should. Yet the sum of Lincoln's meditation is an admission that he did not know the will of God. Both sides might be wrong, he said; and "it is quite possible" that neither side in the war can boast of doing God's will, much less of having God on their side. Only the fact that the war goes on makes the President "almost ready" to say that therefore the continuing war must be part of God's plan. But "almost" and "quite possible" are not certainty; and unlike many lesser minds that fought for him and against him, Lincoln was not willing to presume that he and the Almighty were on the same side.

To pray this petition is to confess our separation from God's will. We might be acting on that will, but usually we are unaware when we do. History and our own lives are interlaced with irony. When we imagine we do God's will, we are probably in trouble. We are more likely to be deluded than not. The working of God's will is usually seen afterward, if at all, and even then one can hardly be certain.

The rallying cry of the First Crusade was "God wills it!" One might say that because those Crusaders were victorious, the slogan was correct. But we are very weak in our understanding of success. The First Crusade did attain its own objectives, but did it attain God's? Success is a frail reed to lean

---

4. Lincoln, *Collected Works* V, 403–4.

Thy Will be Done on Earth as It is in Heaven.

upon when it comes to confirming whether one does God's will or not. I can almost hear the phone trying to ring. There it is.

'Ello, Buddy. You were perhaps expecting moi?

Please do not call me Buddy. I don't like Buddy.

You stray from ze point.

And ze point is?

Zat my followers, ze so-called "Calvinists," have cooked up ze so-called "Protestant ethique" in my name.

You were not responsible?

I merely suggested zat material success might indicate divine favor also in a spiritual sense. Was zat so wrong, avocado?

You know it was, Sir.

Ohh, you wound me. To be rebuked by such an authority! What would you suggest? How shall we know if God favors what we do?

I do not presume to know.

No, you do not know. Nor does anyone else.

Have you used up your minutes yet, Sir?

Click.

That's the thing with Calvin: show him who's boss and he gets in a snit. *Ach,* not again.

I am not in ze snit, Monsieur. Apologize!

Due to limitations of space, I cannot at this time apologize.

If you are one of God's elect, zen any Bozo can be elected.

Bingo. Exactly my point.

I deplore zis "Bingo." It is Catholique!

I do not expect him to interrupt again for a while. For some reason this has turned into a personal issue. I believe it is due to Dr. Calvin's notoriously abrasive personality. And he wears that stupid-looking cap. Oh no.

Hello?

You are now ze fashion authority, Monsieur?

I am not going to answer the phone for a while. A discussion of the will of God should not degenerate into a personal disagreement. But that is what discussions of the will of God usually come to.

*

How do we meditate on the will of God, then? To meditate, one must empty one's mind. Likewise, to long for the will of God is to empty one's will. Our attitude becomes receptive. We ask to receive the will of God. However, we also ask to *do* it.

Jesus does not say, "Father in heaven, do your will." The wording is, "your will be done." This suggests the possibility of agents, intermediaries. We are asking that God's will be done by those who are instruments of that will: you and me. We confess that we do not do God's will and wish for that to change.

We ask not to know God's will, but to do it. It is natural to want to know God's will. We also want to know why. To ask "Why?" is one of our first reactions to tragedy. But there is seldom a good answer. Or the answers are facile. "Why?" is the mind's attempt to heal the heart. But the mind cannot heal the heart, try as it might; and the full answer probably would not be understandable to us anyway. Only love of other people and ultimately the love of God heal us. As to tragedy, we will never know why, as long as we live.

This petition lays our tragedies into the hands of God. It should not be prayed with resignation, but with affirmation. We open our hearts to the healing of God's love. Let the mind be still. Let us rest in the will of God. To meditate on the mysterious will of God is to ask for the flow of God's love into our hearts.

*

This and the previous petition show that Jesus' view of the world is realistic. One might even say it is negative. This world is not God's kingdom. God's will is not done. The world is a lousy mess. If justice were being done, if mercy were the common rule of behavior, if we loved our enemies, then these petitions might not need to be prayed. But as C. S. Lewis reminds us in *The Problem of Pain*, the Christian religion was first preached in a world without chloroform. Christianity understands pain.

One way to interpret this petition is as a call for the end of the world. It is a way of crying, "Enough!" Enough killing, enough famine, enough brutality and poverty and disaster. Bring on your kingdom, do your will. I am ready. We are more than ready. One can hear the anguish of the world in these four words.

Blow it all up; cover us with the rubble. The Book of Genesis says God has rebooted the world once. Astronomers say that we could all be wiped out by an asteroid. Human beings have more than enough nuclear power and chemical and biological agents to put an end to us tomorrow. It could happen so easily. Would God so repudiate this beautiful world? Perhaps it is we, not God, who are the lethal ones. This petition might be a prayer for the preservation of the world, not its destruction.

*

This petition is a testament to the power of unanswered prayer. It recognizes that God does not always do what we ask, and that things are not as we wish—nor, perhaps, as God wishes. This petition is a monument to the failure of Christianity, a monument to the prevalence of pain and evil. Jesus turned everything upside-down, and showed us the delusion of our expectations. This petition is an admission of failure or indifference or powerlessness.

Does God wish for us to pray for God's will? Does God need our help? Does God need our criticism? What kind of a god lets the world go to pot and then asks us to pray for something better? Is this all a joke?

This petition is at the crux of the disjunction between what Jesus preached and religion as we know it. This petition has nothing to do with how God is supposedly running the world or not running the world, and everything to do with the heart of God. What most matters is that our hearts and God's heart meet. This petition is to be prayed until nothing else matters. It asks for the realization of reality.

*

Whatever is pure, whatever is beautiful, whatever is true—of such is the will of God.[5] Where love is, there is the will of God.

It is better to try to define the will of God in these terms than in terms of what should be done in the world. God has created the world; but God's will and not the world is the object of this prayer.

We remember that God's kingdom is already real, though the world still executes John the Baptist and towers still fall on innocent children. Presumably then, God's will is real, and whatever happens is what God has wanted; but such things are true in the kingdom of God, within us and among us in a way perceived by the blessed and enlightened. "Only that day dawns to which we are awake." Or as John Keats put it, "I am certain of nothing but of the holiness of the Heart's affections and the truth of the Imagination—What the imagination seizes as Beauty must be truth. . . The Imagination may be compared to Adam's dream—he awoke to find it truth."[6]

*

---

5. I am loosely paraphrasing Phil 4:8.
6. Letter to Benjamin Bailey, Nov. 22, 1817. Keats, *Letters*, 67.

The concern in this petition is not so much the world as the field where God's will takes place, but us as that field. We are asking for God's will to be done not only *out* there, but *in here*. I ask that I myself do the will of God, not that the world be magically changed independently of my efforts. If Jesus preaches a Copernican Revolution, then *here* is the center of that revolution. We are no longer bystanders in the will of God; we are no longer expecting a big smash-up of the world in which we are enthralled (and vindicated) spectators. That apocalypse is to be achieved first in us.

Therefore the questions of whether or not God's will is being done on earth, and why not, are immaterial. "Seek ye first the kingdom of God, and his righteousness; and all these things shall be added unto you."[7] God's will is our peace. When we pray for God, we receive what we most need and become our true Selves.

It is our affair whether or not the world is going as God wishes. The problem of how God's goodness, omnipotence, and omniscience can exist alongside the world's evil should occupy us as we pray this petition. The petition is our attempt to solve that conundrum. The petition does not ignore, but penetrates, the problem of evil, insofar as it attacks the evil in us.

*

However, there is an unresolved tension in the whole petition, because once we have understood the mystical communion implied by "thy will be done," the next seven words come in resoundingly: "on earth as it is in heaven."

Here we ask for everything to be made right. This aspect of the petition is an outcry, a demand, and a painful protest against the way things are. It is a fierce objection to God's failure to make the world the way God seems to have said it should be. If Jesus healed diseases and insanities, they must be contrary to God's will; but they are still with us. Jesus fed the multitude; yet half the world does not get enough to eat. The one who said the truth shall make us free has not freed the oppressed in this country and in this world. The one who stilled the tempest does not prevent earthquakes, volcanoes, and storms from destroying us. *Do thy will, Lord! Surely this is not how the world is meant to be!*

The cataclysmic, bestial events of the past century, and the threat of what is to come at the hands of crazed humankind, prevent any equanimity, any calm folding of the hands, pertaining to the will of God. This petition is in part a lament. Its background is a terrifying and heartbreaking world.

---

7 103 Matt. 6:33, KJV.

Three thousand years ago, children were burned on altars; in our times children have burned in ovens. Atrocities fuel our argument with God, and this petition is that argument. We want a better world, and assume such a better world is somewhere in God's will, for God is good.

At times there is no room in this petition for apologies for God—such as that our knowledge of goodness is inadequate, or that God's ways are trustworthy though inscrutable. Why did one child die in a gas chamber? Why does one child get crushed by a tank? What kind of God are You? You are a failure. You don't give a damn. You ask for faith and goodness from us, and permit our children to be starved, permit murderous tyrants to kill us by the thousands and millions. You permit the innocent suffering of our brothers and sisters—and ourselves—warehoused in hospital wards. Do You not see? Do You not hear? Do You not care? Or are You powerless to prevent these things? This petition is a wailing wall. All of history moans through its words. We are expressing our disappointment in God; we are raising our fists in anger.

Therefore this petition is a primary expression of belief, a confession of faith. It is a direct engagement with God on a primary level, the level of our pain. In our pain we shout at God. And God is the answer to our objections. God is the refutation of the world's evil. In lament and protest, we go directly to the only meaningful answer, which is not a logical solution or a worldly remedy, but the One whose absence is the source of all our pain and heartbreak.

The Lord's Prayer addresses the absence of God. We do not know why God seems to be absent, but the vacant world is in crisis. What we can do is pray for God's presence. In our spare time we can puzzle over the question of theodicy, but for now, we can pray. And then what? Are we to pray that God fix the world, while we do nothing to fix our own little shed and neighborhood? Complaining and venting might help us, but they do not help the person who needs company, or food, or health, or money, or a job.

Lament is a form of prayer. Complaint is a form of prayer. Action is a form of prayer.

*

To want the will of God done on earth as it is in heaven is to ask as Jesus told us to ask. But to ask for it now is to ask for your and my will to be done. In this way, even "good prayer" can oppose the will of God.

As Jesus framed this petition, there is no timeline. To relinquish our timeline in the face of suffering is to relinquish our own will, and that is a goal of this petition. Sure, we want God's will to be done, but how can we pray for this without hypocrisy if we stubbornly hang onto our own will first? "Do Your will, when I say. This prayer is an order. Over and out."

As such, our petition is a failure. Our prayer does not work. We have been praying it for two thousand years, and we still do not get it.

"Well then," someone could object, "if you do not put a timeline on this prayer, then I guess you could say that the prayer has not failed. There is no way to check it." That misses the point. The petition is not for the world to be changed; it is for the will of God to be done on earth as it is in heaven.

We have neglected the real nub of this petition until now. This is like one of those Ten Question tests where the first sentence is, "Read all the directions before completing any of the steps." Naturally you ignore that command and go through a series of ridiculous steps. "Stick a pencil up your nose." "Use your nose to push your eraser along the floor for three feet." Then when you get to Number Ten, it says, "Do not complete steps 1—9." And you feel like an idiot.

So here we get step ten: "as it is in heaven." We are asking for God's will to be done on earth as it is done in heaven! Why didn't we read ahead? *How is God's will done in heaven?* We do not know. Oh yes, we have crude assumptions, but they all cause us problems. One assumption is that in heaven, God gets everything done the way he wants. Which implies that it is different on earth, where God does not get what he wants. Why not? This question can spawn endless argument and supply innumerable theological kittens with innumerable balls of yarn.

Evil has entered the world. Why? Because God made humankind free. Did God also make humankind perfect? If yes, where did the evil come from? If no, did God do less than perfect work? Well, maybe evil entered not from humans but from the devil. Then where did the devil get his evil? Supposing we can answer that one, the next question might be: Why does God permit evil to thrive? There is nothing wrong with good, clean fun, but these questions have not made appreciable differences in the world for two thousand years and it is not likely that playing with them will have different results in the future. They are conundrums. And although we have wonderful brains, they are small. They are made to solve problems, particular kinds of problems—the thinking of God not being among them.

The bottom line here is that all of our answers are only speculation. We simply do not know how the will of God is done in heaven. Might the will of God be done *willingly* by those who are in heaven, and Jesus means that we should pray for God's will to be done *voluntarily* on earth? It could be. But we do not know.

But one thing seems certain: God's will is not done in heaven in the way that our wills are done on earth. Jesus has worded this petition in the form of a contrast. The way of heaven is different from the way of earth. Here on earth, we do our wills through the operation of earthly power. We want a new SUV that can tow a six thousand pound boat with a motor the size of the Taj Mahal and can negotiate the nearly vertical cliffs of Rattlesnake Canyon—so that we can drive it to the grocery store and put our bags into the back. We exercise our earthly powers to get the vehicle. We exercise the power of our intelligence and negotiate a new contract. Then we get on the Internet (electricity, information; i.e., power) and find out what the SUV costs the dealer, and this gives us a lever on the consultant who sells us the vehicle at the dealership. And since power begets power, we drive the thing home with the power to intimidate other drivers and impress our neighbor, who has the previous model of this SUV. We gas up, harnessing the power of chemistry, and blow the detritus into the lungs of our grandchildren; we continue to obtain the gas due to our military power, which keeps the sea lanes open and assures that oil-producing countries will not get overly huffy. In our small way, we derive power from and assert power within the whole power system of the human world, which we call the global economy. It is wonderful and it has raised our standard of living to where it is today, and as an added bonus it warms the world.

But Jesus is implying that a different economy works in the kingdom of heaven. These various power tools are not only irrelevant and inapplicable, they are of a lower order: they belong to the world of death that is the lot of every mortal. Things of the earth die; things of heaven live forever.

What will heaven be like? We want to get there—if not for the society, at least for the climate, as Mark Twain put it. But have any of us thought about what we will do all day forever without television? Will there be sports? Surely there has to be some kind of entertainment. Hymns and harp-playing might be all right for a while, but is there electricity? Can we play our electric guitars in heaven? Yes, but they won't need cords? Some of us like cars, but will there be roads up there?

We have some clues as to how the will of God is done in heaven. Those clues are present in the life and work of Jesus. Jesus' power was love, which in this perverse world does not look like power at all. Instead of conquering territory by blowing its defenders to rags, Jesus healed the blind, deaf, lame, mentally ill, and diseased. Instead of leveraging capital, Jesus preached good news to the poor. I am not saying that you are dirty if you leverage capital; most of us do it one way or another. I am saying that there are two different power systems in the world and in the kingdom of heaven. This prayer asks that God's will be done according to the heavenly power system, right here on earth.

If we are sincere about the prayer, the conclusion we should draw is that we are to imitate and embody the heavenly power system if we want God's will to be done in us. If we do not, then we are not really praying this prayer but are simply thinking of it as another element of earth-style power. "Where love stops, power begins, and violence, and terror," wrote Carl Jung.[8] If "love your enemies" is not typical of a different power system from what we exercise on earth, what is? Evidently it is how things are done in heaven. (No enemies in heaven? Correct: if we love everyone, we have no enemies in that system. But combine that system and ours, and we have "love" and "enemies:" heaven's power applied to earthly problems.)

A concept of power must connect ability to objectives. If we want to run submarines, then diesel and nuclear power plants are pertinent. If we want to increase the material standard of living of our citizens, worldwide economic influence is an important power. But if we have all the steam power in the world, and our objective is to write sonnets rather than heat buildings or operate choo-choo trains, what we have is not power. If we have nuclear, technological, and economic power, but our objective is to love our enemies and enjoy the kingdom of heaven, then our power is not power. Short- term power has its uses, but we are asking for what lasts.

Power must be connected to whatever we consider success. We want the wrong kinds of power because we have the wrong notions of success. We connect things that should not be connected. This realization makes me need to ring up Dr. Calvin once more.

'Ello?

It's me again, Sir.

"Me"? Who is zis "Me" who should have said "I"? Do you think you are so important zat I should know who you are by ze mere sound of your voice? Really.

It's the Author.

Sacré bleu!

I don't mean the Author of everything. I am the author of this book on the Lord's Prayer.

You seem unable to identify ze sarcasm. What infinitesimal problem is worrying your minuscule brain?

I knew there was a reason I have reservations concerning you. It's that you are responsible for otherwise religious people believing in worldly success. They think if something succeeds, that is God's validation.

---

8. Jung, *Undiscovered Self*, 103. Pertinent to why power is not a good thing in human hands is Jung's observations that "The evil that comes to light in man and undoubtedly dwells within him is of gigantic proportions," and that man "regards himself as harmless and so adds stupidity to iniquity."

We have already dealt with zis issue, guppy man. You have forgotten, perhaps? Too much for ze little gray cells to remember?

We did not deal with it sufficiently.

Sufficiently for whom?

I just want to say that millions of Protestants think that worldly success indicates heavenly validation. We accomplished it; God must have been on our side. They think that in their own lives, God makes certain things work for them to show them that he wills those things.

And what is wrong with zat, lepton?

It is not provable. It is probably a fallacy. I think the gospel witness argues the other way. But we have all gone astray on this issue and I hold you responsible.

And tell me, iota subscript, do you hold your friend Marteen Luthaire responseeble for Luthairans, eh?

Slam. That guy is so smart. He never concedes a point; he's always right. Smug little—

Hello.

You were talking about love, remember, mon petit ami?

Please stop calling me.

Ze phone connection works. It must be God's will, no? Ongk ongk.

I don't know. People think being a writer is easy. Look at what I have to contend with. And because this is a Christian topic, I have to constrain my hostile impulses. I hope that when we get to the kingdom of heaven, all of our theological differences will be washed away.[9]

*

Perhaps this is a prayer that does not touch the world. If the prayer takes place entirely within a world that does not exist, or exists elsewhere, is this petition mere escapism? If this prayer is a conversation between us and God in the kingdom of heaven, where all have their daily bread, all are forgiven, all are delivered from evil, and where the name of God is hallowed and the will of God is done, why pray this prayer now; why not save it until we are dead?

Our consciousness must imitate the consciousness of Christ. I have emphasized what might be called the mystical element of the Lord's Prayer: by mystical I mean that which pertains to our experience of God, our consciousness of God. Surely this is not a misplaced emphasis. The prayer comes

---

9. There is actually a moral here. This episode has shown that we do not exercise the power of love and forgiveness consistently; therefore, we need to pray this prayer earnestly and make conscious efforts to act out what we pray for.

from Jesus, and the primary fact about Jesus' consciousness is God. Jesus speaks from the most intimate relationship with God. That is the source of this prayer, and the goal of our prayer.

Furthermore, the kingdom of God is now. The will of God is done now. There is no later; there is no future being considered. We do not enter the kingdom of God when we die; the will of God is not done in some marvelous future time. We are trying to adjust the world to reality. Only when God's kingdom and God's will are realized in this moment have we prayed the prayer as Jesus intended it. That could be the prayer's success. Moving our consciousness into heaven is how we transform the earth.

We asked Jesus how to pray, thinking of prayer as a way to get what we want or to improve the world, but Jesus answered from an understanding of prayer that is completely different. For us, prayer is asking; but Jesus sees God face to face. Jesus lives within the relational being of God. When Jesus shows us how to pray, he has this face-to-face reality in mind. He is already in the kingdom of God. He *is* the kingdom of God. The goal of the prayer is to place us with Jesus, to put us where Jesus is.

*

But one child cries. And another will cry tomorrow. The day after, an innocent bystander will be shot on a street in Chicago. And the next day, a twelve-year-old will be recruited into an army and given an automatic weapon. If we pray for a mystery, it is also a mystery that we pray.

But it is God's will that we pray.

*

"Keep on trying!" we pray. We shout encouragement to God, as in the old silent films. We are the woman whom the villain has tied to the tracks, and we are shouting encouragement to the hero. Our shouts are muffled; there is a gag over our mouth, but we are frantic. The hero is working hard and working fast.

We ask Jesus what to say, as we lie tied to the track. He tells us. The train keeps coming; the hero works at the ropes. We want the hero's will to be done. We have a warm and active interest in it. The train is real, the tracks are real, the rope is real. The director has told us what to say. Thank God we got the part.

*

Is Christianity intended to be a mystical, otherworldly religion? To the extent that it is a religion, it cannot be. Nor does it desire to be: The Christian religion presupposes a system of ethics that deals with this world as it is. The rest of the world praises Christianity for ameliorating human suffering, establishing hospitals, feeding and clothing the hungry and poor, and converting troublemakers into active doers of mercy and justice. The world condemns Christianity where it does not live up to the ethical ideals of the Founder.

Jesus himself "went about doing good."[10] His teachings are eminently practical, not in that his precepts are easy, but in that they represent the only way of making a better human world: forgiving everyone, loving one's enemies, holding nothing back from those in need, and doing unto others as we would have them do unto us. Are these good things not the will of God? When we ask for God's will to be done, do we not ask that people, including ourselves, do the right and good thing here and now?

Jesus was also a healer. Is it not then also the will of God that the lame walk, the deaf hear, and the blind see? We must assume that such is indeed the will of God. Then we are obligated to pray in this petition for the cessation of earthly suffering. Such a request is both petitionary—asking for ourselves—and intercessory, asking for others.

This petition, then, has two functions, radical and ameliorative. Insofar as Christianity is not a religion but the perception and practice of reality, it is radical. Insofar as Christianity is a religion, this petition is an invocation of power to make the world better. The latter aspect of Christianity is vital, though temporary. As John writes in his first letter, "this world and its desires are passing away, but those who do the will of God live forever."[11]

There need be no contradiction here. Reconciling the two aspects of this petition, Christianity emphasizes not the *happening* of the will of God, but the *doing* of it by believers. The New Testament contains little in the way of prayers for the cessation of hurricanes and the initiation of political peace and harmony, but everywhere it urges belief, changed hearts, and new behavior. The early Church saw the will of God in human terms, as something humans do. We pray, then, for a radical perception of the kingdom of God, for this perception to become widespread, and for human behavior to proceed from that perception. We ask for a new reality—the actual reality—to govern our doings. As we perceive and enter that other world, this world is made better.

---

10. Acts 10:38, KJV.
11. 1 John 2:17, NRSV.

But a change in the world's external circumstances—the ending of droughts and aggressive behavior and so on—without a change in human hearts would be pointless. Such a world, with no conflict and no problems, would feel like hell on earth, the way we are now. We would go mad with boredom. We have restless, aggressive, and desirous hearts. There can be no perfect world as long as human nature remains what it is. Nature would not give us the excitement we crave, people would not give us the stimulation we desire, and material things would be unavailable or would have no appeal: we would have nothing to live for. So when we say, "change the world," we mean, "change us."

*

Liars are elected to office; thieves lounge in the boardroom; the violent man grows old in his wealth while unoffending Lazarus shivers over a heating grate. This is how the world goes. When the will of God is done on earth, will there not be a reckoning?

Jesus' answer to this burning question is that we should both pray for forgiveness and forgive. Because all evildoers, like ourselves, trespass by working contrary to God's perfect will, we are to forgive them all. We can assume no judgment upon them. We should remove the beam from our own eye rather than pick at the mote in someone else's. It might be helpful to note that in the kingdom of heaven, any villain we could name (if he or she is there) would be there as a changed person.

So evil is not to be reversed or punished? Are murderers and hypocrites to be just as well off as anyone else? Will not God's wrath wipe out wrongdoers? Before trying to answer this question, we should be aware of one thing: Righting today's wrongs and preventing tomorrow's would not assuage the grievances of the past or erase ancient outrages. Punishing those who deserve punishment will not bring back the lost children of Rachael.[12] Answering this petition by correcting things will not solve the problem of evil. Were God's will on earth done in this way, starting today, we would still not know why evil has existed all these years in plain view of a just God.

This petition seeks a more thorough answer to the problem of evil, a complete answer that does not leave ancient horrors standing in the foreground of our picture of God. An answer, coming from the timelessness of God ("as in heaven"), would be a total answer to evil. Since past acts cannot be erased, their natures must be changed or revealed. And that can be done

---

12. One always wants to be careful about asking God to punish those who deserve punishment.

only in our hearts. The world is made up not of them, but of us. We have both killer and St. Francis in ourselves.

We must cry out in earnest. We must convey our grief and anger. We must want a changed world. A fresh and acute sense of the world's wrongs is required of every Christian. We must want the killing to stop. We must detest the thievery that oppresses humankind. We must want the devils, if we believe them to be devils, defeated. We must want God's kingdom to come as an earthly kingdom. Let us pray this petition literally and crudely, from our pain.

*

We are not meant to solve the dilemma of whether the kingdom will be heavenly or not, whether earth will become heaven or heaven will become earth; we pray both horns of the dilemma. We are children of heaven and creatures of this earth. So we pray this petition urgently, even angrily, as heathens who want our way. We must pray it more than wishfully. We pray it hotly: *Come now! Overthrow evil, make things right!* We must hunger and thirst after righteousness; we must plead for the suppression of vile, brutal, and godless acts. *Stop this carnage now!* Only when we mean it do we communicate. God talks to us. We shall do the will we cry out for.

This petition covers many activities, including how and why we pray. So let us pray for this earth and let us want its people to be happy—praying as though everything depends upon God and acting as though everything depends upon us. These are the two angel-wings of prayer, and it is our compassion that unites them in flight. God wants honest pray-ers, and how can we be honest about God's changing the world if we do not feel the stab of this world in our own hearts?

This petition, like others, is a paradox, an apparent contradiction, and the only way to deal with this phenomenon is to pray both sides: pray with fire when the fire is burning, pray with bliss when we are in peace. As an active tool, this prayer is a way to put our anguish into words; as a means of meditation, the prayer lifts our vision to God. We are still both material and spiritual beings.

To pray this prayer in faith, either way, is to know that God's will is coming. The time is unspecified. We are to expect God to such a degree as to feel an intimation of God. The more we recognize God's absence and are stung by it, the more we expect God to be here, and the closer we are to the kingdom of God.

Jesus knows precisely what to ask for. He has seen it; he has come from that place. We may ask when, but Jesus tells us simply to pray. For Jesus, the reality already exists. There will be a new heaven and a new earth. It could happen in the first century, or in the fiftieth; it is all the same. Eternity is always here. The will of God prevails.

*

As Mark tells the story, Jesus' understanding of the world included the idea of conflict or warfare between God's power and the power of evil or the evil one. Jesus cast out demons by exerting superior force. The strong man has entered the house, and the demons are diving out the windows. So heavenly power must also take the form of earthly power. This would be expected, since God created all the powerful forces of the universe. Our understanding of power must be complex.

Jesus casts out demons by the sheer power of his authority. Jesus can give orders that demons must obey. Then why did Jesus not cast all of them out? Surely Jesus' authority did not end at the boundaries of those who asked help. The gospels do not answer such questions. All they say is that someone cried out for help, and Jesus rescued. The Lord's Prayer seems to operate the same way.

We ask for the will of God to be done. It is not automatic; it does not spread out across the entire world with one mash of a button. For the present, it leaves most of the work undone. A strange will!

Is there a real battle going on, or is the Marcan struggle against demons a kind of living metaphor, street theatre, an enactment of what is true in one dimension using the terms of another dimension? After all, the world's thought and action are dominated by conflict, war, power; the mode of life that we understand is an arena of conflict, from the food chain to the battle against our own wills. God speaks to us in languages that we know. Yet our languages do not represent the whole reality toward which the Lord's Prayer draws us. The prayer's language must break out of language.

We pray for peace in the language of war. We address the Eternal in the language of mortality. We pray for the heaven of complete and intimate communication in the languages of the world. The answer to the petitions we pray would be to erase the words of those petitions; it would be to transform the metaphor of the world into the pure being of heaven.

The very categories of existence would be gone. We live in a universe whose conditions are time and space. Time and space are not conditions of heaven; God is not limited or formed by them. That is why theologians say that God is everywhere, and knows all things before they happen. They say this not because they believe in a God still more powerful than your average genie, but because time and space are not the stone and mortar of God's house. The universe is a metaphor made of thought.

The kingdom of God is a kingdom of happiness because the conditions of tragedy are absent. Without time and space, there are no circumstances as we know them; i.e., there is no remorseless chain of cause and effect. Being is primary—unconditioned Being. This sounds abstract and it is, because the concrete things that stand behind our language are gone.

For God to be only a little absent would be total catastrophe. It would be impossible. Strictly speaking, we cannot ask for God's presence, because there is nowhere else. The apparent absence of God might be a language, adapted to the world of cause and effect. We cry for God's actions, and awaken to God's presence.

We are asking in language—which is made of metaphor—for Being, the resolution of metaphor. Our thoughts are made of language. Hence God's thoughts are higher than our thoughts, and mystical experience of God cannot be conveyed in human thought and language.

Therefore our petition must also be absolute. We are not asking God to come down and fix some of the world's problems but otherwise not inconvenience us. We are not saying, "Thy kingdom come a little." So to pray that God's will be done on earth as it is in heaven is to be willing for it to happen *now*, and to happen *comprehensively*. We would do well to think before praying this petition, in case we get what we ask for. Whatever we were planning to do tomorrow—we would have to be willing to let it go. Whatever our pleasures, our desires, our routines, and even our responsibilities—we might have to let them go. We are praying for something more radical than the end of the world. There will be no world to reference. The end of the world as we picture it is a worldly end—volcanoes, earthquakes, and fire—but the kingdom of God will come like a thief in the night. That is, quietly, secretly, and unknown; we might not recognize its workings. Perhaps he is already here among us, right in our own house, in this night we live in.

We are asking for a radically new life, saying like Ruth to Jesus, "Whither thou goest, I will go . . . thy people shall be my people."[13] We are asking for God, and most of what we know of God is Jesus. We follow Jesus into that kingdom he represents, the surprising kingdom that is so contrary to the world we know: a new world where the humble are great, where it is happier to give than to receive, where we have no enemies in our heart because all are loved, and a world where earthly power and wealth and success do not count. This kingdom is faithfully represented in the very prayer that we speak.

13. Ruth 1: 16, KJV.

Praying this prayer intentionally is like touching Jesus' sleeve. It is to speak with his mind; it is to will with his will, which is the will of God. Our praying it is the will of God being done on earth, as it is in heaven.

6

Give Us This Day Our Daily Bread

One astute reader of this prayer[1] insisted that this petition refers to Christ himself. "Bread" refers to what we need for life. "Is not life more than food?" Jesus asks.[2] Bread for the larger life, eternal life, is the Word of God; and the Word of God is the Son of God.

> . . . they said to him, "What sign are you going to give us then, so that we may see it and believe you? What work are you performing? Our ancestors ate the manna in the wilderness; as it is written, 'He gave them bread from heaven to eat.'" Then Jesus said to them, "Very truly, I tell you, it was not Moses who gave you the bread from heaven, but it is my Father who gives you the true bread from heaven. For the bread of God is that which comes down from heaven and gives life to the world." They said to him, "Sir, give us this bread always."
> Jesus said to them, "I am the bread of life . . ."[3]

There are other ways to develop the meaning of this petition. Where would we be without the forgiveness of our Father in heaven? God's grace is also our bread. Anything that gives us life, particularly more abundant life, is our bread. Therefore we are correct in praying for these things.

*

---

1. I don't want to name names, but his initials are Martin Luther. *Works* 42, 49–81.
2. Matt 6:25, NRSV.
3. John 6:30–35, NRSV.

But many believe that Jesus was talking about food in the ordinary sense. Matthew has it as "give us this day our daily bread," and Luke has "give us each day our daily bread."[4] Luke's Greek says, literally, "the bread of us belonging to the morrow, give us each day."[5] The word "daily" prevents any grandiose or figurative meaning for bread, so I will assume for the next few pages that Jesus was talking about ordinary food. I might point out here that even so insistent an interpreter as Luther eventually changed his mind: in a relatively early sermon on the Lord's Prayer he spoke nearly exclusively about the spiritual interpretation of the petition, but later in his *Large Catechism* he referred amply to the ordinary meaning. Luther did believe that we should interpret Bible passages first according to their plain sense. And here the plain sense is that Jesus is saying that we may ask for food.

Still, he used the word "bread" so that we would not take the idea of food completely literally. He meant us to see that bread is a metaphor for the necessities of life. Whatever we need for life, that is what we ask for in this petition.

Luke's version differs from Matthew's. As children, one of the first things we learned about making wishes is not to be stupid about that third wish. Suppose you rub a lamp and a genie steams out of it and swells up to gigantic size, saying, "I shall grant thee three wishes." You can wish for any silly thing you want for numbers one and two, but you'd have to be a dummy if you didn't say for number three: "I want an endless number of wishes granted." If the genie doesn't nix that idea, you're in clover. Luke's version appears to differ from Matthew's in the same way: Matthew's version asks for today's bread, but Luke's asks for the day's bread "each day." However, if we are not to be blindly literal about how Jesus means "bread," we ought not be blind about the word "today" in Matthew. It conveys the same request as Luke's version. "Today" means bread for the day, presumably every day: we pray this prayer every day. Each version can be thought of as saying, "Give us the day's bread." Give us what we need each day. Perhaps again Matthew and Luke translated an Aramaic word or phrase in their own ways, and it would be cranky to pick at a problem that does not really exist.

The real issue in both versions is what the petition tells us. It is not only a request; it is a sermon. It involves no less than the contrast between the economics of the present world—the economics of death—and the economics of the kingdom of heaven—the economics of life.

---

4. Matt 6:11, NRSV; Luke 11:3, NRSV.
5. Marshall, *Interlinear Greek-English New Testament*, 20.

"The mass of men," wrote Henry David Thoreau, "lead lives of quiet desperation."[6] He adds, however, that, "it is the characteristic of wisdom not to do desperate things." We are required to be philosophers in order to live well; and Jesus is expressing a philosophy in this petition.

> To be a philosopher is not merely to have subtle thoughts, nor even to found a school, but so to love wisdom as to live according to its dictates, a life of simplicity, independence, magnanimity, and trust. It is to solve some of the problems of life, not only theoretically, but practically.[7]

There is a pattern for living in this petition. The pattern Jesus implies unites the spiritual and physical necessities. Again Thoreau:

> By the words, *necessary of life*, I mean whatever . . . has become so important to human life that few, if any, whether from savageness, or poverty, or philosophy, ever attempt to do without it.[8]

An indispensable part of the question of how we obtain what we need is to be found in its contrapositive: How do we avoid what we do not need? It would be worth our while to study this contrapositive, because it seems we have nearly lost all sense of the warning contained in it.

Jesus, and Thoreau after him, is alerting us to a mortal danger. Evidently the people around him were as susceptible to it as we Americans are; it is only that the United States and the rest of the "developed" world provide a highly visible example of something gone wrong. We do not think there is anything wrong with having more than we need. In fact, we consider it to be a positive good. The more the better. We work for security, to lay up something against a rainy day (but in mega amounts). It is that margin of safety, that sense of an unbreakable safety net, for which we spend our days and nights.

But everything in this world has a price. What is the price of this security? Think about it, and we all know it is false security: we can be wiped out by illness, disease, accidents, terrorism, and even violent weather. It is only that narrow band of relative security that we are after, that economic nest egg that separates us from the people who have to live on the streets. And separates us from ourselves.

There is another way.

---

6. Thoreau, *Walden*, 6.
7. Ibid., 12–13.
8. Ibid., 10.

> Do not store up for yourselves treasures on earth, where moth and rust consume and where thieves break in and steal; but store up for yourselves treasures in heaven, where neither moth nor rust consumes and where thieves do not break in and steal. For where your treasure is, there your heart will be also....
> No one can serve two masters; for a slave will either hate the one and love the other, or be devoted to the one and despise the other. You cannot serve God and wealth.
>
> Therefore I tell you, do not worry about your life, what you will eat or what you will drink, or about your body, what you will wear. Is not life more than food, and the body more than clothing? Look at the birds of the air; they neither sow nor reap nor gather into barns, and yet your heavenly Father feeds them. Are you not of more value than they? And can any of you by worrying add a single hour to your span of life? And why do you worry about clothing? Consider the lilies of the field, how they grow; they neither toil nor spin, yet I tell you, even Solomon in all his glory was not clothed like one of these. But if God so clothes the grass of the field, which is alive today and tomorrow is thrown into the oven, will he not much more clothe you—you of little faith? Therefore do not worry, saying "What will we eat?" or "What will we drink?" or "What will we wear?" For it is the Gentiles who strive for all these things; and indeed your heavenly Father knows that you need all these things.[9]

"But seek ye first the kingdom of God, and his righteousness; and all these things shall be added unto you."[10]

I am putting most of this in Jesus' words and Thoreau's words, because it is humiliating to preach a sermon in your own words when you do not heed them yourself. I happen to like cars. I like them very much. Over the years I have developed a philosophy: all a person really needs is three or four cars. If you have five really good cars, you don't actually need more.

In considering why one should listen to the Sermon on the Mount and *Walden*—the thoughts of a man who lived by himself in the woods for two years—I have focused on what is bad or dangerous about seeking plenty. Jesus says it sharply: "No one can serve two masters."[11] Thoreau puts it this way:

> I think that we may safely trust a good deal more than we do. We may waive just so much care of ourselves as we honestly bestow

---

9. Matt 6:19–32, NRSV.
10. Matt 6:33, KJV. (Italics added.)
11. Matt 6:24, KJV.

elsewhere.... The incessant anxiety and strain of some is a well nigh incurable form of disease. We are made to exaggerate the importance of what work we do; and yet how much is not done by us! or, what if we had been taken sick? How vigilant we are! determined not to live by faith if we can avoid it.[12]

The inevitable result of not living by faith is a life of "quiet desperation." Or perhaps not so quiet. The explosive despair of our society and our world might make Thoreau change "quiet."[13] Hopelessness is another term for "quiet desperation." Without hope, where is life? Why do we ask for the bread of life and then spend most of our time refusing it?

Jesus tells us to ask for each day's bread. There is an unmistakable chasteness in that request. He has pared down our desires to our needs. Ask for our needs only. Avoid having more than we need like the plague it is. No one can serve two masters. Either we will love God or we will love our money. It is very simple. We may disagree, we may try to finesse and fudge the sharpness out of the statement, but there it is: You cannot serve God and money. A house divided against itself cannot stand. We will be servants of God, or slaves of money. Money is a jealous god; it will brook no other gods before it. Our heavenly Father at least will forgive; but Mammon is unforgiving, and it wants our time and our soul. Obsessions enslave us; love of God frees us.

This petition is a very harsh request—harsh for us, and there is no way to temper this or make it funny. We are at war inside, and "war is hell."[14] Jesus wants to free us from the hells we make, and he is doing it here by disciplining us. The Lord's Prayer intends to purify our desires.

If we are not able to pray this petition in its chasteness, we cannot really pray the others. All the petitions are interrelated. Here we see that something is required of the beggar. The beggar is so much the poorer when in his wretchedness he makes idols. One could say that the Lord's Prayer from beginning to end would have us obey the First Commandment. "I am the Lord thy God .... Thou shalt have no other gods before me."[15] We can trust in our luxuries and monetary security, or we can trust God. Jesus is telling us that, "we may safely trust more than we do."

*

---

12. Thoreau, *Walden*, 9.
13. He was, after all, referring to nineteenth-century New Englanders.
14. William Tecumseh Sherman.
15. Exod 20: 2–3, KJV.

Let us pick ourselves up off the floor and consider another issue in this prayer: we are actually asking God to give us food. We are asking for something of this world: physical life. This is not the kingdom of heaven. We should note, nevertheless, that if we pray this petition rightly, with the preceding discussion in mind, we are asking for worldly things from a heavenly point of view.

Is it disrespectful to ask God to give us food? This is the creator of the universe. Should we not ask for something big, if we ask for anything at all? It is not very classy of us to ask the Lord for something. But in fact, God through Jesus has instructed us to ask. By asking, we realize that everything comes from God. If we are too good to ask, then we might also assume that some things we have do not come from God. This request acknowledges the connection between God's grace and our lives.

Asking for food is humbling. A big shot can ask for success in closing a billion dollar deal or victory over the country's enemies; but the same big shot has to eat. When we ask God for food, we have a chance at remembering that we are all little shots.

The prayer asserts our dependence, not our independence. We would rather ask for all the bread we will ever want. We would like to make sure, and cover it all at once. But security and independence apart from God are illusions and idols, so we might as well remind ourselves of it daily. We are never assured that we will always have what we need. An endless supply is not granted at one request. Each day we must ask again; and each day it is to our benefit that we remember where it all comes from.

Tonight our soul might be required of us. We might die in bed, a war might break out; our ship might come in flying the Jolly Roger. We do not possess tomorrow. Yet we lay up our treasures in tomorrow—retirement, a vacation, mending relationships, finding meaning in life, or reading a good book—but some tomorrows never come.

I am not trying to frighten us. These little reminders help us realize that every breath is a miracle. We might as well ask for the next breath as ask for the next meal. It is all one. It all comes from God. Asking for these things is the twin of giving thanks. From the standpoint of this request, every day can be a beautiful day. The necessity of these simple requests enlightens us to the grace behind our needs.

*

For all that has been said about the kingdom of heaven, we must also consider that the petition relates to this earth. Are we treating God like a genie? When we look at the Psalms, we find all kinds of prayer, some of it terrible from a Christian viewpoint. But much of the prayer in Psalms assumes a connection between our requests and God's activities on earth: "This poor man cried, and the Lord heard him, and saved him out of all his troubles."[16] But not only does God answer the prayers of the poor, God answers the prayers of the righteous.

> The face of the Lord is against them that do evil, to cut off the remembrance of them from the earth. The righteous cry, and the Lord heareth, and delivereth them out of all their troubles.[17]

The claims made by some of the Psalms, such as this one, go even beyond deliverance for the righteous:

> Many are the afflictions of the righteous: but the Lord delivereth him out of them all. He keepeth all his bones: not one of them is broken. Evil shall slay the wicked: and they that hate the righteous shall be desolate. The Lord redeemeth the soul of his servants: and none of them that trust in him shall be desolate.[18]

We have here not only trust that the souls of the righteous shall be saved, but that righteous people will not suffer physical injury. Perhaps this psalm is a flawed prayer. In any case, voices throughout the Old Testament assume that God will reward the righteous with earthly peace, prosperity, and health. It is the same thought that stands behind the Protestant ethic for which I have blamed John Calvin: God shows his favor to the "elect" by giving them worldly success. I expect a phone call any moment, but we will push on.

Knock, knock!

Someone is at my door. Excuse me.

Yes? (At my door stands a ruddy, red-haired fellow in a long black coat.) You practically knocked my door to smithereens.

Hoot, man! I trrried to rrrrring yourrrr bell, but it's out of orrrderr.

I was expecting Calvin. You don't sound like Calvin.

Calvin rrrings; John Knox.

It is regrettable that readers must put up with such frivolity, though of course it is unavoidable. On behalf of John Calvin and John Knox, I express the deepest chagrin and profoundest apologies.

I was saying that one line of thought in the Old Testament assumes that the righteous are rewarded. But other Old Testament witnesses find no connection between what one deserves and what one gets: this is the

---

16. Ps 34:6, KJV.
17. Ps 34:16–17, KJV.
18. Ps 34:19–32, KJV.

tragic vision, and we find it most emphatically in the Book of Job. Job has done no wrong in his life, yet afflictions come upon him. His friends try to pry some secret sin out of him, but there is none except the sin of which everyone is guilty, establishing rules for God. The Lord's Prayer deals with this philosophical conundrum simply: ask, and do not make assumptions based on the answers.

We cannot make assumptions because there is never a point at which we stop saying the Lord's Prayer and reflect on what has happened. The solution to an unanswered petition for daily bread yesterday, is to ask again today. The word "daily" in the prayer is our sign that the petitions are to be prayed regularly. Are the righteous rewarded; is anyone righteous; are sinners punished; aren't we all sinners? These questions are made moot by the prayer of a poor child in need. Ask. Just ask.

The one thing that is certainly not said in this petition is that God does not address our earthly needs. For all our words about the heavenly orientation of the Lord's Prayer, we must see that its petitions have one foot on earth. There is a danger that if we were to understand the Lord's Prayer only in terms of the kingdom of heaven and make only lofty spiritual claims for it, we might eventually feel ourselves too good for this world. This petition is a stage hook that jerks us back to earth.

*

The petition is for *our* daily bread, not *my* daily bread, and this reminds us that your and my needs are not different from anybody else's. The executive and the actress must ask for food; the postal worker and the politician must have their daily bread. We are animals who will die without air, warmth, water, and food. "How dieth the wise man? As the fool."[19] The separation we feel from most of the people in this world is not geographic but economic; it is induced by false security. Foolishly we think that our money makes us different. This petition reminds us that we are not different. Although many Americans do not worry about where our meals will come from tomorrow because we have money in the bank and food in the cupboards, tomorrow is not ours. What God gives us is *now*. In this we are like all our brothers and sisters, all children of our heavenly Father, whose lives all hang by the slender thread of breath.

The plural nature of this petition—give *us*—entails the necessity of sharing. Because we are not asking only for ourselves—no child could decently omit her siblings—and because the world's resources are limited,

---

19. Eccl 2:16, KJV.

we agree to refrain from waste and superabundance. The petition does not posit miraculous appearances of food and other necessities in the world. Pop! Here's a burger. No. The petition does not ask for manna; its implications are mundane. We tend to pray this prayer as if it had no realistic implications. What does it mean to pray for enough for everybody? In God's kingdom, where God's will is done, no one would withhold from anyone else the necessities of life in order to store up security against tomorrow. We would all be secure against tomorrow if we all shared today.

It is therefore important that this petition not assume miraculous influxes of necessities. Chevrolets will not drop out of the sky. Consistent with the other petitions, this one assumes a change of heart, a new will in human beings. By praying that others receive their necessities, by restraining our desires and by sharing, we do the will of God and act out God's kingdom.

The prayer assumes that there could be enough food for all. Jesus would not have us take bread from another's mouth. In this sense, it can be difficult for those of us living in "developed" countries to understand and mean this petition. One of the supposed blessings of being an American is that we can have fruits and vegetables out of season, and as much beef as we want. What do such privileges cost the world's population? Trucking our grapefruit up to Minneapolis from Texas burns a lot of resources. Feeding five Americans beef on land that could feed one hundred people rice might not seem fair to ninety-five of those people. I am not trying to make us feel guilty; I am trying to show how the prayer can be more realistic than it seems to be. By the way, the beef cattle of the world blow out enough methane every twenty years to make enough poisonous atmosphere for a small planet. It is surprising what you can learn from a book on "spirituality."

*

There is an ethic of justice in this petition. Not only is the request for *our* daily bread; it is for our *daily* bread. The justification of greed and tyranny is always tomorrow. We need give nothing today to those in need, nor correct their maltreatment, when tomorrow is always available. Tomorrow the world will be fair and people will be just. But this prayer would meet all needs today.

It is easy to miss this point when we pray for *my daily bread*. But properly prayed, this petition makes a crushing demand—not on God but on us. People wonder how it can be said that God is just. In what effective way can God be just? At best, it would seem, God merely prefers justice, helplessly prefers justice, while in the world God created, the unjust prosper, the poor are robbed, and children suffer illness and cruelty. Apologists for God place

His justice in a reckoning at the end. Just wait: all wrongs will be avenged, victims will be compensated, and offenders will be savagely punished after history ends and the world has passed away. Christians will get raptured and everyone else will get theirs.

This prayer does not see it that way. God is just; God will not simply become just. This idea should frighten us, as we sip our morning coffee. It is nonsensical to ask for God's will to be done when I refuse to do it myself, when I do not ask for *our* daily bread but *mine*.

Is there a bit of this problem—starvation—that we can address ourselves? Is there one little thing that I can do to reduce my own selfishness? Why not do it: why not prove that prayer gets answered?

*

If economic progress here can lift others elsewhere, wealth can be a positive good. The prayer implies that we wish to be delivered from the false tomorrow in our heads that is induced by plenty today. It asks for the only tomorrow that exists: it exists not in our plans or our portfolios but in the will of God. Money is only money; but human nature is human nature, and we are easily deluded and come to cherish the illusion that we have conquered time and exceeded our humanity. We acquire possessions and find at last that we ourselves are possessed.

We think more money is better than less money; that more food is better than less food; more clothing is better than less clothing. The Lord's Prayer is not so sure. This little bit of doubt is worth our time.

The Lord's Prayer praises, it intercedes, and it petitions; but where does it thank God? Here, in this petition, thanks are implied, but perhaps not in exactly the way we might think. We can see the value of each day's food, each day's shelter, and each day's clothing. Once we learn to see our provision as a daily matter, we become thankful more easily. Nothing is taken for granted when every twenty-four hours is uncertain. A grateful heart prays one day at a time.

Consider the evils we escape each day. With what grateful relief do we understand that we have been fed one more time! The world does not owe us a living. Why are we fed, and not two billion others? Is it because we work harder than a rickshaw driver, or are more deserving than a malnourished baby?

Really, what donkeys we are. When we have lots of stuff and do not worry about food and shelter, the notion creeps over us that we deserve it all, until we believe it with real conviction. Am I only speaking for myself? I hope so, because then the world's problems will be solved tomorrow.

We should not churlishly refuse our gifts, but it is worth our time to consider the possibility that some of them are obstacles and temptations, and that some advantages so-called are really disadvantages. It is good to have a right hand, but "if your right hand causes you to sin, cut it off and throw it away."[20] Give us our daily bread and lead us not into temptation. Give us what we need but deliver us from evil.

If we should not refuse our gifts, neither should we trash them. What child, receiving a new toy, smashes it up? Bad child, eh? You know what I am about to say: If our food and breath and drink are precious, it would be poor thanks to waste or pollute them. It would be shabby of us to ask for a toy, destroy it, and demand another. What right do we have to ask for things we mistreat or waste?

Sometimes our complaints about unanswered prayer sound tinny. Excess makes thanks sound obscene, as it deprives others of the justice we look for. Our needs for today are limited; our desires for tomorrow are unlimited. We can never have enough for tomorrow. Our desires are infinite, but the world's resources are finite. This introduces conflict—more to blame God for. Your hunger for food comes from my craving for security.

So Jesus warns us that if we call down for ourselves the goods of a thousand tomorrows, we will call down their evils as well. Nothing in this world comes unmixed: if we invoke more goods than we need, we might get more evils than we can handle.

*

We fail to recognize the limited sense of this petition when we confuse gods with God, and when we confuse endless time with eternity. We want immortality, not eternal life. That is, we want to live more or less as we are, forever. But we will die. That cannot be avoided, and it is no good to worry out the reasons why. There will come a change, and then the unknown. But instead of that, we want the known to continue forever. Jesus reminds us that we have to run this risk, no matter how much stuff we collect. Our stuff is not our immortality, though we may stock our tombs and embalm ourselves in plastic, electronics, and the preservatives in our foods.

God does not promise us immortality, but eternity. In this way, the petition for our daily bread is at the heart of the Lord's Prayer. It illuminates our relation to God, our creatureliness, our falseness in everyday life, our idolatry, and our need for God. You do not ask a reasonably invented god for daily bread: you ask for chateaubriand, forever; you ask for the defeat

---

20. Matt 5:30, NRSV.

of your enemies, everything you ever wanted—everything. But here we are reminded of whom we pray with and for—our brothers and sisters—and whom we pray to: our Father in heaven. Our little petition reminds us of our little selves. We are nothing apart from God. We must understand our shared poverty in order to receive everything. This paradox is at the heart of Christianity.

*

"Our help is in the name of the Lord."[21]

Many of us receive our daily bread without asking. (And many of us recite this petition without mindfulness and earnestness.) God makes the rain fall on the just and the unjust. So what is the relationship between getting and asking? The question goes to the heart of this and all prayer.

Here is one way to think about the question. To us, who are in time and space, prayer comes first, and the answer follows. But to God, outside time, the chronological order does not apply and can be handled any way God invents. Indeed, to use the term "answered prayer" at all might be to commit the *post hoc, ergo propter hoc* fallacy: "after this; therefore because of this." It rains after we have washed our car; therefore we caused the rain by washing the car. We prayed for our daily bread, and we received it; therefore our prayer was answered.

Whereas God, who knows our every need, gives us bread and prompts us to ask for it—beforehand, as we see it—in order to give us what we need still more: a sense of miracle, a perception of the Father's relationship with us. So what is efficacious prayer? Prayer that gets what it asks for? No. Efficacious prayer is prayer in which we realize that God is with us. Prayer is not the tool; food is the tool.

When we feel the connection—know that God meets our need rather than we ourselves, our country, or even our parents—we perceive the true state of affairs. In fact, we would not receive any daily bread, or need it either, had not God made us, did not God sustain us, did not God want us for His kingdom.

*

Why does Jesus not say, "*Please* give us our daily bread"? I would think we may inject the "please" if we want to. Some languages do not have words for "please." The only Aramaic I know comes from reading baseball scores in Aramaic newspapers, so I cannot speak to this issue. Only, it seems that

---

21. Ps 124:8a, KJV.

the whole prayer inculcates an attitude of respect, awe, reverence, and love that render our little word unnecessary. There is an eagerness and directness about omitting the word that might be desirable. The word drops out of intimate discourse.

*

We might pray, "Give us what we need." In this way the physical and heavenly aspects of this petition join. "Bread" causes us to retain a proper perspective, but who has prayed this prayer and always meant the same thing each time, in each of the petitions? Give us what we need: forgiveness, help, strength, instruction, love, food, rest, insight, wisdom, companionship, humility, and shelter. *Give us what we need: all things come from You.*

*

Does God withhold food if we fail to ask? No more than do we, as parents. But there is something about taking things for granted that we do not like to see in our children. It is not good for them.

*

Under normal circumstances, we do not ask strangers for food. But if we are all beggars, is God not the compassionate stranger? Perhaps yes, until we discover in this stranger our parent.

*

A final note: Referring to Deuteronomy 8:3, Jesus said, "Man shall not live by bread alone, but by every word that procedeth out of the mouth of God."[22]

---

22. Matt 4:4, KJV.

7

Forgive Us Our Trespasses [Debts/Sins] as We Forgive Those Who Trespass [Sin] against Us [Our Debtors]

We might as well skip this one because we do not forgive. Let us move on to the next petition.

Oh my, it's the telephone. Hello?

What did you say just now?

I said, let's move on to the next petition. This one's impossible.

Where do you think you get off, trying to dodge this petition?

It's my book. Can't I do what I want?

!!##@!!

Is this Martin Luther?

No, it's Pocahontas. Why can't you stick to business?

Could we resume this conversation some other day?

You can't extract Dr. Luther like a tooth. Once a Lutheran, always a Lutheran. What's this Knackwurst *about skipping the petition?*

It's too difficult!

It's easy.

Say what?

"Say what"? Before you are sitting down to write a book, maybe you should take a writing class or two.

Herr Doktor Luther, Sir, what do you mean this petition is easy? I know for a fact that I'm deficient in this forgiving business.

But you have forgiven.

Once or twice. A few times.

Quite a few. In fact, just last week an old friend of yours apologized for not writing or calling you in six months, and you told him to forget about it.

You know a lot, Dr. Luther.

That's why they call me Luther.

OK. But I'm not sure how my telling my old buddy to forget it—

The way you forgave, that is how you wish the Father to forgive you. I told you it was easy.

[The two sing:]
Ohhhh, Lutherans Lutherans Lutherans
Are the happiest people on earth.
Ye-e-e-es Lutherans Lutherans Lutherans
know God can forgive us at birth.
At baptism's font
we get what we want;
let's party for all that we're worth.

That was fun, Dr. Luther. You're a real *mensch,* Sir. Dr. Luther?

Hmm. Perhaps Martin Luther was not really on the phone. Good insight, though.

*

Rrringgg.

Hello?

This time it really is Martin Luther! What was that all about?

What's the loud thumping noise?

It's me pounding this table I'm sitting at! How dare you speak for me! How dare you put words in my mouth! How dare you attempt to sing?

But wasn't I right? Doesn't God forgive like that? I mean, easy as a breeze? "Don't mention it!" "Forget it!" If friends do that, doesn't God do it all the more, because he loves us infinitely more?

Free does not mean easy! God forgives out of love, and sometimes love costs the agony of crucifixion. Click.

I must confess to being relieved that he hung up. I am ashamed for being so facile about God's forgiveness, and so casual with Martin Luther.— Oh nuts, there goes the phone again.

Hello.

Guess who.

Squishy hat, strange eyes, lute player?

Bullseye.

I'm sorry, Dr. Luther.

Forget it, muchacho. *Don't mention it.*

*

What is our motive?

Because we are human, with mixed and cloudy motivations, we ought to go one step back behind the petition for forgiveness and figure out why we are asking. And then let us take a step behind *that* and clarify *what* we are asking.

If we are asking for escape from hell fires and the torments of eternal damnation, we are Baal worshippers.

If we are asking for immortality, it amounts to the same thing.

What if we ask for nothing? What if we already have what we need? Then the element of adoration sounded by the first petition is here also. Perhaps adoration is an element of wakefulness; it is certainly related to being truly present.

In asking forgiveness, we are declaring ourselves present and asking for God's presence also. "Cast me not away from thy presence, and take not thy holy spirit from me," are the words of a penitential Psalm.

> Create in me a clean heart, O God;
> and renew a right spirit within me.[1]

*

Matthew and Luke record different versions of this petition.

Matthew: "Forgive us our debts, as we forgive our debtors."

Luke: "Forgive us our sins, as we forgive our debtors."

Some denominations stick with the Matthew version and pray "debts" in church; others employ a compromise that suggests both sin and debt: "forgive us our trespasses, as we forgive those who trespass against us." It does not require a dumpster full of scholarly monographs to establish the fact that there is no essential conflict here: it is clear that even for Luke, "sins" means "debts."

Why not the same word in both gospels? The Lord's Prayer is a kind of poetry, and Robert Frost defined poetry as that which is lost in translation. Let us assume that there is no exact Greek equivalent for the Aramaic word Jesus used in this petition. Each author translated the word in the way that made most sense to him, in view of his background and purposes. It is probably fortunate that we have two different Greek words, because the original word used by Jesus was poetic: efficient and suggestive, perhaps entailing nuances of debt, offense, injury, and sacrilege.

---

1. Ps 51:11–11, KJV.

A good deal of doctrine is revealed in this array of words. Primarily, Jesus seems to have associated sin with debt. Once again, our everyday notions are put into question. We usually think of sin as an offense, actively committed against God or some human being. I do not have to tell my readers what sinful offenses are. Most of you are hard cases.

Not that sin is a laughing matter: one glance at that suffering figure on the cross and we understand. I am not making light of sin, but of the way we often think of sin. I do so because this petition assumes that the real heavy-duty sin lies in what we have failed to do, rather than in what we have done. And I do not mean that we have failed to read the Bible regularly, pray, and visit the sick. These failures might be lamentable, but they do not reveal the vast abyss of separation.

We walk around starving in multifarious ways, surrounded by people who could feed us, but who do not. Nor do we ourselves feed the hungry. We are insanely callous toward each other, and in general ignore God as well. Instead of caring for God and each other, we are encapsulated in our own little worlds, bubbles, and cells. The world sometimes seems to be a vast asylum populated by the criminally insane, all of us mumbling savagely, clutching our mean possessions and lashing out when something swims into view. Compared to an actual mental institution or prison, of course this world is not what I described; but perhaps compared to the kingdom of heaven, it is. We can know "the better angels of our nature,"[2]—that is, our deep Self—but the love that would cure us makes the artificial self fearful, and so our awareness is painfully constricted. In such an earthly Inferno, sin is the condition of withholding the love, kindness, help, care, understanding, listening, feeding, sacrificing, seeing, believing, trusting, praying, and talking that we might give God and each other.

This condition cannot be addressed by the usual means. By "usual means," I refer to the little things we do to assuage our consciences. If we have a bad conscience, we buy if off by doing good things. And then we feel better. That is why the conscience can be misleading. It does not touch the great separation; it fools us into thinking that sin consists of infractions that mere conformism to superficial laws can reverse. One might say that the devil is an accuser in that there almost seems to be an intention to distract us from the real problems. We can fix these little sins ourselves.

But the vast separations within us, between us and other people, and between us and God, cannot be overcome by means that touch only the apparent self and not the deep identity within us. We have withheld ourselves

---

2. The phrase is from Lincoln's First Inaugural Address, in *Collected Works* IV, 271. It might be observed that his appeal to "the better angels of our nature" was unsuccessful.

from God and each other, which is a profound and radical condition of debt. Praying more, having more unselfish intentions, refraining from religious and civil violations—these once again are only dressings on the wound. Of course they are good, as far as they go. But if efforts in these directions make us forget our condition, they are the worst kind of sin. They are righteousness that proves to be evil. So Jesus hammered at the scribes and Pharisees, the religious people of his day. They did not have to be smarmy or self-righteous, because the wrong is much deeper than anything we can see. We are to be more righteous than they were.[3]

Good behavior is still good behavior. Neither Jesus, Paul, nor Luther said that we should not behave well. Of course we should behave well. But good behavior will not cure our condition of sin. No behavior of any kind addresses the underlying problem. We have to change our thinking as to what "work" or behavior is, related to God:

> Then they said unto him, What shall we do, that we might work the works of God? Jesus answered and said unto them, This is the work of God, that ye believe on him whom he hath sent.[4]

What is believing in Jesus? Not merely accepting a factoid: Jesus is the Son of God. "The devils also believe, and tremble."[5] Believing in Jesus results in an awakened heart, in communion with God. Belief in this sense is a vehicle of love.

*

In the sense that debt is unpaid restitution, we owe those we have injured. In that way, this petition includes active sins or trespasses against someone, and does not refer exclusively to omissions. When we rob someone, we owe that person what we have taken plus reasonable compensation for injury, time in court, and whatever else.

But there are crimes we commit that cannot be compensated for, no matter how remorseful we become, and no matter how much we want to make things right. Most of the offenses we commit are like that. We can verbally abuse someone and apologize later. Yet we have done damage. We can betray someone's confidence and later restore the relationship if that person forgives, but how can we replace the precious trust that our friend has lost? Her view of the world is a little darker now; there is an injury somewhere

---

3. Matt 5:20.
4. John 6:28–29, KJV.
5. Jas 2:19, KJV.

deep inside. How can we make restitution to our children for inflicting psychological damage when they were growing up? We are debtors.

We owe people for things done and things undone, for things said and things not said. We have perpetrated offenses against ourselves, other people, and God—in thought, word, and deed.

It is not morbid to pause for a moment and dwell on our sins; it is irresponsible to leave wounds untreated. Every injury we commit wounds us; everything we owe others we have lost in ourselves. If this were not so, we would not have to pray for forgiveness. We could go on blithely, ignoring our wrongs, confident that God has stamped our passport for the wild blue yonder. Has Christ not covered our sin and paid our debt? Why go on praying this petition? Everything's cool.

We are not praying for salvation every day; we request healing for others and for ourselves. We are praying that God finish our creation. Do we want to be saved just as we are?—show up at the feast in the kingdom of heaven dressed like Dracula? God might love us just as we are, but we do not. God's love is still transforming and awakening us, and we wish for that awakening and transformation to be completed. Because we still sin, though saved,[6] we must continue to ask for forgiveness. The most rudimentary good manners would prevent us from presuming on God's forgiveness, saying, Oh yes, I did touch off that conflagration down at the Sons of Sweden Hall this afternoon, and I know it was wrong, but God has covered all my sins and I can do what I want to those oafs any time I choose.[7]

The believing heart regrets every wrong committed and every opportunity neglected. Married couples offend and forgive each other throughout their lives. Children are not detached from their families every time they mess up. The more saved, the more conscious we are of our faults and the more contrite.

Discovering and admitting our wrongdoing is very helpful to us. Were we persuaded of our righteousness, we would fall into the worst sin possible: replacing God with ourselves. Only God is good. We, who are evil—as Jesus says[8]—cannot get anywhere by mistaking righteousness for blessedness. But to remember who and what we are, and to remember our need for God, is a kind of blessedness.

---

6. *Simul iustus et peccator* is Luther's phrase, meaning "at the same time saved and sinner."

7. Do not be led astray by this book. It is WRONG to abuse Swedes for being oafs; do not do it. [Editor's note.]

8. "If ye then, being evil, know how to give good gifts to your children, how much more shall your Father which is in heaven give good things to them that ask him?" Matt 7:11, KJV.

*

We may pray this petition in whatever way is pressing. We are not always going to be so theological as to have the profound depth of sin in mind; more often we are going to have specific sins in mind. Fortunately, we do not over-theologize when we suffer. The commission of wrong is a royally good occasion to suffer; it should be, unless we have lost all compassion for other people.

Only the strong can admit mistakes, can accept responsibility for wrongdoing, and can stand the truth. Only the strong can face their weakness before God. This is a strength that comes from love.

*

If anything is a spiritual law, it is that we are forgiven as we forgive. We should not confuse forgiveness with salvation. We could speculate: we could imagine that the saved are all in their places in heaven, some happy and some unhappy. The saved who have not forgiven are isolated and miserable, surrounded by green grass and fragrant meadows but clutching their knees.

Such crude pictures do not solve the basic conundrum of why the forgiven still need to forgive and be forgiven. Let us leave the paradox as it is. Jesus tells us that we cannot expect forgiveness from God unless we forgive our own debtors. Something is left up to us, and the more we give and forgive, the happier we shall be.

There is a practical requirement or law here. We have to forgive. It does not seem fair that the injured party must forgive. Someone has damaged our body, perhaps taken away our hearing or sight through drunkenness or carelessness—and on top of suffering the permanent injury that is nearly impossible to reconcile ourselves to, we have to *forgive* that person also? It is not fair. We all know that life is not fair. The simple truth is that we suffer if we nurse resentment, and are healthier and happier if we forgive. Perhaps the psychological and physical phenomena are instructive images of a spiritual phenomenon. We cannot complain about fairness if we do not play fair ourselves: we have been given everything, so we in turn give the grace of pardon.

Workbook-type questions:

1. Where is St. Petersburg? Can you find it on a map?

2. Draw a picture of a favorite pet or animal.

3. Think of something that hurt you recently. Who did it? Why did they do it? Write a letter to that person telling them about how you feel.

Forgive Us Our Trespasses as We Forgive Those Who Trespass against Us

4. Did you spell everything correctly? Now tear the letter up.
5. Answer this question: Do you forgive that person? Why or why not?
6. If the answer to Question 5 was "No," pray to God for help in forgiving, even if you do not see why you should forgive.
7. Repeat Number 6 until you can answer Question 5 "Yes."

*

The following are some experimental thoughts pertaining to sin and forgiveness:

The words "sin," "trespasses," and "debts" can cover legal misbehavior as well as spiritual illness. So perhaps it is good to keep in mind that the kingdom of heaven removes everything from the legal frame of reference. That is the effect of speaking of Christ as both our judge and our advocate.

When we forgive, we turn away the cup of poison from which we had been drinking.

A crime or hurt committed against us is only the commencement of its evil. The stain from such acts spreads like ink on a napkin. The only thing we can do to stop and reverse the growth of that stain is forgive.

If we are concerned that disreputable people will take advantage of God, we can rest assured that someone in hell will be assigned the job of rewriting endless lists of who has cheated the Almighty. Lots of cheaters will sneak into the kingdom of heaven—and then realize nobody was at the doors taking tickets.

The difference between our sins against God and other people's sins against us is not one of degree, but one of kind. We did not create those other people.

When we can forgive without feeling a sting, then we have forgiven.

Forgiving others has restorative power.

The person in charge of admitting you to heaven will turn out to be the person you have hated most in this life.

Your bitterest rival on earth is your best friend in heaven. This person has accepted the assignment of being your most bitter rival here because no one else loves you enough to do it.

If your worst enemy is yourself, then forgiving others is exercise in forgiving yourself. You are in charge of admitting yourself to heaven.

Perhaps "forgive us our trespasses" and "as we forgive those who trespass against us" are two ways of saying the same thing.

*

What if guilt is a social mechanism?

I ran an experiment on this item. I took an assortment of variously colored balls into my back yard and called my neighbor's terrier, Exxon-Mobil. When Exxon-Mobil took the yellow ball in his mouth I reproached him by saying "*Shame* on you!" "How *could* you?"—and the like. Eventually whenever he picked up the yellow ball he slinked off with it, hanging his head, and eventually went inside and hid under a desk. I repeated the experiment on our local congressman, with similar though less dramatic results. From this I have drawn the following conclusion: The sense of guilt can be inculcated socially and arbitrarily. Because this is not a science book, I will not include the complicated and arcane mathematical calculations leading to my conclusion.

I am suggesting that praying for forgiveness is a healthy thing to do; nevertheless, the connection between feelings of guilt and actual sin is unproved. We might need a sense of God's forgiveness to heal us psychologically, just as we need God's physical healing power. A connection between guilt and bodily sickness is not news, but we must rely on something we cannot feel when it comes to salvation.

Therefore we pray this petition on at least two levels. One is the level of immediate healing, the removal of felt guilt. We can come to this prayer for relief. Another level is the depth of sin in us, felt or unfelt—the gulf of separation that we deny, or have begun to feel as the pain of longing. We need help with the invisible, spiritual distress we live with. So it is good to pray this prayer at all times, even when, or especially when, we do not feel particularly guilty. The prayer deals with sin but not always with guilt.

*

The foregoing consideration can be frightening. If we cannot feel our fundamental separation, how do we know that God forgives us? An answer to this fear comes in the petition itself: Jesus tells us to pray this petition. That is enough to assure us that God wishes to forgive us our sin and heal us, overcoming our separation and awakening us. We would not be told to pray for forgiveness if God had no intention of forgiving.

How then do we know whether the prayer has been successful? Well, the prayer itself is not successful or unsuccessful. A yardstick for measuring our forgiveness is the one given by Jesus: to the extent that we forgive, we can be assured of our own forgiveness.

In the *Inferno*, the first part of Dante's *Divine Comedy*, we read descriptions of horrible punishments being suffered by the damned in hell. They are lurid and awful and disgusting, as hellish punishments should be. For example, some are engaged in endlessly biting the flesh off other people's backs. These are the Wrathful, the people who were obsessed with anger while on earth. God did not devise such a terrible punishment: in each case, the sinner goes where his earthly obsession leads him. He gets what he truly wants, without earthly limitations. Everyone fulfills and acts out his obsession, forever.

In the same way, we establish our own spiritual condition. God has saved us, offers us the kingdom of heaven, wants us to be present but will not force us. We're in. But we can remain unconscious of the beauty around us if we focus on revenge. If justice is what we want, justice we will get. God offers us love and mercy; or we can face our own wrath.

Sometimes it is beyond our power to forgive others. We might then pray this petition with the sense of asking for help forgiving. "Lord, forgive my sins, and help me forgive those who wrong me." It might be still better to pray, "Lord, forgive my sins, and help me forgive So-and-So." We could include a person we cannot forgive in our prayers—pray for *something* in relation to that person, something we can honestly pray, even if it's "May John not go hungry today," or "May Joan not suffer cancer." We can still detest them, but not want them to be bitten by a deer tick or need their stomach pumped. Little by little, we may identify their humanity and learn bits of compassion for them. Forgiveness might come.

But what if forgiveness never comes? I do not see how we can expect a parent ever to forgive the murderer of their child. Yet the power of God works beyond expectations, and this most difficult forgiveness is probably achieved sooner or later. We simply cannot enjoy the kingdom of heaven fully if there is someone present with whom we are not reconciled. It is not easy, it is not right, it is not fair; but it is necessary, and we can count on help that is more powerful than our own pain. That pain of ours will finally cease to torture us when we are able to forgive.

*

"Against thee, thee only, have I sinned."[9] That art thou: the God within. Ultimately, we sin against ourselves.

*

This prayer can be prayed individually, of course. But it seems to be primarily a communal prayer. We have to pray this prayer together with other people in order to fully understand and appreciate it. Imagine yourself

---

9. Ps 51, KJV.

in a quiet room with several people, or in a church, praying "forgive us our trespasses." We are praying for each other.

Sometimes the beauty of this strikes home. If you have been a member of a church for a long time, you know the people fairly well. You have had arguments with a stubborn church board member; you have resented the minister's political remarks in sermons; you have been irritated no end by the entitled kids in your Sunday School class; you have loved the Christmas programs, though, and there have been times when you have been grateful to know these people. You have played golf or gone caroling with them; you have served food in the church basement at funerals, and have helped those who are grieving and in need of your comfort. You have planned a wedding in this church; the preacher has come to visit and pray for you in the hospital. These are imperfect people but under God, you have become a kind of family. You are now praying for each other.

Perhaps you are attending a small weekday prayer service. You do not know these half dozen people around you, but together you say the prayer, and the realization comes over you that you are now together with all Christians at all times and places, saying the words of this prayer. Hypocrites and saints have said this prayer with us; centuries of suffering mortals have trusted the Lord of this prayer and have prayed with us. The poor, the kindly, the wise, and the patient, have all said this prayer and we are all praying for each other: "forgive us our trespasses."

We acknowledge that we have all done wrong. We confess this to each other, in each other's presence. You and I are admitting fault, letting it be known that we are not what we try to look like. (What an unburdening!) Our disagreements and little aggravations are gone for a moment, and we say these words with a kind of humble love for each other. In the little moments of this prayer we are a family. Even if our love is understood only during this sentence, the connection point is made; we have prayed for each other. We have prayed that we be ushered together into the kingdom of heaven.

This is the Church; it is not a group of people with one particular point of view or another. The Church is all who ask God in the name of Jesus to forgive us our trespasses and our debts, as we forgive each other.

*

Anyone who has helped distribute communion can understand what the communal nature of this petition means. Anyone who has handed out the bread or wine of the Lord's Supper has seen the humility that is forced on us at times in church, especially if one has done this where people must come up front and kneel, and hold out their hand for the bread or wafer, and receive the cup. We are all humble and impoverished mortals underneath our everyday roles, dying every day. Who will be absent from this rail six months from now? Who has come up here with tears in his heart? A big, hefty man whose suit is too snug for him comes up and holds out a thick hand; a woman bejangled with fifty-year-old jewelry thinks of someone who used to kneel beside her at this rail; a boy in tennis shoes not knowing or caring why he is here kneels with a lifetime of trouble ahead of him; the president of the church council is speechless for once and respectful of the gift; the man and woman in uniform are trying to fasten on to the courage of the faith: and here is the prom queen not wearing the mask of her dazzling smile, the professor not hiding behind his knowledge, and the doctor wanting only some peace and quiet in her life. We all receive together. We all live for a moment in the kingdom of God, together. "Forgive us our trespasses, as we forgive each other."

The communal nature of this petition can mean that the Church in its best moments bears our burdens of forgiveness. We might be unable to forgive someone who has injured us, but the Church in Rwanda and in Pennsylvania's Dutch Country has forgiven murderers. As we, the Church, have forgiven, so may we, individuals within the Church, be forgiven.

The wider we can say this prayer, the better. Why not include a child we have not seen, dying of tuberculosis in Calcutta or New York City? Why not forgive the crowds pouring along the streets of Tokyo and Hong Kong? But the real test might come with those we have seen, with those whose faults grate against ours every week in our own neighborhood and our own church. Perhaps someone in our family is next to us. If we can receive the Lord's Supper humbly together, then we have forgiven and have been forgiven more than we know.

*

All the other petitions are easy to pray, compared to this one, or so it seems. This is the only one that requires something extremely difficult, if not impossible. But consider:

We do not always hallow God's name. The first petition should be null and void most of the time we pray it.

We do not want God's kingdom to come. We either imagine a false kingdom that does not inconvenience us, or we really mean for it to come later, at some fictional future time when we have satisfied all of our plans.

We do not want God's will to be done, because that means we are calling fire down onto our own desires.

Do we want the bread of heaven? We can pray the small part of this petition and ask for our physical bread, but do we really want what we need?

We are imperfect in praying all these petitions. Perhaps they carry only one percent of their possible weight when we pray them. But the Lord's Prayer does not depend on being prayed perfectly. When it can be prayed rightly, we will no longer need to pray it. Jesus has told us to pray like this, knowing full well that we are imperfect and that we will pray imperfectly. Maybe our praying will be ninety-nine percent sin and only one percent beatitude; but so what? God overcomes sin. Faith the size of a mustard seed can move mountains. This prayer is a gift. It is a golden trumpet handed down from heaven. Shall we not practice because the first notes will be squawks? The instrument is perfect even though we are not; it will sound better and better until, perhaps after a lifetime of practice, we use it to make heavenly music. This prayer is an answer to prayer.

*

Pray this petition now with one other person in mind, as if you and she or he were kneeling side by side at the communion rail. Let it not be an enemy or a victim this time, but let it be someone you love—the person you love most in this world. Imagine that person beside you, and pray, "Forgive us, as we forgive." This is only a single step, but it is wonderfully important. The two of you, in the words of the old liturgy, are "together with angels and archangels and all the company of heaven."[10]

---

10. *Book of Common Prayer*, 334.

8

Lead Us Not into Temptation

Does God lead us into temptation? Perhaps He must, or Jesus would not have taught this petition. But if this is true, we might need to re-arrange our thoughts rather fundamentally.

Or perhaps Jesus is telling us to ask, "Do not let us make you into the idol of our fears." Dispel the jealous, wrathful, vengeful, tempting God of our nightmares. Do not allow us to project our false selves onto the screen of the firmament.

*

This petition could be the most unsettling and disturbing clause of the Lord's Prayer. Behind it could be an understanding of God that remains consistent with the general biblical witness, although it is at odds with the more philosophical concepts of God which we carry around with us, often unknown to ourselves. That is, many of us accept without reflection a dualist view of reality: there are two forces in the universe, good and evil, light and dark, God and the devil. These forces are nearly evenly matched. Dualist philosophies and religions that were in competition with the Jewish, Christian, and Muslim faiths have managed to inject some of their ideas into our everyday thinking. However, most of the Bible does not speak of God as having a competitor. Its demons and devils are all inferior powers, only temporarily able to exert their influence on earth.

But because we have sentimentalized our understanding of God's love, this petition contradicts what we think we have figured out about our heavenly Father.

Excuse me; I need to answer this.

Hello?

Mmmm, yes, this is the Operator. I have a conference call for a Mr. Grant, ah, Graham Grant.

Yes . . . go on.

Can you certify that you are actually Grant Graham, Graham something, whatever?

Yes, whatever.

All right. Go ahead, you two.

Hello? That you, Gramm? This is Luther. We were just putting one over on the operator. A little humor.

Humor is out of place in a book on the Lord's Prayer.

I know, Gramm. Just shut up and listen. I've got James here.

Helloion. Amped.

James! You mean, *James?* The author of the Epistle of James?

Autone. That's me, Dude.

Sir! This is such a privilege. May I ask whether you actually wrote that epistle? Are you really the brother of Jesus? Did you know that Dr. Luther called your letter "an epistle of straw"?

Noik?

Ach, Gramm, shut—

Yes, he did.

Interrogaton? Major rail bang, Bro!

Because he said your letter preaches works instead of grace. You say we should work for our salvation.

Dirty lickings, man. Facterion?

I said it and I still say it; but—

I'm sure he didn't mean it. Did you, Dr. Luther.

Of course I meant it. Here I stand. Sit.

Actually, he makes an interesting argument, Mr. James.

Hey, you call that mushburger an argument? It's chowder, man!

I don't need you to apologize for me, Gramm! This is no brother of Jesus. The guy is from Milwaukee. His Greek is an outrage. You're surrounded by imposters, Gramm. But the real James's letter is an epistle of straw!

Totally aggro, paddlepuss! Frube! Goat-boater!

Sirs, I feel that this is not constructive. Why are we having this conference call?

Exclamaton! Almost forgot, Dude! Bro Martin here agrees with me that you're hooked in a riptide with this temptation idea.

You and Dr. Luther agree?

It's a weird world, Dude. But there it is.

Dr. Luther?

Not kidding here.

Please tell me then, what have I got wrong?

Since you memorized my Shorter Catechism *you shouldn't have to ask. You haven't forgotten?*

Oh no. It was drummed into me.

Recite. The section about "lead us not into temptation."

All right. "God tempts no one to sin—"

Hold it! Say it again? Repeat it?

"God tempts no one to sin."

Right. Go on.

Ahem. "God tempts no one to sin, but we pray in this petition that God may so guard and preserve us that the devil, the world, and our flesh may not deceive us or mislead us into unbelief, despair, and other great and shameful sins, but that, although we may be so tempted, we may finally prevail and gain the victory."[1]

Good. What do you think, Jimmy? Not bad, eh?

Not bad for a grommet.

Beg pardon, gentlemen. With all due respect, what if Dr. Luther was wrong?

You'd be calling me wrong too, Dude. Here's chapter and verse: My letter, chapter one, verse 13: "No one, when tempted, should say, 'I am being tempted by God'; for God cannot be tempted by evil and he himself tempts no one." Carve that, Dude.

What if you are the one who's wrong, eh, Gramm?

I feel like you're piling on. I want to hang up.

We should be so lucky.

Haw! Epic guffaw, Bro! Epikos!

But let's see if he's got an argument. I don't mind a debate now and then.

This barney couldn't debate his own boardies, Bro Marty.

Sirs, I didn't come here to be insulted.

No? Where do you usually go?

Cowabunga! You oughta do comedy, Bro!

I say if Dr. Luther wants to be a funnyman, let him write his own book on the Lord's Prayer.

Okay, time to bail, Dude. Getting gnarly. Hear this. God doesn't tempt people. Debate over. Alohaion. Endless summer to you both. Click.

Dr. Luther? Are you still there?

I'm still here.

---

1. Tappert, *Book of Concord*, 347–8.

Do you really think a book in the Bible should be called "an epistle of straw"?

Why not?

Because it's in the Bible.

You're going to tell me that the Bible is the Word of God and it's infallible. Listen, the Word of God is Jesus Christ; and the Bible is infallible insofar as, and only insofar as, it testifies to Jesus Christ. Got that? Now go memorize it.

Memorize what, Sir?

The Bible.

The *whole* Bible?

I did. If you're smart enough to disagree with me, you should be able to memorize the Bible too. And write fifty books. And maybe start your own reformation.

Sorry, Sir.

You live in Amerika. You're free to disagree. You're free to act like a gorilla.

I do disagree, Sir.

Then I expect you to explain yourself to these good people. Click.

Well, my friends, Good Readers, Martin Luther himself has told me to explain why I think God tempts us, so I shall. Here goes:

In both Matthew and Luke, the wording is clear: "Lead us not into temptation." Even if you translate the Greek word as "trial" instead of "temptation," you have the same problem, the same issue. Therefore we should assume that Jesus said "lead us not into" whatever the danger is.

Why? Surely Jesus would not have said this if, as Luther's catechism and the Epistle of James say, "God tempts no one." I am sure that most readers can accept the possibility that Luther was wrong (though not merely on my authority); but many readers will not be prepared to think that there is a mistake in the Epistle of James. If you accept the idea that the Bible is inerrant, the following will make no sense: There is a contradiction between what Jesus says in the Sermon on the Mount and this passage in the letter attributed to James. All I can say is that regardless of how inerrant the Bible might be, we ourselves are imperfect; and as long as we must rely on human reason, we will find contradictions in the Bible. One of them is right here. I cannot explain it, nor can I explain it away. It is just that I choose to go with Matthew and Luke's rendering of what Jesus said.

What Jesus said assumes that God indeed leads us into temptation: that is why we ask God not to.

We may find the idea of God leading us into temptation not only terrifying, but philosophically repugnant. However, everyday human experience tells us that God subjects us to temptations and trials. Even Luther says that life "is nothing more than one great trial . . . . This is and will ever remain a life of trials."[2] If these trials, or temptations, came only from devils and other evil forces, Jesus would have said "*save us from* temptation." But he said, "*lead us* not into temptation." You and I know that we are tempted and tried all the time, and we feel that God is not a helpless bystander.

To put it in old-fashioned, everyday language, trials make us stronger. This world presents us with trials because God intends for us to learn and to grow in wisdom, strength, and discretion. These trials are not sadistic experiments, but constitute occasions and tools for spiritual development— not in order to earn salvation, but to learn salvation, to make us fit for the salvation God has given us. All this is virtually a platitude, but let us carry through with the thought, at least as an experiment.

God gives us trials. In other words, God presents us with choices. We are constantly given options that strengthen our ability to concentrate on the kingdom of God. Each of these options conveys risk: we might well, and often do, choose wrongly. We fail constantly, but we learn.

Probably one of the temptations is to think of temptation as harmless. A way to do that is to restrict its meaning. Why do we think of temptation as always sexual?—or if not that, something having to do with calories? Both of these avenues of evasion trivialize temptation. As if we could avoid the devil by staying away from sex in thought, word, and deed. To think so is to fall into deep trouble, to bask in a false security, and to slide into an absurd but poisonous pride.

The world is writhing in violence; people are starving by the millions; selfishness and greed in the hearts of powerful people keep the majority of humankind from decent work and happiness; women and children are sold into slavery; diseases are rampant that should have been eradicated years ago; families abuse each other, lie to each other, and steal from each other; prisons are full and churches are empty—and we think the word "temptation" means *sex*? That is the easy way out. Something has us fooled.

The problem is with love. We do not give it, we do not have it, and we do not receive it. We do not know what it is but we cannot survive without it. And love has everything to do with this petition.

Jesus tells us to pray against God. He tells us to pray that God desist from doing what God is doing. "Stop!" we cry, even though it is God's will to bring us into temptations and trials. Perhaps temptation is situational Zen: it can awaken us; it can prompt us toward enlightenment. Is God going to stop? Look around. We have been praying this petition for two thousand years and the world is still on its way to hell in a handbasket.

---

2. Luther, *Works* 42, 71.

What is this petition for, then? *It is for us.* Why should we pray this petition? *Because we want temptation.* Or rather, we want the objects that tempt us.

If we want temptation, we are going to make the wrong choices. We are going to become weaker, not stronger, if we seek the very illusions that tempt us.

"Temptation is sweet." Some clichés have frozen themselves into our language because they are indisputably true. Oscar Wilde said he could resist anything but temptation. Tempt me with a higher salary. It's a nice problem to have. Tempt me with more reasons to buy this luxurious car, to invest in a showy house, to spend my time watching garbage on television; tempt me to look at you with serious intent to forget who I am. Tempt me with power. Tempt me to kick your butt. Tempt me to become glorious. I will make my own decisions. I want these choices.

I want these choices because happiness lies in those directions. Happiness means having these choices; it's waiting for me in wealth, power, sex, fame, comfort, excitement, assertiveness, and success. So without these options, I can't grab happiness. Without happiness, how can I grab immortality?

So Jesus says, "Lead us not into temptation."

We are not praying against God after all; we are praying against our desperation. We pray, Do not show us these things! We do not want them. We are weak and will fall for them; but we know better. We want God. We want the kingdom of God. This petition, like the others, intends to purify our desires. We pray: Temptation is sweet, but I do not want it. Keep it away!

I thirst for the shallow, alcoholic joy of possessing things—or her—or him. Let this cup pass! I crave winning; I crave money in the bank and numbers in my portfolio; I am hungry as a wolf for beating that guy to the contract; I will devour your country's resources; I will chew you up. *Starve me!* I am surrounded by sleek electronics and glittering jewelry on graceful people, by fast elevators and quiet automobiles, by well-filled uniforms and by entertaining churches. *Put me into the wilderness!*

God will give us all the temptation we want. If that is the way we must learn, then so be it. However, "The paths of glory lead but to the grave."[3] So Jesus says, "Seek ye first the kingdom of God, and his righteousness."[4]

"Lead us not into temptation" is a way of saying,

> As the hart panteth after the water brooks,
> so panteth my soul after thee, O God.

---

3. Gray, "Elegy," 2445.
4. Matt 6:33, KJV.

My soul thirsteth for God, the living God . . .[5]

Thus this petition embodies the whole Prayer.

Do not hide your face from us. Hear us when we cry. Make us strong enough to come to ourselves. May our temptations look like enemies. Turn us to You. Lead us not into temptation.

*

We may look for a little help with this word "temptation" in the three gospel passages pertaining to Jesus in the wilderness.[6] Matthew, Mark, and Luke say that Jesus was led or driven by the Spirit into the wilderness to be tempted. So much for the idea that God tempts no one.

But the word for "to tempt" or "to put to the test" is used again, by Jesus, within the narrative itself. According to Matthew:

> Then the devil took him to the holy city and placed him on the pinnacle of the temple, saying to him, "If you are the Son of God, throw yourself down; for it is written, 'He will command his angels concerning you,' and 'On their hands they will bear you up, so that you will not dash your foot against a stone.'"
>
> Jesus said to him, "Again it is written, 'You shall not put the Lord your God to the test.'"[7]

By this very prayer, we could be led into temptation. When we pray, "deliver us from evil," we are tapping the train of thought that says, "He will command his angels concerning you," and "On their hands they will bear you up, so that you will not dash your foot against a stone." Then we could be tempted to tempt God, or to put God to the test. We are not to pray to see whether God will deliver.

To tempt God is to ask God to act, not for the sake of what we need, but for the sake of proving that God is God as we conceive him. It would be like seeing whether we can invoke a towering power by saying "abracadabra." When we pray this petition we confess our weakness. We are not even asking for strength to resist temptations; we are asking to escape them. This is the same as asking for love. God's righteousness is love, and this righteousness delivers us from temptation. Temptations are empty substitutes.

For Matthew, Jesus is the Son of God. He is divine; he is not the son of God as a human being can be the son of a Greek deity, but he is "of God."

---

5. Ps 42:1–2, KJV.
6. Matt 4:1–11; Mark 1:12–13; Luke 4:1–13.
7. Matt 4: 5–7, NRSV.

Jesus and the Father are one in the gospels. So when the devil tempts Jesus in Matthew, he is asking God to prove that he is God. Instead, God rejects the challenge. God has acted like not-God in allowing himself to be tempted, or challenged. He not only refuses to respond to the challenge; he has acted contrary to what is asked. To challenge God is the work of the devil, however we conceive of that term or name. When we see the evil of the world as an argument for the non-existence of God, when the world's evil blinds us to God, we are being tempted. We ask God to keep us away from this. We ask God not to take our measure, not to bring us to judgment.

I think that sometimes God offers us what we desire. This is temptation—to use the power of God to get what we want. Once we receive it, we learn that our fulfilled desires are only ashes in our mouths. "And I polluted them in their own gifts."[8] The disillusionment we experience is part of the education God offers us. But we ask that this step be short-circuited. In trust, we give up a desire; we waive the use of God's power. We will do without, and leave the results to God.

*

What is temptation? If we know something is wrong and want to do it anyway, we are tempted. Temptation always tests our strength—strength of character, or moral strength—and as such it causes a conflict in our will. What we call moral strength is the trained will—trained by society, the Church, school, our parents, our beliefs, or our heroes. Temptation brings the pain of anticipated guilt or the pain of frustrated desire.

Temptation is therefore a trial or test, an ordeal spotting one kind of strength against another. The Lord's Prayer assumes that what we are tempted to do is an evil: "lead us not into temptation, *but* deliver us from evil." Perhaps the prayer implies that we will fail this test of strength—that we will proceed from trial to crime.

What we are tempted to do must be acts that separate us from God, judging by the consistency of the rest of the prayer. We could be separated from God by our own guilt rather than by some misconduct; indeed, that seems more likely, as God offers forgiveness for our sins. But our own consciences may be the obstacles; furthermore, the evil implied could be very straightforward: we give in and do things that hurt us and other people.

Our first task is to pray this petition as if there were no philosophical problem. We simply ask that no trial come. We simply ask that God not bring us to the test.

---

8. Ezek 20:26, KJV.

There is inherently little more problem in the idea of God leading us into temptation than there is in the idea of evil. Evil must exist by God's permission if God is all-knowing and all-powerful. So the idea that God would cause temptation or permit evil assumes that God could make a trial-free, evil-free world if he chose to.

Except that *we* are here. Given the nature of the world's personnel, how can we expect a perfect world, or expect perfection to feel perfect? Troubles are inevitable when human nature is involved.

Then why pray against them? Are not the troubles and tribulations of this world tools by which we are taught, obstacles that force us to grow? We cannot be left as we are; therefore, "man is born to trouble, as the sparks fly upward."[9] God will use the materials at hand; but we pray that other means be used, and we pray that each of us would hallow God's name and do God's will.

Anyone who does not wish to avoid trials of strength is suffering from pride, a murderous obstacle between us and God. We might have confidence in the Judge and in our Advocate, but who would not rather settle out of court? To pray this petition is to acknowledge our weakness, our frailty, and our humanity. It is to call upon God's strength.

*

The first step toward praying this petition rightly is placed within the petition itself. We pray, "Lead *us* not into temptation." We are praying not for ourselves alone, but for others. We have reached out from ourselves and have prayed for someone else. We can pray this petition with a particular person in mind; we can pray it with a few people in mind, such as our family and friends—or or our team or our congregation or our country—or for everyone. The prayer works on us within these circumferences. We can pray it any way we want, as long as it is honest. Eventually we will pray this prayer as largely as it is meant to be prayed, for everyone in the kingdom that has no boundaries. Then we will be free of that last and worst enemy; then we will have overcome the last and most corrosive temptation; then we will have shattered the only real idol in the world—our false self.

*

I trust readers to use discretion and go with Luther regarding this petition if it seems best; however, I will venture another experimental thought or two. I wonder whether this petition defines temptation, by implication.

9. Job 5:7, KJV.

That is, perhaps Jesus intends something different from the common idea of temptation. Perhaps he must, unless we are willing to believe that God will do us evil unless we ask Him not to.

This petition implies that God would act in a certain way, but it is also our heavenly Father's will that we ask Him not to. God would, and would not. What is it God's will to do, that God prefers not to do?

Judgment comes to mind. To entice to sin is to desire a judgment. God is just; God is merciful.

I wonder whether the apparent conflict or contradiction between God's justice and God's mercy takes place only within the human mind. It reflects human nature, which is divided and in conflict with itself. Two things that should be harmonious are in conflict when taken into the divided human mind. This petition allows both sides of the mind to be expressed.

Or—to look at this problem in terms of traditional Christian theology—both judgment and mercy come together in Christ. Judgment is absorbed, taken in and suffered, by Jesus in his passion and on the cross; mercy is radiated outward by his suffering and forgiveness; the two are triumphantly affirmed by the resurrection. Of course this has not been the only Christian way to think of the crucifixion: this way assumes that Jesus was the sacrificial substitute for us, receiving on himself the wrath and judgment of God. Some find this to be a crude throwback to the idea of a tribal god who exacts vengeance, retribution, and sacrifice. It should be noted here, however, that sacrifice seems to be an essential element of life, as every parent and soldier knows.

Luther wrote of the "alien work" of God. This is the work of darkness, terror, and condemnation: the work of the Law. God's apparent righteousness demands this. This righteousness always tests, because it is a standard. Against this standard, we fail and are condemned. Therefore we pray: *Do not bring us to the test. May Your merciful will be done instead.* Thus, according to this meaning of "righteousness," a just God would hold us up to and against the holy standard, measuring and testing us. We pray to be delivered from this. But according to the righteousness of God's kingdom—the righteousness by which things are made right—the heavenly Father in love and mercy transforms us. It is not that God has two wills, or that God's will is conflicted; it is that from the standpoint of the law, or under the consciousness of our sin and guilt, the justice of God looks terrifying. But the justice by which the judge declares us innocent is God's righteousness seen in the light of grace. If this judge says that we are polished as a pearl, then that is what we are. Perhaps it is the prism of our world that apparently splits the single light of God's will.

We ask not to pass the test, but to be spared the test. In doing so we confess our weakness and imperfection, and our reliance upon God. We know we cannot pass. "Temptation" or "test" or "trial" comes from the left hand, the alien work, of God: the law would certify us as righteous if only we could follow it, so outside the kingdom of God the law can only be a rule of death. God's righteousness has two aspects: one, inside the kingdom, reveals God's way of making things right—grace and good will and peace; the other, outside the kingdom, accuses, condemns, and appears to us as wrath. In the law, God meets us an enemy who would test us, prove us, and damn us. He is implacable, perfect, and inescapable. The ultimate trial presided over by God's justice outside the kingdom is therefore to us an evil, from which we pray to be delivered.

Some Christian thinkers have seen Christ as a sacrifice who satisfies justice in our place; others see Christ as victor over the satanic forces of evil, which he defeats not by force but by offering himself in love. Either way, love proves to be powerful, releasing us from slavery to evil. Evil and forgiveness do not co-exist. Still another point of view sees Jesus' suffering and death on the cross as a demonstration by God that we are loved and forgiven beyond our wildest imaginings. We accept this divine love and we live out our gratitude by showing love and mercy toward others. But ultimately, the cross is a mystery in and though which the law is transformed to grace, and the justice that tests becomes the justice that transforms.

The crucifixion stands at the center of the Christian story; like the horizontal and vertical beams of the cross, the crucifixion demonstrates wrath and mercy, defeat and triumph, suffering and glory. This petition arises out of the center of the conflict between two apparently opposing views of God. God tempts, afflicts, and judges; God is loving, merciful, and forgiving.

We are trapped within this conflict because of who and what we are. Our minds will not deliver us. We can ask, with this petition, for God to deliver us. We take up the cross and follow.

*

Because we live in the everyday world, however, we may pray this petition in the familiar sense: help us when we are tempted. Perhaps it amounts to the same thing. In everyday usage we ignore the difficulties of this petition, glide over the idea of God leading us into temptation, and associate temptation and evil with something outside of, or against, God.

While this understanding of the petition might be limiting, and to pray it would be to pray a different prayer, perhaps it has its uses. But we must recognize that it posits a force opposing God. This force need not be equal to

God (dualism is not necessarily entailed), but it must operate against God's will whether or not in the long run it remains inside that will. Jesus combats devils in the New Testament. They operate with at least temporary impunity unless God's help is called in.

This petition can be prayed as a call for constant help against such enemy forces. If this is what we mean when we pray the Lord's Prayer, this is what we mean, and it may be what we get. While there might be no harm in praying this sense, and quite possibly there is good whenever we realize that God hears and delivers, we deprive ourselves when we fail to apprehend the larger meaning. Again, we can pray the whole prayer in the usual senses: Praise You, God; make the world better; give us what we need to live in this world; forgive us for the wrongs we do; keep us out of moral trouble; and prevent us from being hurt. Such a prayer unites us with religious people of all times and places. It is not a bad prayer; it is just a small one. It is like being given a ticket to the kingdom of God but getting off the train in New Jersey.

Jesus indicated that this prayer is larger than what we ordinarily pray when he used the words "Father" or "Papa" and "thy kingdom." As the people around Jesus did, we can ask for bread and fishes, physical sight, and the clear wine of a blessed wedding. Our Father might desire to give them to us. But these gifts can always be a means of transferring our attention to a greater gift.

We might look at life as a battle between two powers, God and evil, but Jesus is after the difference between the world and the kingdom of God. He wishes us to be wise as serpents, but innocent as doves: we should be savvy enough to defeat the present evils without losing our childlike citizenship in the kingdom of God. Victories in the present conflict will be evils themselves if they distract us from the larger disparity between the world and God's kingdom. Enjoy lovely Hackensack; then get back on the train.

Jesus did address our need for short-term help. He fed the hungry; he healed the sick. He did not, would not, preach the kingdom of heaven without first doing good, without feeding people who could not listen to preaching because of the gnawing pain in their stomachs. We may assume that Jesus wishes us to go and do likewise. We will die. Our hungers will come and go, as will the bodies that experience them. Our thirsts will kill us or pass. Like the woman at the well, we ask for living water, water from the kingdom so pure that once we drink it, we shall never thirst again.[10]

*

---

10. John 4:5–26.

This petition in particular makes it seem that the Lord's Prayer might be at least two prayers. One is the prayer that Jesus prayed, fresh from the kingdom of heaven. It expresses the consciousness and the will of God on earth. And the other prayer is prayed by us. We are simply ashamed of our sin, afraid of the evil we might do or that might happen to us, anxious about where our next meal is coming from, and we believe that God will hear us and make us, our lives, and the world better. We need earthly things.

We should not feel bad about praying this way. These requests are not unworthy to make, for evidently God does not deem such earthly help unworthy to give. After all, we are expected to give it to each other.

Many praying people know that God hears, answers, helps, and saves, even in—and perhaps especially in—the little things of life. We might not be able to figure out why God has not helped other people out of disasters, but this puzzle does not interfere with our own perceptions of miracles, our experience of God's love and God's earthly power. We know that God is great enough to change the small things of our minuscule lives. God is greater than the creator of the universe needs to be: in coming into our immeasurably small places on this infinitesimally small planet, God exhibits greater power than we can imagine. A god too great to notice us or care about us would be too small for Jesus.

Let us not be hesitant, then, about praying for food or help when we need them. We may pray the lesser Lord's Prayer in full assurance of God's love. If we know that a greater prayer exists in the Lord's Prayer, let us pray it whenever and however we can; but meanwhile, the same loving Father listens and loves us not at all less because of our inadequacies. So be it: We pray "not as we ought, but as we are able."[11] God seems willing to deal with that.

The other prayer, the ideal prayer, is also prayed. The Spirit of God intercedes for us, making articulate the inarticulate groans beneath our daily needs—the sighing for God, the timeless longing hidden behind our momentary needs. *Lead us not into the temptation of thinking we are nobler than our needs.*

We might not fully understand this petition. But we do not offend God by praying it, even if we believe wrongly about God leading into temptation. Jesus gave us this petition. If nothing else, it reminds us that we are never above temptation. We always need God.

The whole prayer is beyond us. The best way to understand it is to pray it.

*

---

11. Lutheran Church in America, *Service Book*, 35.

But after all, considering "Lead us not into temptation" by itself might actually be a translation mistake. Possibly "lead us not into temptation, but deliver us from evil" is one statement, not two. In the manner of Hebrew or Aramaic parallelism, one side of a double-worded statement clarifies, emphasizes, or completes the other. So perhaps "Lead us not into temptation" means "deliver us," the way we might say, "Don't go *there,* come *here!*" The first half is hypothetical, showing what we don't want as a way of emphasizing what we do want, and not a way of saying that we think the first statement is complete in itself.

Therefore Luther's frank statement, "God tempts no one to sin," could have been based not merely on his assumptions about God, but upon his knowledge of biblical languages and rhetoric. To forestall an insultingly congratulatory telephone call from some anonymous party, I should confess that this is probably an obvious point, and I have belabored "lead us not into temptation" for nothing. Oh, oh.

Hello?

Krankin,' Dude! Kowabunga!

Dr. Luther?

Click.

Well, let me offer a paraphrase of this petition. *Lead us away from temptation.* In other words, *Do not lead us into, but out of, temptation and the evil that results.* We would say to a child, "Don't go without your jacket and catch a cold; put your jacket on!" The child might never have gone to school without his jacket in the past; it is just our way of nagging him, of emphasizing our statement. *Don't let me get sicker, Lord; please make me well!* Don't lead us into temptation, but away from evil.

9

But Deliver Us from Evil

HERE IS A PLACE to remember that the Lord's Prayer is plural: deliver us. It applies properly to others in proportion to me to the degree of about six billion to one. God is *our* Father. If we want someone we love to be delivered, we know that God hears our love for him or her and feels it also.

Deliver them from what? From evil. The request is not for deliverance from illness, accidents, starvation, or violence—but from whatever is real evil, whether as a consequence of poverty or wealth, failure or success, danger or security. From whatever is evil in what might befall us, or in what we do, we ask for deliverance.

If we are detached from the fruits of our actions, we are not susceptible to their evils. If we do our duty, endure our pain, do our good, without the evil of cause and effect sticking to us, then we are above their evil. But in this world, full of double meanings and irony and unforeseen, unrecognized consequences, we do not know what to pray against. We do not know what, specifically, is evil in what meets us, or in what we do or think. We ask God to deliver us from whatever is evil in life—things we do not perceive well enough to name. We can trust God to sort it out. We ask not to be delivered from this and that, but from the evil in this and that.

*

This petition, being one with "lead us not into temptation" as it probably is, means both *prevent us from doing evil* and *defend us from evil done to us*.

*

" . . . all the prayers in the Psalms and all the prayers which could ever be devised are in the Lord's Prayer."[1] This petition, which ends the prayer in most ancient manuscripts of the Gospel of Matthew, not only sums up all prayer, but sums up the Lord's Prayer. As has been mentioned previously, each petition tends to contain the whole of the Lord's Prayer; this is most obviously true of the petition asking that we be delivered from evil.

Were there no evil, the Lord's name would be hallowed, God's will would always be done, there would be no want and nothing to forgive, temptation would be absent, and we would live in the kingdom of God. But as with the other petitions, this one can be prayed with many different things in mind; and to pray this petition can be to summon a genie or it can be to take a step toward the kingdom of heaven. We should give some thought, therefore, to what we are praying; because how we define evil goes a long way toward defining us and revealing what we think of God.

What is evil? To answer this question, we should refer to the first half of the petition. The whole unit is as follows: " . . . and lead us not into temptation, but deliver us from evil." As was suggested in the previous section, this sentence follows a parallel or dual pattern common in biblical poetry:

> A time to weep, and a time to laugh; a time to mourn, and a time to dance.[2]
>
> For our soul is bowed down to the dust: our belly cleaveth unto the earth.[3]
>
> Thy word is a lamp unto my feet, and a light unto my path.[4]

Therefore, we might be able to learn what Jesus means by evil if we keep temptation in mind. "Do not lead us into temptation: but deliver us from evil." If temptation refers to choices presented to us, then evil refers to self-inflicted damage.

Of course there are other ways in which the temptation/evil pair can be understood. For example, "temptation" refers to that which is placed in front of us; likewise, "evil" refers to that which is thrown at us from outside of ourselves.

On the other hand, "temptation" can also refer to the inner reality that is affected by our choices. We resist something that *for us* is a temptation.

---

1. Luther, *Works* 42, 180.
2. Eccl 3:4, KJV.
3. Ps 44:25, KJV.
4. Ps 119:105, KJV.

A new car would not tempt the neighbor, but it might tempt you or me. The inner reality, not the external means, is what matters. Likewise, "evil" does not apply to an injury or illness necessarily, but to the effect of it on our heart and mind. We might get the flu like millions of other people, and it is neither good nor evil in itself; but if the flu prevents us from enjoying something we wanted, we might blame God for our perceived misfortune, and so the result is a little bit of evil. We are asking to be delivered from the evil consequences of the things that we do and the things that happen to us.

We could pray for the opposite. Getting the flu could be our ticket out of some temptation that otherwise would have come our way. Getting the flu could give us time to think over our life and how we are wasting it. The effect can be magnified by something like a heart attack, which is *prima facie* evil but can have beneficial results. In other words, we can be praying that God turn evil to good. That can be a delivery from evil. Even something intended toward us as evil, such as someone giving us Chicago Cubs tickets, might be turned to good in some unlikely and unforeseen way.

In large terms, this petition—understood as a prayer for God to turn evil to good—is a prayer for the redemption of the world. As someone has said, " . . . this life is nothing but one accursed evil."[5] All this can be turned to good by the power of God, or so we confidently pray if we mean this petition. The bad things that have happened to people cannot be reversed, but their effects can be transformed.

In one sense, we do not know what evil is. There is an old Chinese story about a man who has caught a beautiful, healthy wild horse.

"That's good," says his neighbor.

"No," says the farmer, "it's bad. My son tried to break the horse and was thrown off and snapped his leg."

"Oh, that's bad!" says his neighbor.

"No, it's good. The army recruiter came along today and didn't take my son."

Judging the short segments, we can decide what is bad and good, but as events develop we see that our judgments are limited. Therefore this petition does not enumerate specific evils, but leaves the definition of evil up to God. Whatever evil is, and whatever temptation is, we wish to escape them.

If we were more specific, we might sometimes pray an evil prayer. Suppose we pray for deliverance from the obvious evil of losing a major battle in a war. The other side is praying the same prayer. Perhaps it would be wrong not to pray for our troops; but to do so, as Mark Twain pointed out in his *War Prayer*, is to pray many other things as well, things that we would think

---

5. Luther, *Works* 42, 76.

of as evil. What would God have to do, to deliver our troops from evil? Burn a hundred foreign tank crews? Incinerate ten thousand civilians? You see, this petition leads to sensitive considerations, but the very difficulty of coming up with comfortable examples of what to pray for shows that we do not have a reliable understanding of evil. That is one of our human failings, an evil in itself from which to beg deliverance. What did good, pious German Christians pray for during the Second World War, and what would their prayers being granted have meant to American boys? To be delivered from evil is a vast prayer, encompassing perhaps a few knowns and a multitude of unknowns.

In another sense, the only evil that can hurt us finally is our own. No enemy machine gunner can damn us; no disease can deny us happiness in the kingdom of God. If the greatest enemy in this life is our voracious false self, then the direction of this petition is clear; and once again it contains within itself the first step out of our predicament, because the prayer is to deliver not *me* but to deliver *us* from evil. We are praying again for others. Even as we look inward to see what we really mean by "evil," we are also looking outward and asking for relief from evil's results.

In a further sense, we pray this petition against God's laws. No one has the power to destroy our soul, only God.[6] This is the ultimate evil, considered from our point of view: to be lost and never more to know God is the worst thing possible. So in asking deliverance from this evil we ask that God not judge us according to the law. We ask that God not lead us into temptation. We ask that God forgive us our trespasses. We ask that we hallow God's name and that God's will for our rescue be carried out.

The most miraculous event conceivable is our salvation or inclusion in the kingdom of God, because miracles suspend or contradict the natural order, and violate the rules of necessity. The clearest necessity is the logic of our illusions. Effects follow causes, but we pray for a miracle. What greater miracle would there be than the bestowing of God's forgiveness, by which our heavenly Father overcomes his own laws and his own justice? God can do the impossible.

*

Another thing Bro Marty said on that day in 1528 was,

> We do not pray the petitions like clods, who pay no heed to the magnitude of the things we pray for, who seek only food for the

---

6. And perhaps ourselves?

belly, gold, and so forth, not caring about how we may become good.[7]

"Magnitude"? We forget that the things we ask for and receive have consequences and can change the world. The statement continues: " . . . there is great need to pray for the bread we eat, for grain, cattle, and the like, and for all that we have, in order that we may know that all this comes to us from God."[8] The second part of that sentence is the operative element: "in order that we may know" that all this comes from God.

I have been saying that our prayers sometimes are no different from pagan prayers. Some might object that *to whom we pray* separates our prayer from pagan prayers. A pagan prays for gold; we also pray for gold (financial security, success in business, a good pension, or whatever). The difference is that we pray to God, not to an idol.

But what we ask for in large part defines to whom we pray. Pray to the Living God, the Creator of the Universe, our loving heavenly Father in the name of Jesus—for money? Well, maybe. But it depends on what the money is for. For having more than other people, or more than we need? So that we can support our families, do good, or be delivered from want and anxiety? Because we are hungry? Of course. We would ask our dad for money if we needed it. But a Mercedes-Benz?

What evils do we ask God to pull us away from? If we were to make a list of evils, we would be getting to the bottom of what we believe in; we would be outlining our values. We are revealing our fears and hopes. Read the list for its opposites, and perhaps we are writing some of our dreams.

We would each make different lists at first, but they would probably converge as we think about them and erase the bad items. At bottom, anything that hurts us and others is evil; and what hurts us separates us from God.

Jesus said a hard thing: pray for your enemies. Whatever is on that list is going to have to do good for our enemies too. The difficulty of this shows that we are here, and not in the kingdom of heaven. Ultimately, we pray for ourselves, because our only lasting enemy is ourselves—speaking again not of the deep and genuine Self, but of the self that has been made by our fears and desires and the pressures of the world to be something other than the child of heaven inside.

So we are invited to pray like children of our loving heavenly Father, instead of like "clods."

---

7. Luther, *Works* 51, 181.
8. Ibid., 181.

"You . . . who are evil."

Both Matthew and Luke report that in the same sermon as the prayer, Jesus tells us that everyone who asks receives.

> Is there anyone among you who, if your child asks for bread, will give a stone? Or if the child asks for a fish, will give a snake? If you, then, who are evil, know how to give good gifts to your children, how much more will your Father in heaven give good things to those who ask him![9]

When he said that "you . . . are evil," Jesus was not singling out a pernicious subgroup among his listeners. He was talking to his disciples, other listeners, and presumably to us. In a matter-of-fact way, Jesus was summing up human nature from the standpoint of the kingdom of heaven. Sometimes the offhand comment of a person reveals a whole world. In this case, the remark about our being evil was a small, subordinate element of the point that because God is good, we can trust our heavenly Father to give us good things when we ask. We not-so-innocent bystanders are contrasted with that goodness. Even we, who are evil, give our children good things. That is just the way it is: we are evil. Jesus was no sentimentalist; his view of human nature came from great height and great immediacy and was therefore a clear assessment. There is no bitterness in the assessment, and the listeners were not meant to feel insulted. Just clarified.

Is it possible that some of us are less evil than others, and God loves those who are less evil more than God loves those who are more evil?

> But I say to you, Love your enemies and pray for those who persecute you, so that you may be children of your Father in heaven; for he makes his sun rise on the evil and on the good . . .[10]

If we, "who are evil," are to love our enemies, how much more God must love them—the evil and the unrighteous, the enemies of the kingdom of heaven! It would seem here that there are both evil and good for God to love; but the previous statement, made from a different perspective, lumps everyone into the evil category. God's love means that justification and salvation are not moral categories, but the condition of those whom God loves.

There are two usages here, which indicates that Jesus was not splitting philosophical hairs in defining evil. It is a flexible term, which could be used

9. Matt 7:8–11, NRSV.
10. Ibid., 5:44–45.

to differentiate one kind of people from another; and it could also be used to characterize humankind's basic condition relative to the kingdom of God. Perhaps the very point is that the word "evil" cannot be used precisely, and we would not get the kind of answer we want from Jesus were we to ask him, as the young lawyer asked about the word *neighbor*, "What exactly is evil?" Or perhaps we would ask, "Who is evil?"

Going by the Good Samaritan story, we might conclude that Jesus would answer the question, "Who is evil?" by saying, "Do what is good." And perhaps if we asked, "How can one tell who is evil and who is good?" the answer might be, "Take the beam out of your eye, go, and sin no more." However, this is all guesswork. Jesus was not willing to call even himself good. Only God is good.[11]

Jesus certainly was and is a healer. In New Testament days his healing drew crowds. He exorcized demons—cast them out of people with a word of command. Perhaps exorcism was simply a first-century understanding of healing psychological disorders; perhaps there were and are real supernatural beings that possess human beings. In either case, the healing power of God in Jesus is a force that illness or demons cannot withstand. Presumably these elements that must be opposed by God's power are evil.

A glance back over the last century or two of history, or a look around us today, quickly encompasses vast and appalling evil. Let us pan back over a century of machine gun fire and smokestacks spewing plumes of human ashes, and focus in on the small city of Johnstown, Pennsylvania in 1889, as a towering wall of water from the South Fork Reservoir hurtles eastward. Freeze the frame with the wall five hundred yards from the edge of town, and consider how this has happened. It has rained heavily, so perhaps the "forces of nature," ever indifferent and impersonal, are to blame. In some books, that means God is to blame. But then, the South Fork Reservoir has been held at bay by an earthen dam that was known to be weak. Nothing has been done about its weakness: the reservoir was built to provide recreational opportunities for a sporting club whose wealthy men do not want to look bad or to spend money on safety for other people. As the wall of water is suspended, people in Johnstown are doing what they normally do on a weekday. Mothers are hanging out wash; bankers are examining mortgage applications; children are out playing, and two sisters are dressing their dolls.

"Deliver us from evil." All right, let it go. In a few seconds, a thousand people are mauled, crushed, drowned by the massive bolt of water and the churning debris of trees, boulders, houses, and horses. The flood is

---

11. Matt 19:16–17, KJV.

not through with Johnstown yet. Hundreds of people clinging to pieces of houses are swept downriver. At a sturdy railroad bridge the debris of the city smashes against the structure and piles up an immense crush of furniture, carriages, walls, and roofs. Here people are battered and mangled, but hundreds of survivors hold on with desperate energy—until the stacking mass somehow catches fire. The screams and agony last only minutes.

None of the wealthy club members was ever prosecuted on behalf of the more than two thousand innocent people who died horribly. Some of the poor were doing evil work too, however, lest we come away with the impression that human nature is unevenly distributed: before the bodies were even cold, men went among the piles of corpses with pocketknives, cutting off fingers to steal gold and diamond rings. Some of these scavengers, in turn, were caught by enraged vigilantes, who understandably but criminally lynched these ghouls without trial, defense, or ceremony. Plenty of evil to go around, and most of its victims were innocent as far as we can tell. At one point two little girls were seen on a raft—not for long, as one slipped off and the other remained with her doll, crying, sweeping along until she was thrown up against the crush. The image of one little girl with her doll, sitting on a piece of roof in the rain as she rushes toward the flames, is enough to smash any theology.[12]

Right now, the earth is moving at unbelievable speed. The air is not so good any more. We who are in control of the earth have our differences; there are stockpiles of chemicals and germs that could take care of all of us many times over, and of course we have nuclear devices that could make short work of all life on the planet.

St. Augustine coined the term *massa damnata*, which means that we are all victims of each other's sins. A man gets drunk and an elderly couple driving home in the dark pay with their lives; a power plant in eastern Europe releases tons of toxic particulate matter into the air each day and a child in Mexico City coughs blood. A politician decides to play it tough with his nuclear weapons. A wretch somewhere in a busy city decides that his ideology is worth a few thousand civilians' lives. Bank executives play fast and loose with bad mortgages; elected officials balance job losses against carbon emissions; chemists come up with a cheap way to make infant formula. Security is an illusion. Evil is everywhere. I once heard a preacher say, "Nobody takes the time to pray, and we wonder why the devil is loose." Human nature is certainly on the loose.

Perhaps there is an asteroid out there with our name and the date August 14, 2077 written on it. Perhaps there is a young man or woman in Kabul

---

12. See McCullough, *Johnstown Flood*.

or Peoria whose righteous intelligence will find a way to ignite us all. Maybe a test tube will break.

Nature or human nature and the kingdom of God are on a collision course, and we had better pray for the world of the Lord's Prayer before the other world becomes fully operational. There are always two expectations in life: one is the expectation that we will be killed by accident or design or disease, and the other is the expectation of a savior who will be called Wonderful, Counselor, The Mighty God, The Everlasting Father, The Prince of Peace.[13] Whatever evil is—whether we even use the word or not—it is opposed to the kingdom of God. We will never figure evil out. What we can do is live the life of this prayer, and pray it.

We cannot overcome evil by ourselves. Both elements, evil and goodness, seem to be within each of us. We do not have the luxury of choosing whether we will combat the evil inside us or the evil around us: they are one evil. To convert ourselves, and study the Word, and sing praises to an Awesome God, meanwhile letting the misfortunes of life grasp other people's sleeves, meanwhile letting the *massa damnata* come down like a wall of water—is to be the very evil we pray God to deliver us from. To combat the world's injustice and poverty but not address the darkness inside our own souls is to magnify the lie that kills millions in the name of truth. There is one evil. Perhaps that is why the text in Matthew says literally, "deliver us from the evil one." The demons of the world might be legion, but they all work for the same master. Whoever and whatever is not of God, is of the other side. What we think of as a middle ground is really a battleground. Either we pray to our heavenly Father and work for our earthly neighbor, or we fall down before the great abomination and throw the children of the world upon its altars. No one can serve two masters.

Whatever the nature of this battle is, it has not been won. But in this prayer we can at least decide. This warfare is going to decimate us all; there will be no survivors. But we can fall into the arms of God.

*

This is a dangerous world. The Lord's Prayer cannot always be prayed in a calm and peaceful tone of voice. This petition about evil is not always soothing. Sometimes the way to say it is the way a soldier in a foxhole prays. For dear life!

*

---

13. Isa 9:6, KJV.

The paradox of this prayer and of all prayer cannot be resolved in this life. On the one hand, the Lord's Prayer is to be prayed within the context of the kingdom of God. The world's evils will never be defeated or erased and to pray for earthly relief rather than for the fruits of the kingdom of heaven is to pray only a small part of the prayer. The persistence of evil in the world is evidence for this. Surely we are not meant to believe that hunger and evil and temptation will go away. On the other hand, experience also tells us that God answers prayer and defeats evil for us. We can see that people are healed, and we would be blind to miss the fact that we have been delivered from many evils—even as we define "evils" in our own ways. So this prayer, which should not be prayed solely for earthly benefits, should certainly be prayed for earthly benefits.

Perhaps we may simply go ahead and pray the prayer. Perhaps it is a helpful comment on the limitations of the human mind that God commands the impossible, that God violates God's own inviolable rules, and that while we are drowning in evil of our own and others' making, God baptizes us into eternal life.

Or it is all a delusion and a lie. Certainly something is a delusion and a lie. Either the kingdom of this world is a lie, or the kingdom of heaven is a delusion. They are in conflict. Everything we do is an image of this paradox. Life and history are characterized by the irony of double meanings. We are all sinners with the prayer of Jesus on our lips. We are saints polluting our grandchildren's air. We pray not as we ought, but as we are able: "Deliver us from evil."

*

We may pray this petition as a request to be saved from bad things happening to us. Certainly we may pray this petition to deliver *others* from such earthly evils. When it comes to praying for others, we should not be too fastidious. We do not take chances, we do not become theoretical; we cover all the bases and pray like a shotgun, trying to hit everything. We can fiddle around trying to make ourselves better and more spiritual, but when we pray for our children, our church members, and for our enemies, we are to pray flat out with everything we have.

Sometimes we fear for their safety. Or we have compassion for their hunger. So that is how to pray at that time. The word "us" saves us from too much wisdom. We ask God to help us and others escape floods, fires, murder, accidents, starvation, and sickness—things that, rightly or wrongly, we consider evil. Insofar as we understand things, we know that to be sick is worse than to be well, to be thirsty is worse than to be satisfied, and to be starving is good for nothing. We may pray this petition according to our understanding of good and evil, as they relate to our interests and the interests of others. The more truly we understand those interests, the better we will pray this prayer. We will never get a full understanding. Offering up our compassion and our fears is more important. We can pray this petition in confidence that God loves and hears, because Jesus told us to pray this way. We may pray that God will act in response to our imperfect requests if it is God's will to do so—and perhaps for all we know, even if it is not God's will. But we cannot always pray in confidence that God will prevent all the evils that might come to us. Nor can we be sure that our definitions of evil match God's. We simply have to pray in our own condition, which is ignorance and uncertainty and sin. We might go out and do the very evils we pray against.

All we need in order to pray is an honest request. The dishonesty of a withheld request is worse than the confession of an unworthy desire. If it is important to us to escape a danger, or to be healed in some way, or to be given courage or wisdom, then we should pray for this. For what is a wish unprayed? It is an offering to the idol of despair, or the idol of unbelief, or the idol of self-sufficiency. Any desire we have is to be shown to God. A desire worth having is to be offered as a request; the others are offered as confessions and then posted to the junk-heap of forgetting. The One is closer than any earthly father: all desires are known to God; no secrets are hidden. This prayer will cleanse our hearts and minds; it will do the work of confession; it will supply material for communication between two persons who love one another.

*

The words of the Lord's Prayer are set in the text of Matthew, yet they change in meaning from one person to another, and from one prayer session to another. If we were perfectly consistent beings, then the prayer would be immovable like Gibraltar; yet we have our good or bad moments of unselfishness and anger. And we seem to have no fixed and complete idea of who God is, to whom we pray.

The Lord's Prayer is the Lord's Prayer. But a great deal depends upon to whom we are talking and the context. The prayer becomes more emphatically the prayer of Jesus and less the prayer of an angry, fearful child as we contemplate God and listen less to the machinery of our minds. We pray for better things, we drive closer to the root of evil, the more we pray to our heavenly Father and the less we pray to a tyrannical and abusive figure of our fears. The more we pray the good prayers, the more we talk to the living God; the more we talk to God the better we pray.

*

I have a confession to make. My conversations with Luther and Calvin might be apocryphal. Comic relief might have value, and perhaps some points were clarified by the use of dialogues, but these invented conversations have an additional purpose: they show that even when we know that something like a movie or a novel or a dialogue is made up and entirely fictitious, we sometimes give it a little bit of our belief, as if it were reality. We half believe in Huckleberry Finn, or perhaps more than half. Jesus made up the parables. And of course, when God decided on a universe, he just made it up.

That goes for us, too. God did not discover us; God made us up. This is an important realization. It is human nature bred in the bone to think of ourselves as discoveries. But maybe God could just forget us.

Is it possible for God to forget? Some might argue that if for God all things are possible, then God can forget. However, forgetting is not a capability but a lack. The philosopher's God cannot fail, because philosophical concepts of God usually involve the idea of perfection. Therefore the philosophic God forgets nothing; in that way everything that ever existed must still exist—and the human soul, in the mind of God, is immortal, imperishable. And sin is durable. But the heavenly Father of the Lord's Prayer is not necessarily the philosopher's God.

The Memory of God was the subject of a recent Luther-Calvin Colloquy held in Stubb, New Hampshire. As the convener of these annual colloquia, I was privileged to moderate the final session, part of which I reproduce here from transcript, at no charge:

Moderator: Gentlemen, the previous session ended inconclusively as to the question of human immortality, because no agreement was reached as to the nature of God's mind, or as to the relationship between God's memory and our actual being. May we resume discussion of these issues?

Calvin: *Certainment.*

Luther: *Knackwurst und sauerkraut!*

Moderator: Excuse me, Dr. Luther?

Luther: The discussion is nonsense! A lower order of being cannot conceive of its existence within a higher being. A thought of mine can't turn around and regard its thinker.

Calvin: Ah! But zat is *exactement* what we can do, as ze human beings—because unlike all other beings, we have ze self-reflective capacity, *non*? It is ze image of God, who is self-reflective: zat is what ze Trinity means.

Moderator: An excellent point, Dr. Calvin!

Calvin: Get off my side immediately.

Moderator: Of course. What do you say in reply, Dr. Luther?

Luther: Who says we are self-reflective? Our notion of self-reflection is *Wurst*.

Calvin: Then what do you call zis capacity to regard ourselves, eh?

Luther: Consciousness. We have no idea of whether we are self-reflective. We only flatter ourselves that we are. Are we each little trinities? What we see is not really ourselves.

Calvin: Ah, but it *should be*, Dr. Luthaire; it *should* be. We have been damaged. Our image of God has been tarnish—how you say, smudg-ed, broken.

Luther: You picture consciousness as a mirror, but there is no one to regard the mirror. Either we look, and there is no mirror; or there is a mirror, but no one to look.

Moderator: But what do we see when we look into a mirror?

Luther: *Ach*! It isn't us looking into a mirror; it is only a figure of speech pertaining to the mind—a mirror floating in the air, with nothing but another mirror to see it. But now that you mention it, who knows what we see when we look into a mirror? We suppose it is ourselves that we see, but who can verify it? We see an illusion, that makes us think we are self-reflective and therefore gods; but it is not real.

Calvin: Ah, *Frere Martin*, what is real, eh?

Luther: It is impossible for us to know. What is essential is invisible to the eye. Only God knows.

Moderator: Dr. Luther! I never suspected that you were such a radical skeptic when it comes to human knowledge, or that you would quote St. Exupéry, or that Dr. Calvin, you could be so personable.

Luther: That's because you made me up!

Calvin: *Moi aussi, idiot!*

Luther: I died in 1546! How could I be here at your colloquy in a town that doesn't even exist?

Calvin: Zis, zis Stubb, it does not exist?

Luther: And no one else is here, just the three of us—

Moderator: Our publicity was poor this year.

Luther: The three of us in your imagination.

Moderator: Then, if I felt like it, I could make you disappear just by ceasing to imagine you.

Calvin: No—wait ze moment! [*Poof!*]

Moderator: So, it's just me and you, Luther.

Luther: *Ja*. But for God, what is imagined becomes real, solid like a rock.

Moderator: Could not God, who is free in a perfect way, as we are not, choose to un-imagine us? Then we would not exist.

Luther: Brilliant, Grant! You are ever so much better a theologian than either Calvin or I!

Moderator: And?

Luther: And better looking, too!

Moderator: That is what I wanted to hear. Luther!

Luther: Hmm?

Moderator: What is that behind your back? Fingers crossed?

Luther: Wait—wait, no—[*Foop!*]

This is my way of saying that perhaps God could forget us, and like Shakespeare's Prospero, "leave not a rack behind."[14] We have no life outside of God's mind; so ultimately it is either life in God's reign, or no life at all. God is not only Creator but Sustainer. The human being is not immortal, does not exist on its own. We either become the Self that God has imagined, or we lapse into the only evil that is perfectly evil—separation from God, non-existence. But it can also be claimed that our real Self is somehow in God, of God, one with God; and our being is in God's being. In either case, all temptation pulls us away from our real Selves, which are in God. To be tempted is to gaze into a mirror that offers illusion; to be delivered from evil is to see God face to face. We are nothing, or we are the image of God. These temporary bodies, our houses and cars, our money, and our romances, will not protect us from oblivion. Just as I could forget those characters, God could forget our illusions. Then where would we be, with our great achievements, our money, our security, our cleverness, our piety, our big muscles, and our beauty? Poof.

"Deliver us from evil" means, *Give us life with You, life in your light, life in your kingdom, life in your life!*

> ... Man being in honor abideth not: he is like the beasts that perish. This is their folly: yet their posterity approve their sayings. Like sheep they are laid in the grave; death shall feed on them; and the upright shall have dominion over them in the morning; and their beauty shall consume in the grave.... But God will redeem my soul from the power of the grave; for he shall receive me.[15]

"I shall be satisfied, when I awake, with thy likeness."[16]

---

14. *The Tempest* IV, i, 156.
15. Ps 49:12–15, KJV.
16. Ps 17:15, KJV.

*

To be delivered from evil is to be delivered from the logical consequence of the *massa damnata*. The consequence is death, real death, permanent death: separation from God. We ask deliverance from this evil. Why? Do we love life? Are we merely expressing an instinct for self-preservation? There is no life apart from God, so to ask for life is to ask for life in God. Life in the kingdom of heaven would not be a mere continuance of life as we know it, but it might be life as we pray it. That life is a world of goodness and not evil; it is a world where everyone is good and no one needs to be great, a world where love is the only wealth, and where kindness and not power is success. Therefore:

It is better to be sinned against than sinning.

It is better to suffer evil than inflict it.

It is right to love our enemies.

The merciful, the peacemakers, and the pure in heart are blessed.

The whole Sermon on the Mount and the Christian message could be spun out as consequences of realizing that the only life is life in God.

*

The writer of the Book of Job takes a mighty risk when his main character asks, "If we accept good from God, shall we not accept evil?"[17] What if God were the author of both? This question can move the problem of evil to the problem of perception—that is, from the West to the East. In the scriptures of India, the troubles of the world are real but reality itself is prestidigitation.[18] To awaken out of this entire circle of misperception, misexperience, is the goal of religious discipline. To be lifted out of the painful nightmare is to be released from trial and delivered from evil.

*

This petition, though no more than any of the others, can suggest a thought experiment. Would we pray this petition for everyone, in such a way as to assume that we ourselves would not be led out of temptation or evil unless everyone in the world were excused from temptation and evil? Suppose that were the condition upon which this petition would be granted. Is this not actually a realistic supposition? Would not praying the petition

---

17. Job 2:10, REB.
18. I am referring to the concept of *Maya*, illusion.

with this understanding go a long way in delivering us from temptation and evil?

Suppose God's name would not be hallowed unless everyone hallowed it—and therefore everyone were equally good. Suppose no one could do God's will unless we all did it. Suppose we could not have the kingdom of God arrive in us and for us until it comes to everyone. Suppose God would feed all of us or none of us. Suppose we must refuse to accept misfortune, pain, humiliation, and chastisement for everyone in the world before we could escape them ourselves. That would be an inward condition of malice toward none, and charity for all. It would show in us the change we want everywhere. If in some ultimate sense we are not only our own worst enemies, but our only enemies, and the only ones who can do us lasting damage is ourselves, then to mean the last petitions in this way would be to have God's will done in us and to be delivered from evil. Being friends of God, we would befriend ourselves and all of our fellow parts of the Living Flame of God.

*

Religious authorities came to Jesus asking him for a sign: something that would prove who he was—something that would validate his actions and his teaching. Probably they asked him as a challenge, as a skeptical insult, and as mockery. But also, some must have wanted a sign just so they could know, so they could be sure.

Jesus' answer was blunt: "No sign will be given to this generation."[19] And no sign has been given since. How do we know that any of this is real? How shall we know that in this prayer God has spoken to us, and that all of this has not been mere wishful thinking? How shall we *know* that God is on the side of good and not evil, and that our heavenly Father wills only goodness for us? There will be no sign.

When God appeared to Moses and commanded him to confront Pharaoh, God said,

> I will be with you, and this shall be the sign for you that it is I who sent you: when you have brought the people out of Egypt, you shall worship God on this mountain.[20]

After we have prayed this prayer, and lived this prayer, and have entered the kingdom of God, then we shall know. Not before. Meanwhile, the closest thing we have to knowing is believing, and belief means to pray and

---

19. Mark 8:12, NRSV.
20. Exod 3:12, NRSV.

work for the kingdom of heaven. Here on earth, we make a choice: I am going to live as though the kingdom of heaven is on its way; I am going to live as though God is good; I am going to try to be kind instead of cruel, giving instead of selfish; and I wait for God. Or we can choose to live for our two minutes on the nightly news. We will not know which choice was the more realistic until afterwards. But which way do we want to live? Who do we want to be? What divinity shall we worship—the idols of this world, or the loving God of Jesus?

Suppose that the world is up to us. It will become whatever we make it. The reality for us is what our minds construct. What we decide is real, *is* real. God is our invention and heaven is of our making. Heaven is whatever we want, with no limitations. If we want money, then our afterlife is money unlimited; or if we want fame then we get the effects of unlimited fame; or if we want sex then we get it unlimited, which means at the exclusion of everything else.[21] If we want God, then the reality of our mind, heart, and soul is God, unlimited. Which would we rather have forever, unlimited, infinite: money, fame, power, security, sex, glamour, or God? None of these can be infinite and still leave room in us for any of the others. Which do we choose? And if we choose God, do we choose the god worshipped by the demons of our dreams and of our world, or do we choose the God of Jesus? What, and who, is the Lord of the Lord's Prayer?

The Lord's Prayer, and all prayer, is about making something real that is not yet real. One way or another, we all pray without ceasing. Jesus says, Let it be *this* prayer. Because you are my friends, *this* is how to pray.

---

21. Another name for such "heavens" is hell. There is a map of it in Dante's *Inferno*.

10

[For Thine is the Kingdom, and the Power, and the Glory, Forever.]

WE ARE FINISHED WITH the Lord's Prayer as it probably was given. Most of the ancient sources of the Gospel of Matthew known today do not record anything after "deliver us from evil." Later manuscripts insert the doxology we say in church to conclude the prayer. It would seem that Church usage finally asserted itself enough to become a part of the Greek text.[1] This praise is an appropriate conclusion, however, particularly in view of its return to the idea of God's kingdom.

It is a fitting reminder that the Lord's Prayer has assumed that God's is the only real power and glory, and it will be so forever and ever. Jesus' prayer was not given in a liturgical context; but when adapted for Church use, it needed a conclusion, something that would distinguish it from other elements of group worship. Here ends the Lord's Prayer—amen—and now we move on to the communion or the benediction.

It is certainly appropriate to say this as a part of the Lord's Prayer in our private use. In the first place, the prayer that Jesus gave was meant as a pattern, not intended to exclude other prayer. Christians have used this part of the prayer for two thousand years both in and out of church.

The doxology at the end reminds us that the kingdom of God is not simply an entity out there, or a fixed reality operating on its own. It is of God, issues from God; it is the capstone of creation and its goal, as far as we humans can conceive. The kingdom is an extension of God's will.

---

1. The Bible has come to us through the hands of the Church.

[For Thine is the Kingdom, and the Power, and the Glory, Forever.]

"Kingdom," "power," and "glory" have been redefined by the prayer. God's power and glory are events and conditions in the heavenly kingdom. The kingdom, while imagined to be a place, is God's will in action, God's loving will come into being.

But this doxology is part of a prayer, not part of a lecture, and its function as a reminder is secondary. It is our confession that power and glory and kingdom are of God and defined by God: we confess our faith. Our faith is in God: we subscribe only to God's power and glory. We not only confess, we praise; not only do we praise, we give thanks. We express awe.

We have prayed to our heavenly Father for God's kingdom to come. Here we confess that it is becoming a reality to us. Earlier we said, "thy kingdom come"; now we say God's *is* the kingdom. We declare ourselves to be willing children and residents of that kingdom. We declare its existence.

So the Lord's Prayer, in the hands of the Church and on the lips of the Church Universal, ends with a confession of faith. The doxology is a faithful people's response to the prayer, the first struggling fruit of its reality. We need not be frightened or deterred by the term "faithful people." We all know, or should know, that we are not faithful people but people struggling to be faithful. We need to act and think and pray better. We might be called saints by the Church, but we are sinners too, and in quantity. We are included anyway, because it is not up to us, and the glory and the power are not ours or the world's. But they are ours because they are God's: the kingdom and power and glory.

11

Amen.

WE HAVE PRAYED FOR ourselves and for everyone whom God loves. We have prayed for life, to know and be ourselves, to be fulfilled, to love and be loved, and to see: to see God, to be with God. We have prayed to breathe the breath of the Eternal.

"Amen" is not to be found in the oldest reliable manuscripts of the Gospel of Matthew, but it has been used by the Church for two thousand years as the conclusion of the Lord's Prayer. It means "May it be so," or "Let it be so."

"Amen" can also be an assertion of truth, an emphatic assent, or an insistent agreement. Sometimes we use the word not to mean "let it be so," but "it *is* so!"

The word can be a wish, an assertion that something *should* be, an expression of support, or a declaration of faith. On one end, it can be the solemn, massed statement of an immense congregation standing in a hushed cathedral; on the other end, it can be the sigh of peace uttered by a solitary person in prayer. It is an affirmation.

However we might define our "amen" at any given moment, we are aligning ourselves with the Lord's Prayer. We are affirming all the things we prayed for: the hallowing of God's name, the coming of the kingdom of heaven, the forgiveness of ourselves and others, the providing of daily necessities and the ultimate satisfying of our need for God, and the deliverance from temptation and evil. We want all things to be in God's hands.

*

"Amen" does not express confidence in the prayer we have prayed, but in the prayer God answers. We are not saying, "And there You have it: a fine prayer." Saying "amen" is quietly and humbly placing our prayer into the hands of our heavenly Father. We would not want to pray imperfectly for our family, friends, or church; so we say, "Let it be so, as it ought to be."

Nor should we be stymied by thinking too much about how foolish and sinful we are. "Amen" is a statement of confidence in the instruction of Jesus: "pray then in this way." We cannot be so humbly penitent that we do not dare to pray, because prayer is not presumption. We do not rely on our own perfection, but on God's. We are confident not of our goodness, but of God's. Our assurance comes not from the one who prays, but from the Teacher who taught us to pray, and from the One to whom we pray.

One more point along this line.

> And finally someone may say, "What am I to do if I cannot believe that I am heard?" Answer: Then follow the example of the father of the child possessed with a dumb spirit. When Christ said to him . . . "Can you believe? All things are possible to him who believes," the father cried with tear-filled eyes, "O Lord, I believe; help my faith if it is too weak!"[1]

*

Most of the time we say the "amen" as an exit. It would not be entirely wrong to use the term that way; however, we tend to mean it in the sense of "We're done." To the God to whom all thoughts are known and from whom no secrets are hidden, we say "Stop listening." We are going about our daily business again, thinking our usual thoughts again, and we do not want any observing or tuning in. "The End. Now I can get back to being myself." We unfold our hands, come out of the pleasantly dreamy facial expression, open our eyes, and turn the key in the SUV of our minds. Cough.

We have just crumpled up the page of our prayer and thrown it into the trash. "Amen" in this case has meant, "I didn't really mean it. Disregard. Ignore." But sometimes we are reluctant to let go, which is probably how it should be. We wish to stay within the consciousness of God's presence. We wish to make the world of our prayer into the world of everyday consciousness. "Amen" can mean, "let it *be;*" "let it *come into existence*"; *"let it be our daily world."*

All of our life is a prayer, a communication with our heavenly Father, and a language of thought and activity. The Lord's Prayer should be like

---

1. Luther, *Works* 42, 81.

a transfusion—an infusion of love and power that heals, strengthens, and revitalizes the rest. Our lives are opportunities to make the language of existence consistent with the words of this prayer. We live to hallow God's name. We go on forgiving, wanting to escape temptation, trusting God to deliver us from evil no matter how dreadful our prospects, and we are coming to realize that the only real power and glory are God's. In God's power, we bring the kingdom of the Lord's Prayer out into the world. The intinction of the kingdom into our lives spreads like frankincense. In saying "amen," we declare not an end but a beginning.

*

"Amen" reminds us that this can be a prayer of acceptance. If we think "let it be so," rather than "may it be so," then we can feel a hint of the acquiescence implied in the first half of the prayer: "thy will be done." This is probably the highest form of petitionary prayer.

Anyone who has fought their way to acquiescence in God's will where the life of a loved one is concerned knows what a prayer of acceptance means. If the person you love most is lying in the emergency room after a serious automobile accident, your first effort—if you pray—is to beg and implore God to save the person's life, perhaps also to preserve his or her limbs, wholeness, and mental capacity. Here one almost understands the description of Jesus praying in the garden of Gethsemane: beads of perspiration like blood were strained from his agonized brow. It is a life and death prayer, and all our emotional force is wrung from us. The same is true before an operation; in fact anything large or small that draws upon our deepest attachment, terror, or hope can jolt even a non-praying person into wild supplication.

Second to the Lord's Prayer, the most memorable example of prayer that Jesus gave us is his prayer in the garden, just before his arrest. Jesus anticipated his betrayal, his being handed over to the so-called authorities. He knew that his sentence would be crucifixion.

Before him was not only shame and unimaginable pain, but also the end of his work, the end of his healing and teaching, and separation from the ones he loved. "Father, if thou be willing, remove this cup from me!" After crying out from the depths, Jesus acquiesced. "Nevertheless, not my will, but thine, be done."[2] That is Jesus' answer to the problem of pain, his own pain. No explanation is asked or given.

---

2. Luke 22:42, KJV.

Jesus' supplication in the garden turns into communion with God, in which the supplicant reaches a point of acquiescence, relinquishment, and trust. At the end, the separation between God and the Forsaken One is overcome.

The agony in the garden shows also that Jesus did not have a theological approach to prayer. His prayer was straightforward and intimate. It did not posit philosophical assumptions about prayer nor acknowledge prayer's difficulty as a logical activity.

Some might say that the Gethsemane prayer all took place within Jesus himself. For our own praying, such a location would mean that prayer is completely a psychological phenomenon—we move ourselves to a better state, in which our conscious and unconscious minds talk to each other. For Jesus, if one wishes to retain a traditional Christology, such internal-only prayer could be said to mean that both natures in Jesus—human and divine—came into dialogue. Prayer brings our surface self and our deep Self face to face, out of which deeply healthful work comes unity. Acquiescence might be a state of integration and peace. Perhaps we should pray until this state is reached. We know we have been heard.

*

The portrait of God that I have painted using the colors of the Lord's Prayer might not be the picture you see, nor the portrait intended by Jesus. From now on, you are the artist whose work comes more and more into perfection with each prayer. I am not speaking for Jesus, and I leave my errors on these pages for you to sort through in hopes that I have said something worth your thought. These reflections on the Lord's Prayer were written by a student of the prayer, not by an authority on the prayer. They were written in well-intended ignorance that he hopes the reader will sift for herself or himself. Understanding or misunderstanding, we pray together to our Father in heaven.

*

The "amen" at the end of the Lord's Prayer can be a statement of trust in God to fulfill the unspoken and unknown intentions of each phrase. We cannot keep it all in mind at once, nor can we fully understand the petitions. We pray much of the prayer wrongly. In all this we call upon the Spirit of God, who intercedes for us and makes our shallow, spotty, and infrequent prayers full. With "amen" spoken in confidence, we can imply a request that the wrong in our prayers be forgiven and transformed.

Prayer can be a guide to meditation—hence this book's dwelling on the words and phrases; but even meditation is not itself the goal. Ultimately, prayer is not about thinking the right thoughts, but is the heart's response to the love of God. Prayer rises to adoration, to communion. It moves from words to song to silence, "wordless as the flight of birds."[3]

*

Perhaps we will awaken to find the dream is true. Call it salvation, call it enlightenment, call it Buddha-consciousness, or call it love: the kingdom of Heaven is already here. We need only to wake up to it. "Only that day dawns to which we are awake."

> You must not imagine that you are drawn against your will, for the mind can also be drawn by love . . . .
> Show me a lover and he will understand what I am saying.
> Show me someone who wants something, someone hungry, someone wandering in this wilderness,
> Thirsting and longing for the fountains of his eternal home . . . .[4]

*

The Lord's Prayer describes a parent beyond our dreams who is closer than we know. This is someone different from many of the figures portrayed by popular religions: the designer of sacrifices, the dictator of minute and exacting laws, the punisher of innocents in unrighteous nations, the party to exclusive covenants, the executor of vengeance, or the slayer of heathen. All these gods might exist in the world as the laws of physics exist, but the heavenly Father of Jesus is the heart and glory of a different kingdom. This is our Beloved, who forgives, provides, calls, gathers, enlightens, saves, and loves without reason or boundaries. If this universe was dreamed up, why not the kingdom of God also—the next dream and a newer creation? What if love and imagination lie behind the laws of physics, and the universe is essentially a dream? Then perhaps the prayer of Jesus is a vision of the Dreamer's dream. Let us then love God and one another and ourselves, for we are witnesses of that vision and children of that dream.

---

3. MacLeish, *Poems*, 106.
4. Augustine, "St. John's Gospel," 1.

A Note of Appreciation

My thanks to Elizabeth Gramm, without whose conscientious editing and astute observations this book would be a continuous stumble; and to Sarah Gramm Behof, whose many thoughtful suggestions are reflected in the text. And I am grateful to my wife, Camelia Maianu, for her support.

Works Cited

Augustine. *Confessions*. Translated by Henry Chadwick. Oxford: Oxford University Press, 1991.
Augustine. "The Homilies of St. Augustine on St. John's Gospel." In *The Inner Journey: Views from the Christian Tradition*. Edited by Lorraine Kisley. Sandpoint, ID: Morninglight, 2006.
The Book of Common Prayer. New York: Church Publishing Incorporated, 2007.
Dickinson, Emily. *The Poems of Emily Dickinson*, edited by R. W. Franklin. Cambridge, MA: Harvard University Press, 1999.
Faulkner, William. "Nobel Lecture." In *The Portable Faulkner*, edited by Malcolm Cowley. NY: Modern Library, 1971.
Frost, Robert. "The Death of the Hired Man." In *Robert Frost: Collected Poems, Prose, and Plays*. New York: Literary Classics of the United States, 1995.
Gray, Thomas. "Elegy Written in a Country Churchyard." In *The Norton Anthology of English Literature Volume 1*. Edited by Stephen Greenblatt. New York: W. W. Norton, 1979.
Jung, Carl. *The Undiscovered Self*. New York: Signet, 1958.
Keats, John. *The Letters of John Keats*. Edited by Maurice Buxton Forman. London: Oxford University Press, 1931.
Kempis, Thomas á. *The Imitation of Christ*. New York: Catholic Book Publishing, 1977.
Kittel, Gerhard. *Theological Dictionary of the New Testament*. Volume 1. Translated by Geoffrey W. Bromily. Grand Rapids, MI: Wm. B. Eerdmans, 1964.
Lincoln, Abraham. *The Collected Works of Abraham Lincoln, Volume 5*. Edited by Roy P. Basler. New Brunswick: Rutgers University Press, 1953.
Luther, Martin. *Luther's Works*. Edited by Martin O. Dietrich. Philadelphia: Fortress,1956.
Lutheran Church in America. *Service Book and Hymnal of the Lutheran Church in America*. Minneapolis: Augsburg, 1958.
MacLeish, Archibald. *Collected Poems, 1917–1982*. Boston: Houghton Mifflin, 1985.
Marshall, Alfred. *The New International Version Interlinear Greek-English New Testament*. Grand Rapids, MI: Zondervan, 1976.
Merton, Thomas. *New Seeds of Contemplation*. New York: New Directions, 2007.
Saint-Exupéry, Antoine. *The Little Prince*. Orlando, FL: Harcourt, 2000.
Shakespeare, William. *The Complete Works*. Oxford: Oxford University Press, 1988.
Tappert, Theodore G., ed. *The Book of Concord: The Confessions of the Evangelical Lutheran Church*. Philadelphia: Fortress, 1959.

Thoreau, Henry David. *Walden: An Annotated Edition.* Edited by Walter Roy Harding. Boston: Houghton Mifflin, 1995.

Twain, Mark. *The Autobiography of Mark Twain.* Edited by Charles Neider. New York: HarperPerennial, 1959.

Wiesel, Elie. *Elie Wiesel at the National Press Club/Cassette.* National Public Radio, 1988.

www.ingramcontent.com/pod-product-compliance
Lightning Source LLC
Chambersburg PA
CBHW062042220426
43662CB00010B/1619